Calvinist Humor in American Literature

st Flannery O'Connor Nathaniel Hawthorne Ma
k Twain Ernest Hemingway Herman Melville N

n William Faulkner **Calvinist Humor** Ernest He
el West **in American Literature** Flannery O'Con

Michael Dunne

Louisiana State University Press
Baton Rouge

Published by Louisiana State University Press
Copyright © 2007 by Louisiana State University Press
All rights reserved
Manufactured in the United States of America
First printing

Designer: Barbara Neely Bourgoyne
Typeface: Chapparel Pro, text; Avenir, display
Printer and binder: Thomson-Shore, Inc.

Library of Congress Cataloging-in-Publication Data

Dunne, Michael, 1941–
  Calvinist humor in American literature / Michael Dunne.
      p. cm.
  Includes bibliographical references and index.
  ISBN 978-0-8071-3260-9 (alk. paper)
  1. American wit and humor—History and criticism. 2. American literature—History
and criticism. 3. Calvinism in literature. 4. Wit and humor—Religious aspects—
Christianity. 5. Comic, The—Religious aspects. I. Title.
  PS430.D86 2007
  817.009—dc22

                                                                    2006039570

The paper in this book meets the guidelines for permanence and durability of the
Committee on Production Guidelines for Book Longevity of the Council on Library
Resources. ♾

Contents

Preface

This is not my first encounter with what I am calling "Calvinist humor." In the summer of 1990, I attempted to derive a seminar from my musings on some bleak American authors. The title I chose, "The Power of Blackness," was stolen from Harry Levin's 1958 study of Poe, Hawthorne, and Melville. To some degree, the seminar got at what I was interested in, but its title falsely suggested to too many people that I was teaching a class about Richard Wright and Ralph Ellison. Then, for the fall 1997 semester, I proposed a seminar with the more accurate title "Calvinist Humor." Even before the semester began, greater problems than those caused by my appropriation of "The Power of Blackness" title began to arise. First of all, the scheduling center, a bureaucratic institution of considerable power, informed the schedule maker in my department that the course should more properly be called "Calvinistic Humor." When I was asked to accept this grammatical correction, I willfully insisted on my original title: "Calvinist Humor." However, the folks at the scheduling center eventually won out even while seeming to acquiesce cordially in my intransigence. When the course bulletin was finally published, the seminar was listed as "Calvanist Humor." Spelling brought on the last laugh—at my expense. In retrospect, the whole experience has come to seem to me merely another manifestation of Calvinist humor. Imagine someone presuming to resist what every sensible person recognizes as the irresistible powers of an academic bureaucracy! Such a worldly-wise perspective might recognize in the creator of this seminar (me) a vainglorious bumpkin, perhaps along the lines of one of William Faulkner's fools. Of course, I was less experienced in the ways of Calvinist humor at that time and probably less willing to be amused by it when it developed at my own expense, and so I wrestled and wrestled with the problem of finding a definition for a concept that I was pretty much sure existed. Eventually, my experience with the scheduling center and other influences—such as my repeated reading of Flannery O'Connor's fiction—convinced me that there are two strains of Calvinist humor. As the writing of William Bradford and Nathanael West implies, there is a Calvinist joke entailed when we recognize that other people are fallen from perfection without any admission that we may be in the same boat ourselves. In the second form, epitomized by my encounter with the scheduling center as well as by numerous literary manifestations, we acknowledge that we are all equally far from some putatively better state. When something is only to be expected as a part of everyday human nature, it represents the perception of this second form of Calvinist humor. This, at any rate, is what I think today.

Years ago, several students and colleagues asked me to explain just exactly what Calvinist humor was/is before the course in Calvinist humor began. Since I have always been professionally committed to answering all questions, I responded to these inquiries at considerable length—if not clarifying the issues, at least foreclosing further questions. Then, at the first meeting of the seminar, this questioning resumed—naturally enough, and perhaps taking on by that time somewhat greater urgency for the questioners. Again I, and the members of the seminar, offered answers, the consensus being that Calvinist humor is "very hard to define" but that it definitely—or very probably—exists. Throughout the semester, we returned to the topic frequently, asking the same questions, providing some of the same answers. Like the men in Wallace Stevens's "The Idea of Order at Key West," "we knew / It was the spirit that we sought and knew / That we should ask this often . . ." (ll. 18–20). In the end, I think we emerged with our intuitions definitely strengthened but still without a final definition. And so, I resolved to try in this book once more, and at much greater length, to say just what Calvinist humor is.

My efforts to define and illustrate this concept have, naturally enough, involved me in debts to many others. My students over the years have been my most helpful advisors. The students in my "Calvinist Humor" seminar—Kelli Allen, Carol Contos, Jean Corey, John Greer, Julie Morgan,

David Pierce, Leigh Pettus, Stephanie Pullen, and Seth Sparkman—were especially helpful and patient. Professor Larry Mintz told me about some authors who connected religion and humor. Ava Leavell Haymon shared with me her unsurpassed experience and knowledge of southern fundamentalism. Pat Bradley helped me track down some information about Robert Penn Warren, as Allison Ensor did about Mark Twain. Roger Rollin supplied me with a copy of his sterling article about John Milton's humor. Debbie Flanigan put me in touch with her husband, Rabbi Rami Shapiro, who guided me through some scriptural quagmires. Tom Byers and Dennis Hall arranged for me to give the Commonwealth Center for the Humanities and Society lecture at the University of Louisville about Flannery O'Connor's humor. M. Thomas Inge printed my essay about Nathaniel Hawthorne's Calvinist humor in *Studies in American Humor* and graciously granted me permission to revise and reprint it here. My son Paul solved several computer problems for me. My colleague and wife of forty years, Sara Lewis Dunne, read my completed manuscript and made several very useful suggestions for improvement. Professor Thomas Van also read the manuscript and generously suggested corrections and improvements. Marie Blanchard's copyediting helped me say what I hoped to say. I am grateful to all of these people for their support and assistance. The errors that remain are entirely my own.

Calvinist Humor in American Literature

1 Calvinist Humor

For many years I have been interested in a concept that I am calling "Calvinist humor." I know! I know! Like most people who hear the term for the first time, you are eager to point out that the term *Calvinist humor* is something of an oxymoron. Actually, this is itself an example of Calvinist humor: the very normal and only-to-be-expected perception on the part of nearly everybody that there is something odd in the locution and that he or she is the very first one to have noticed this. When something is only to be expected as a part of everyday human experience, it represents the perception that we are all alike, especially in the sense that none of us is perfect, that we are all—in the terms favored by the French Protestant reformer John Calvin (1509–1564)—fallen from prelapsarian perfection into the messy condition that we call real life.[1] In this condition, we are likely to engage in all sorts of imperfect behavior, such as thinking that we are the only ones smart enough to figure out something that is actually evident to everyone. This recognition animates one tendency of the American mindset that I am calling Calvinist humor. It is the voice we hear when Mark Twain writes, in the epigraph for chapter 2 of *Pudd'nhead Wilson*, "Adam was but human—this explains it all. He did not want the apple for the apple's sake, he only wanted it because it was forbidden. The mistake was in not forbidding the serpent; then he would have eaten the serpent" (6). "Aren't people—including ourselves—just like that!" we observe with a comfortable Calvinist chuckle.

The other strain, the other side of the Calvinist coin, shows us that other people are fallen from perfection without any necessary recognition that we may be in the same boat ourselves. As H. L. Mencken writes about the Puritanically inclined, in "Puritanism as a Literary Force," "[T]he sinner who excited his highest zeal and passion was not so much himself as his neighbour [sic]; to borrow a term from psychopathology, he was much less the masochist than the sadist" (232). This is the self-righteous voice we hear when William Bradford writes, in *Of Plymouth Plantation,* about the Indians who have stood in the way of total Puritan domination of New England, "For it pleased God to visit these Indians with a great sickness and such a mortality that of a thousand, above nine and a half hundred of them died, and many of them did rot above ground for want of burial" (270). Bradford obviously feels that these Indians got pretty much what they deserved, and this understanding of divine retribution seems to bring a satisfied smile to Bradford, and—as he clearly expects— it should to us too. Whether adopting the less censorious view of Twain or the harsher view of Bradford, we are left with the conviction that human beings—including American human beings—can be more easily described and defined in terms of their failings and shortcomings than by their limitless potential for good. The Calvinist humorist both embraces this assumption and finds its implications humorous. As Walter T. Herbert, Jr., argues in his book *"Moby Dick" and Calvinism,* "Calvinist faith expressed [a] skeptical view of human nature in general" (29), and this skepticism often results in literature displaying Calvinist humor.

Calvinist humor consists in the perception of imperfection. When we perceive that only others are imperfect, we participate in the form of Calvinist humor preferred by William Bradford and Nathanael West. When we perceive that others are imperfect, as we all are, we participate in the form preferred by Mark Twain and William Faulkner, for example. The two strains of Calvinist humor are alike in making the faults of others more important than their virtues. They differ in terms of what we might think of as the writer/perceiver's disposition: his or her willingness to recognize the same faults in him- or herself. John T. McNeill writes in his introduction to Calvin's *Institutes,* "Since all of us have faults and suffer from 'the mists of ignorance,' we should not renounce communion with others on slight grounds" (lxi). When a fictional character does so, readers are treated to a double laugh, both with and at the character making this sort of judgment. In the theocratic world in which most American writers and critics work, whether or not the observing mind goes in for self-inclusion in the indictment depends on how closely the divine mind is thought to echo the judgments of this observing mind. William Bradford feels that God is in full agreement with him that these clearly sinful Indians deserve suffering in this life and—most probably—damnation in the next. Twain sees Adam to be like himself—like most of us, in fact—in his wrongheaded pursuit of the very thing that is theologically worst for him.

Interestingly enough, this willingness to see and dwell on the shortcomings of others persists in American writers even after the theological underpinnings of religious orthodoxy have been removed. Loris Mirella cogently claims that "Calvinism is more than a set of religious values; it is also, crucially, a complex structure of beliefs and attitudes that, operating systematically, functions as an intellectual framework for articulating certain attitudes and emotions" (21). Thus, despite their often-confessed repudiation of orthodox religious belief, Nathanael West and Ernest Hemingway are as likely as Bradford or Twain to write scornfully of others. In a sense, this is the essence of American literary modernism. Doris Kearns Goodwin is only one of many to recognize the modernist character of this antireligious shift. In *Lyndon Johnson and the American Dream,* for example, Kearns Goodwin conventionally observes, "In retrospect it can now be understood that World War I was a great watershed, the beginning of a period of dissolution in which established landmarks of thought, value, and the social order would be replaced" (60). True enough, we might concede, and therefore—surprisingly enough—while Hemingway and West may not echo the religious sentiments of Michael Wigglesworth and Jonathan Edwards, what will not be replaced in their thinking is the tendency to perceive human behavior in terms of Calvinist humor.

A few minutes' reflection should bring us to the realization that—whether or not we found our judgments in religious belief and whether or not we include ourselves in the indictment—human behavior will seem unsatisfactory mostly when it can be contrasted to some theoretically preferable mode of behavior. To the Calvinistic, or to the Calvinistically influenced mind, this preferable mode of behavior is that of the unfallen, prelapsarian human being. This is the happy, unfallen condition described in Genesis 1.26–27: "And God said, Let us make man in our image, after our likeness: and let them have dominion over the fish of the sea, and over the fowl of the air, and over the cattle, and over all the earth, and over every creeping thing that creepeth upon the earth. So God created man in his own image, in the image of God created he him. . . ." Many years later, Ralph Waldo Emerson recaptures this prelapsarian consciousness in his first book, *Nature:* "Standing on the bare ground,—my head bathed by the blithe air and uplifted into infinite space . . . I become a transparent eyeball; I am nothing; I see all; the currents of Universal being circulate through me; I am part or parcel of God" (11). Emerson's reinvention of the prelapsarian experience apart from its theological origins in the Old Testament is, perhaps, attractive, but it provides only the first pole of the Calvinist contrast between the "real" and the theoretically possible. To get the whole story, one must proceed to Genesis 3.17–19: "And unto Adam he said, Because thou hast harkened unto the voice of thy wife, and hast eaten of the tree, of which I commanded thee, saying, thou shalt not eat of it: cursed is the ground for thy sake; in sorrow shalt thou eat of it all the days of thy life. Thorns also and thistles shall it bring forth to thee, and thou shalt eat the herb of the field; In the sweat of thy face shalt thou eat bread, till thou return unto the ground; for out of it wast thou taken: for dust thou art, and unto dust shalt thou return." To the Calvinist mind, utterly convinced of the irreversible fall of man, the third chapter of Genesis seems to be telling a story with which all of us are bitterly familiar. It is, then, a favorite Calvinist joke to watch real or fictional characters acting as if this story is untrue, as if we actually can have things the way we would prefer.

Even when American thinkers fail to accept the Calvinist view wholeheartedly—even when the relevant vision is decidedly secular—there is still a tendency to see some version of Calvinism as the more attractive alternative to what we might think of as the optimistic, sunny view of life. Thus David W. Noble writes sarcastically, in *The Eternal Adam and the New World Garden,* about the arrival of American Transcendental optimism: "It was proclaimed, in the United States of 1830, that every man had transcended the human condition to achieve perfect freedom in harmony with redemptive nature" (4). Noble's unquestioning acceptance of the unsatisfactoriness of the "human condition" as an unarguable fact of experience testifies to how deeply Calvinistic perceptions have entered into the American imagination. His mockery of claims to the contrary points to the presence of Calvinist humor. This disposition is evident as well when R. W. B. Lewis is trying to lay some groundwork for his valorization of Hawthorne, Melville, and other adherents of "the party of Irony" in *The American Adam*. On his way to pursuing a middle-of-the-road argument, Lewis cannot forgo ridiculing those who belong to the Emersonian "party of hope": "As the hopeful expressed their mounting contempt for the doctrine of inherited sin, the nostalgic intoned on Sundays the fixed legacy of corruption in ever more emphatic accents; and centers of orthodox Calvinism, like Andover and Princeton, became citadels of the old and increasingly cheerless theology" (7). The "hopeful," in this view, are comic or pitiable because of their "contempt for the [Calvinist] doctrine of inherited sin." The nostalgic are simultaneously too extreme in their orthodoxy. In light of this conviction, the wise compromise between two extreme ideologies, in Lewis's view, is what he calls "tragic optimism," a position that avoids both the foolish and unfounded expectations of the party of hope and the theological "gloom" of the party of memory in favor of a more "sensible" position grounded in an acceptance that life is tragic. This position is also, by the way, an ideal one from which to launch missiles of Calvinist humor. Note, along the same lines, this description of "the reflective and responsible [literary] theorist" from the epilogue to Cleanth Brooks and William K. Wimsatt's *Literary Criticism: A Short History:* "He is sure, however, that facing up to it ["evil itself, or division, or conflict"], facing up to the human predicament, is a desirable and mature state of soul and the right model and source of a mature poetic art" (743). This Calvinistic perspective on "the human predicament" may bring one a good deal of unwelcome bad news, but it can also lead to the grimaces, nods, smiles, and even guffaws of Calvinist humor, while the more optimistic perspective cannot.

The simplest, and most un-Calvinist, alternative to this kind of pessimism would be to expect everybody to do the right thing most of the time and thus to expect that everything will eventually work out for the best. Such expectations are often thought of—ironically enough—as exercises

in a typically "American" form of optimism. This is what the Frenchman
Alexis de Tocqueville explains as a peculiarly American disposition in his
Democracy in America (1835–39): "Every man sees changes continually taking place. Some make things worse. . . . Others improve his lot, and he
concludes that man in general is endowed with an infinite capacity for
improvement. His setbacks teach him that no one has discovered absolute good; his successes inspire him to seek it without slackening. Thus,
searching always, falling, picking himself up again, often disappointed,
never discouraged, he is ever striving toward that immense grandeur
glimpsed indistinctly at the end of the long track humanity must follow"
(453). Of course, de Tocqueville is writing as an outsider about what we
might call the American soul. From a perspective more securely within
the American tent, the very American F. Scott Fitzgerald makes the same
point at the end of *The Great Gatsby* (1925): "Gatsby believed in the green
light, the orgiastic future that year by year recedes before us. It eluded us
then, but that's no matter—tomorrow we will run faster, stretch out our
arms farther. . . . And one fine morning—" (141). No positive character
in Flannery O'Connor's work or Ernest Hemingway's would be any more
capable of this sort of optimism than the sinners in Jonathan Edwards's
congregation. This Emersonian sort of happy expectancy is very often
ridiculed by many foreign observers of American life and foreign policy
and also by those Americans who are more profoundly influenced by
John Calvin than by Ralph Waldo Emerson.[2] At the same time, we must
realize that a happy vision of "life" is too monistic to produce wry or bitter laughter, and so this more optimistic vision cannot produce Calvinist
humor. That is why I do not discuss it in this book. My subject is dictated
by those authors who understand sunny expectations to be foolish food
for Calvinist laughter.

One of the most frequent subjects of Calvinist humor in American
literature is the recognition that all human beings—irrespective of their
optimistic aspirations to spiritual transcendence—are inescapably rooted
in the physical world, through what we might think of in Calvinist terms
as the corruptible body. As Robert Penn Warren's character Willie Stark
typically says in *All the King's Men* (1946), "Man is conceived in sin and
born in corruption and he passeth from the stink of the didie to the

stench of the shroud" (72). Of course, Warren's plot makes Stark heav-
ily invested in this proposition as a way of rationalizing his own corrupt
politics. Even so, he shares the Calvinist perception that would recognize
the inescapable physical nature of Indians who rot above the ground and
of prelapsarian humans who eat apples, and these perceptions often appear as what I am calling Calvinist humor. Of course, the Calvinist is not
alone in this perception. The Russian critic Mikhail Bakhtin directs our
attention to other writers' exploitation of what he calls "the grotesque
body." According to Bakhtin's *Rabelais and His World,* "The essential principle of grotesque realism is degradation, that is, the lowering of all that
is high, spiritual, ideal, abstract; it is a transfer to the material level, to
the sphere of earth and body in their indissoluble unity" (19–20). Among
the many American writers who have pursued this mode of investiga-
tion are those usually called humorists of the Old Southwest. As Kenneth
Lynn explains, the Old Southwesterner "could not be bound by traditional niceties in his humor, because life itself was neither traditional
nor nice" (27). Thus, the Southwest humorists often depicted characters
and physical incidents that "nice people" didn't talk about—or want to
talk about. These characters and incidents challenge "nice people" so insistently because they force readers to acknowledge the corruptible body,
the physical limitations that stand between actual human beings and any
imagined state of perfection. This is essentially John Calvin's argument
when he writes, in *The Institutes of the Christian Religion,* that "unless the
soul were something essential, separate from the body, Scripture would
not teach that we dwell in houses of clay and at death leave the tabernacle of the flesh, putting off what is corruptible . . ." (185). Augustus
Baldwin Longstreet brilliantly illustrates this disposition to focus on the
corruptible physical body in his description of a brutal fight in *Georgia
Scenes:* "Bill presented a hideous spectacle. About a third of his nose, at
the lower extremity, was bit off, and his face so swelled and bruised that
it was difficult to discover in it anything of the human visage, much more
the fine features which he carried into the ring" ("The Fight" 62). There
is nothing prelapsarian or perfectible about Bill; he is most definitely a
corporeal entity. Longstreet's "The Gander Pulling," from the same collection, makes this point in terms of the lower animals, recounting that

"[w]henever either of them came round [in this savage competition], the gander's neck was sure of a severe wrench" (117). This practice is probably cruel and disgusting, but it is certainly physical, and that—to some degree, at least—is the author's joke.

The consensus of most commentators on this literary mode is expressed by Mary Ann Wimsatt and Robert L. Phillips when they call George Washington Harris "the most original and gifted of the antebellum humorists" (155). Milton Rickles provides another reason for including Harris in this discussion by explaining that all of this extremely physical humor was "reinforced by [Harris's] strict Presbyterian upbringing" (21).[3] Rickels says that years later "[t]he Harris family had its own pew in the First Presbyterian Church of Knoxville, where for many years Harris was an elder . . ." (27). Therefore, Harris's character Sut Lovingood may be seen not only as the ultimate expression of the Southwestern humorist's recognition of the corruptible body—even to the point of physical cruelty—but also as a lively exemplar of Calvinist humor. Wimsatt and Phillips note in Harris's Sut Lovingood stories "their emphasis on pain, humiliation, and physical grotesquerie" (155). Consider, for example, Sut's description of the title character in "Parson John Bullen's Lizards": "He weighed ni ontu three hundred, hed a black stripe down his back, like ontu a ole bridil rein, an' his belly wer 'bout the size and color ove a beef paunch, an' hit a-swingin out frum side to side . . ." (211). Parson Bullen seems disgusting, perhaps because he is seen from the outside, but in "Blown Up with Soda," Sut is equally candid in reporting all of the unpleasant physical details of his own reaction to an extreme dose of baking soda: "I wer a-feelin the bottom ove my paunch cumin up arter hit, inside out, jis' like the bottom ove a green champain bottil" (216). Since this sort of commitment to physical reality will surface again in the work of such diverse American artists as Mark Twain, Nathanael West, William Faulkner, and Flannery O'Connor, we may be onto something important when we recognize the presence of the physical in many forms of Calvinist humor.

For my purposes here, this Calvinistic strain may reveal itself either in the squeamish recognition of the physically corruptible in others or in the perception that we are all, ultimately, physical creatures, no matter how much we might wish otherwise.[4] Edmund Wilson reads Harris's fiction according to the first option, and so he observes, in *Patriotic Gore:* "It takes a pretty strong stomach nowadays . . . to get through it in any version. I should say that, as far as my experience goes, it is by far the most repellent book of any real literary merit in American literature" (509).[5] Sut helps us to recognize the second perspective himself when he admits, in "Contempt of Court—Almost," "An' yere's anuther human nater: ef enything happens sum feller, I don't keer ef he's yure bes frien, an' I don' keer how sorry yu is fur him, thar's a streak ove satisfackshun 'bout like a sowin thread a-runnin' all thru yer sorer" (240). It is sad if this estimation of human nature is accurate, but it apparently is true nevertheless. As Sut continues, "Yu may be shamed ove hit, but durn me ef hit ain't thar" (240–41).

Edmund Wilson goes on to explain that "[t]his kind of cruel and brutal humor was something of an American institution all through the nineteenth century" (509). In Harris's case, we may consider Sut's observation that "Dad cudent see the funny part" of being chased into the creek and stung by hornets, in "Sut Lovingood's Daddy, Acting Horse" (205). Sut is well situated to appreciate this very physical scene, though, and also the one in which Parson John Bullen discovers lizards in his trousers: "He gin hisself sum orful open-handed slaps wif fust one han' an' then tuther, about the place whar you cut the bes'steak outen a beef. Then he'd fetch a vigrus ruff rub whar a hosses tail sprouts; then he'd stomp one foot, then tuther, then bof at onst" (209). Parson John Bullen is a creature entirely under the influence of his corruptible body here, rather than of his soul. As we shall see later on in connection with Mark Twain's Calvinist humor, insisting on the physical is a way to resist the force that gentility powerfully trained on American life in the nineteenth century. This is what Harris is up to—at least in part—in "Mrs. Yardley's Quilting" when Sut explains, "[Q]uiltins, managed in a morril an' sensibil way, truly am good things—good fur free drinkin, good fur free eatin, good fur free huggin, good fur free dancing, good fur free fitin, an' goodest ove all fur poperlatin a country fas'. Thar am a fur-seein wisdum in quiltins, ef they hes proper trimmins: vittils, fiddils, an' sperrits in 'bundance" (226). Dwelling on the physical and decidedly earthly in this way also resists the pull of transcendental optimism. It is consequently hard to think of many notable nineteenth-century Americans who could articulate Sut's description of Sicily Burns: "Sich a buzzim! Jis' think ove two snow balls wif a straw-berry stuck but-ainded intu bof on 'em" ("Blown Up with Soda" 212). When all is said and done, however, it seems to me that the indisputably physical humor of the Southwest humorists is primarily a way to assert that, in all of its corruptible earthiness, human existence falls far short of anyone's definition of human perfection. As Rickels concludes, "The effect of images of flayed and butchered animals, of diseased and vermin-ous insects, of fatness and thinness, of occasionally seductive women fills the Yarns with a sense of the ever-present flesh" (116). Rickels does not conclude, but I will, that the ever-present flesh is an ever-present reminder of human imperfection, of human nature fallen into an undeni-ably corruptible physical condition. Like the other writers treated in this book, Harris frequently finds this fact funny, and this perception of the imperfect produces a kind of Calvinist humor. And Harris is not alone. As Ed Piacentino explains, in *The Enduring Legacy of Old Southwest Humor*, "Grotesque portraiture, exploiting the body and bodily functions for comical purposes, abounds in the humor of the Old Southwest" (19). As Piacentino's collection demonstrates, and as our own reading confirms, this form of Calvinist humor did not die out in the antebellum period.

Sophisticated observers of American literature have long noted, in the works of America's most distinctive authors, and not just in the works of Twain, Bradford, and the Old Southwest humorists, the presence of values and attitudes associated with the ideas and practices of John Calvin. Herman Melville may speak for many when he observes in his highly appreciative review "Hawthorne and His Mosses" (1850): "Certain it is . . . that this great power of blackness in [Hawthorne] derives its force from its appeal to that Calvinistic sense of Inner Depravity and Original Sin, from whose visitations, in some shape or other, no deeply thinking mind is always and wholly free. For, in certain moods, no man can weigh this world without throwing in something, somehow like Original Sin, to strike the uneven balance" (837). Putting aside this judgment's pertinence to the tales and sketches in Hawthorne's *Mosses from an Old Manse* and his literary career more generally, the most striking element of Melville's remarks is his assumption that any rational observer would come to the same conclusion about the influence of Calvinism in life-as-we-know-it, and life-as-we-know-it is life in America.

Later developments suggest the validity of Melville's assumption. As Agnes McNeill Donohue writes, in *Hawthorne: Calvin's Ironic Stepchild*, "[N]o American writer, conscious of his country's religious past, is able to ignore his Calvinist inheritance, despise it though he may" (342).[6] In support, we may recall that when Henry James wants to warn his readers in *Daisy Miller* (1878) of Frederick Winterbourne's unsuitability as a lover for his heroine, he goes beyond the young man's highly suggestive last name to explain that Winterbourne is a citizen of Geneva, the site of Calvin's theocracy: "But Winterbourne had an old attachment for the little metropolis of Calvinism; he had been put to school there as a boy, and he had afterwards gone to college there—circumstances which had led to his forming a great many youthful friendships. Many of these he had kept, and they were a source of great satisfaction to him" (2). When all is said and done, and Daisy Miller has died from the combination of Roman fever and Winterbourne's inadequate emotions, James sends the latter back to Geneva, solidifying his readers' condemnation through a sort of geographic symbolism. The touchstone of Calvinism may simply be assumed.

Skipping ahead many years in order to simplify a literary history that might easily be expanded,[7] we may pause to notice Robert Lowell's poem "Children of Light" (1944). In this ten-line poem published during World War II, Lowell develops his recurrent themes of antimaterialism and pacifism in one of the densest examples of New-Critical poetry that I am familiar with. After combining the historical ancestry of New Englanders with an allusion to the Lord's Prayer, Lowell puns on the words *stocks* (both investments and Puritan forms of punishment) and *stones* (geographic markers of the New England landscape, as in the poems of Robert Frost, and the unattractive alternative to "bread" in the New Testament book of Matthew).[8] He also protests the burning of grain to keep up wheat prices, even while echoing the biblical symbolism of grain, as well as parodying the cliché that people who live in glass houses shouldn't throw stones. At the same time that he is piling up these abstruse references and allusions, Lowell assumes—as easily as Melville and

James have done—that the merest gesture in the direction of Geneva is enough to communicate a sense of Calvinism's omnipresence to readers immersed, as we all are, in the same quasi-Calvinist American culture.[9] Therefore, he writes that the American Pilgrims of the seventeenth century were "unhouseled by Geneva's night" (l. 4) in the sense that they pursued a fundamental form of Protestantism rather than the Catholicism that Lowell embraced in those days.[10] All of these examples attest that a Calvinist dye suffuses the national literary fabric so thoroughly that it does not need to be referenced specifically.

Certainly many literary critics writing long after the deaths of Melville and James—and also after the conclusion of the war that Lowell so strongly opposed—accept the premise that all Americans share in some sort of Calvinist heritage. In *Rappaccini's Children: American Writers in a Calvinist World* (1981), for example, William Shurr discusses American writers ranging from Jonathan Edwards and William Cullen Bryant to Robert Frost and William Faulkner in chapters with such revealing titles as "The Persistence of Calvinism" and "Calvinism and the Tragic Sense." The popularity of the topic is also apparent in such widely ranging article titles as "John D. McDonald and Calvinism: Some Key Terms" by Frank L. Vatai (1990) and "Samuel Davies and Calvinist Poetic Ecology" by Jeffrey H. Richards (2000). The focuses of *"Moby Dick" and Calvinism: A World Dismantled* (1977) by T. Walter Herbert, Jr., and Donohue's *Hawthorne: Calvin's Ironic Stepchild* (1985) should be obvious enough. In short, an impressive consensus exists that American literature often exhibits evidence of what Shurr calls "the persistence of Calvinism." Furthermore, we may easily agree that only when Calvinism persists in the blood can writers and critics alike summon up the energy to produce Calvinist humor.

Of course, as George M. Marsden writes in his biography of Jonathan Edwards, *Calvinism* "is and was an imprecise term" (86) which people are inclined to toss around without any specific agreement as to its meaning. Even so, it is likely that our sense of orthodox Calvinism—however imprecise—is at least partially influenced by the authentic Calvinist doctrines enunciated by the Synod of Dort (1618–19), which can be represented by the acronym TULIP. That is to say, our sense of what Calvinism *is* usually entails some assumption that Calvinists believe in: (1) the total depravity of human nature, perhaps because of the sin of Adam (2) the unconditional election of those chosen by God for salvation, irrespective of their unworthiness (3) Christ's limited atonement—only for those elected for salvation (4) the irresistibility of saving grace for those so elected; and (5) the perseverance of the saved in the paths of salvation despite all temptations to the contrary.[11] Of course, few readers today—or at chosen intervals in America's past—are likely to endorse such doctrines entirely and wholeheartedly. As Max Weber notes in *The Protestant Ethic and the Spirit of Capitalism,* Calvinism evolved even from its fairly early days: "The Calvinism which fought the English Civil War, still more the Calvinism which won an uneasy toleration at the Revolution, was not that of its founder" (9). Nevertheless, many of the theological assumptions associated historically with Calvinism would be enough to produce a bleak outlook on everyday experience, sin and/or salvation notwithstanding. Focusing on the first three, a person might be likely to form the sour expectations about human nature that we have seen already in the works of Melville, Twain, James, Lowell, and others from all sections of the United States.

This is because, as Marsden writes, "[a]fter the American Revolution, New England Calvinism with a deep Edwardsian imprint emerged as one of the most influential movements shaping the new American voluntary religious culture" (8). Or, to use Alfred Kazin's formula, in *God and the American Writer:* "In the beginning at New England our writers were Calvinists . . ." (3). But, as we have already seen, New England was not unique in this respect. As H. L. Mencken—no partisan of Calvinism in any form—wrote in 1917, "What could be more erroneous than the common assumption that Puritanism is exclusively a Northern, a New England madness?" (205). In support of Mencken's argument, we might cite W. J. Cash's observation about the typical southerner in his highly influential *The Mind of the South:* "And of the intellectual baggage which he brought from Europe and managed to preserve on the frontier, the core and the bulk consisted of the Protestant theology of the sixteenth century and the Dissenting moral code of the seventeenth. . . . The sense of sin, if obscured, continued to move darkly in him at every time—not so darkly, not so savagely, not so relentlessly as in the New Englander, it may be, but with conviction nevertheless" (54). In the judgment of many, this continues to be true of Americans long after the end of frontier days, and not only of southerners or citizens of New England. As Aliki Barnstone, Michael Tomasek Manson, and Carol J. Singley write, in their revealingly titled collection of essays *The Calvinist Roots of the Modern Era*, "In this [twentieth] century, Calvinism appears as a psychological construct, a cultural institution or artifact, a habit of mind, or a sociopolitical structure" (xiii). In literary terms, this means, according to these editors, that "Catholic, Jewish, and African American writers . . . although not in direct lineage from the Puritans, engage Calvinism through their experience as Americans" (xiii). In other words, as Loris Mirella points out in "T. S. Eliot's Calvinist Modernism," an essay in this same collection, "Calvinism is more than a set of religious values; it is also, crucially, a complex structure of beliefs and attitudes that, operating systematically, functions as an intellectual framework for articulating certain attitudes and emotions" (21). In one sense, there is certainly something comic about all of this: that citizens of the country foreseen as the city on a hill, the land of the free and the home of the brave, Eden regained, should think and write as if everyone is in the same lamentable situation of never measuring up to a standard that he or she was born never to reach in the first place. And that is another key to the nature of Calvinist humor: that there is something laughable in all of this seemingly bad news. Norman Foerster writes in his *American Poetry and Prose* (1947): "Three words, it is said, were carved by a former occupant over the mantel of Nathaniel Ward's house in Ipswich, three words summing up the Puritan ethics: *Sobriety, Justice, Piety,* and to these Ward added a fourth—*Laughter*" (8).

First of all, there is the more benign form of this laughter. When something is only to be expected as a part of everyday human nature, it represents one strain of Calvinist humor. Mark Twain and William Faulkner, for example, often root their humor in their recognition that we human beings are all in the same boat. Thus, most readers can easily recognize themselves in Twain's characters and in Faulkner's. Most of us, that is to say, can enter imaginatively into Huckleberry Finn's discomfort when he goes to church with the Grangerfords in chapter 18 of Twain's famous novel:

> Next Sunday we all went to church, about three mile, everybody a-horse-back. The men took their guns along, so did Buck, and kept them between their knees or stood them handy against the wall. The Shephersons done the same. It was pretty ornery preaching—all about brotherly love, and such-like tiresomeness; but everybody said it was a good sermon, and they talked it over going home, and had such a powerful lot to say about faith, and good works, and free grace, and preforeordestination, and I don't know what all, that it did seem to me to be one of the roughest Sundays I had run across yet. (148)

The Christian hypocrisy of churchgoers who engage in a murderous feud is surely an object of Twain's satire here, but the sense that any of us might react to this sermon as Huck does is also powerfully and comically present. The same may be said of the passage in Faulkner's *The Hamlet* when one of Flem Snopes's wild mustangs runs into V. K. Ratliff's bed-room in Mrs. Littlejohn's boarding house:

> Ratliff, in his underclothes and one sock and with the other sock in his hand and his back to the door, was leaning out the open window facing the lane, the lot. He looked back over his shoulder. For an instant he and the horse glared at one another. Then he sprang through the window as the horse backed out of the room and into the hall again and saw Eck and the little boy just entering the front door, Eck still carrying his rope. It whirled again and rushed on down the hall and onto the back porch just as Mrs. Littlejohn, carrying an armful of clothes from the line and the washboard, mounted the steps. (307–8)

During this episode Flem Snopes is engaging in economic skulduggery by exploiting the egos of the male half of Jefferson's population, and that is immoral—by Faulkner's standards and the reader's—but Ratliff's situation is laughable on its own account. He is as astonished at finding a wild horse in his bedroom as any of us might be. When Ratliff (understandably) says about the horse: "[I]f he saw just half as many of me as I saw of him, he was sholy surrounded" (314), we all recognize our own probable reactions in his. What follows this recognition is Calvinist laughter. In the words of C. Hugh Holman's *A Handbook to Literature,* the essence of humor for these American Calvinistic authors is "a sympathetic recognition of human values [that] deals with the foibles and incongruities of human nature, good-naturedly exhibited" (467). Obviously this is the mode preferred by Twain and Faulkner, and yet, if these two writers—and others we will later mention—are to be recognized as Calvinist humorists, these "foibles and incongruities" must be accepted as universally shared.

On the other hand, Nathanael West and Flannery O'Connor always seem to be looking down on their own fictional characters for these characters' perfectly ordinary humanity. In this respect, their ironic authorial distance lends full support to F. H. Buckley's assertion in *The Morality of Laughter* (2003): "Laughter signals our recognition of a comic vice in another person—the butt. We do not share in the vice, for we could not laugh if we did" (4). Putting aside the inapplicability of Buckley's remark to the previously cited examples from Twain and Faulkner, we can see its pertinence to the works of West and O'Connor. This grisly mode of humor can be seen in West's writing when, for example, Peter Doyle, one of the desperate correspondents seeking advice in *Miss Lonelyhearts,* writes at the end of his letter: "Please write me an answer not in the paper because my wife reads your stuff and I dont want her to no I wrote to you because I always said the papers is crap but I figured maybe you no something about it because you have read a lot of books and I never even finished high" (111). Like Twain, West surely has satirical intentions in his book. There is definitely something wrong with a culture when, as West's character Shrike says in the novel, "The Susan Chesters, the Beatrice Fairfaxes and the Miss Lonelyhearts are the priests of twentieth-century America" (62). Despite this serious satire, there is also recognizable Calvinist humor in *Miss Lonelyhearts.* Anyone reading West's novel—not to mention the Brown University graduate who wrote it—can feel superior to Doyle in terms of education and articulateness. Furthermore, such readers probably assume that they would never be so gullible as to seek spiritual guidance from a newspaper columnist like Miss Lonelyhearts. That is to say, West is looking down on Doyle, his own fictional creation, and encouraging us to do the same. This is a tendency he shares with Flannery O'Connor, who writes about the young mother who is soon to be murdered in "A Good Man Is Hard to Find" that her "face was as broad and innocent as a cabbage and was tied around with a green head-kerchief that had two points on top like rabbit's ears" (137). O'Connor provides an equally unsympathetic description of Ruby Hill in "A Stroke of Good Fortune": "Standing up straight, she was a short woman, shaped nearly like a funeral urn. She had mulberry-colored hair stacked in sausage rolls around her head . . ." (184). O'Connor also resembles West in having more serious philosophical issues in mind, mostly issues concerning faith and salvation. At the same time, she just cannot resist a malicious swipe at her own fictional characters. Both West and O'Connor thus epitomize what I have discerned to be the other, harsher strain in American Calvinist humor.

John Moreall focuses on this second dimension of Calvinist humor, in his *Comedy, Tragedy, and Religion,* when he writes, "In the Calvinist vision, not only the damned but even the saved seem to lack human dignity" (116). Moreall's perception—like O'Connor's and West's—can be easily traced to Calvin's own writings. In *The Institutes,* for example, Calvin notes "what mean and lowly little men we are," and he goes on to add: "Before God, of course, we are miserable sinners; in men's eyes most despised—if you will, the offscouring and refuse of the world, or anything viler than can be named" (12). It only makes sense to wish that there were some way to rise above this pathetic (fallen) condition so as to look down on others who are still mired in it. To some Calvinist humorists, like West and O'Connor, there is such a way and this way is to engage in the harsher form of Calvinist humor.

Both of these strains are exhaustively illustrated by some of America's most distinguished authors, and this is the subject of my book. William Bradford is not alone, for example, in epitomizing a Puritanical form of Calvinist humor. Especially in the works of Michael Wigglesworth and Jonathan Edwards, Bradford's highly censorious form of humor lives on. Both Wigglesworth's poem "The Day of Doom" and Edwards's famous sermon "Sinners in the Hands of an Angry God" joyfully predict the sufferings of the damned even while confidently sparing the speakers these torments. The Puritan settler Mary Rowlandson understandably shares some of these same attitudes, especially toward the Native Americans that she calls "wolves" and "hell-hounds," but in her account of her own

Indian captivity she frequently allows us to see also the kind of common human failings in her own behavior that Twain and Faulkner are so attracted to. My next chapter, then, will point to examples of both sorts of Calvinist humor in the writings of some distinguished American Puritans.

As an ideological descendant of the Puritans, Nathaniel Hawthorne is the subject of the following chapter—chapter 3. Since Hawthorne is less univocal in his Calvinist humor than most of his predecessors, it will naturally turn out that his depiction of these issues will be more ambiguous than the historical records. In his shorter fiction and in his novel *The Blithedale Romance,* Hawthorne repeatedly finds humor sometimes in recognizing common human failings of fictional characters like Adam Forrester and Lilias Fay and sometimes in looking down on the failings of characters like Richard Digby and Young Goodman Brown, whom he has himself created. Hawthorne is, then, unquestionably a Calvinist humorist in both senses of the term that I have been using.

Hawthorne's friend and onetime neighbor, Herman Melville, is the subject of chapter 4. Basing my argument on Melville's later works, *The Confidence Man* and *The Piazza Tales,* I explore in this chapter what one critic has called "Melville's quarrel with God"[12] in order to see if this quarrel produces any Calvinist humor. When we see the passengers on the *Fidèle* foolishly falling prey to the confidence man or when we watch Amasa Delano confidently assuming in "Benito Cereno" that he cannot be in mortal danger from the rebellious slaves aboard the *San Dominick* because he can clearly remember his innocent childhood as Jack of the Beach, we must conclude that the various ships of fools that Melville writes about amply supply our needs for this kind of bitter amusement. Melville is clearly a Calvinist humorist.

Mark Twain definitely belongs to this fraternity of humorists, too, as I have already indicated, and so it is only appropriate that he serve as the subject of chapter 5. Sometimes, as in the horrific occurrences depicted in his shorter fiction, Twain emphasizes the distance from perfection common among men and beasts. Whether his fictional characters are trying to deal with jumping frogs or what they believe to be human corpses, they display the failings common to most human beings. Also, in the astringent depictions of human nature presented in his very disturbing novel *Pudd'nhead Wilson* and in the bitter reflections on human nature attributed to Pudd'nhead Wilson's Calendars in this novel and in *Following the Equator,* Twain makes Calvinist jokes about the sorry condition in which we all frequently find ourselves. Other texts by Twain, including *The Mysterious Stranger* (1900) and "The Man That Corrupted Hadleyburg" (1900), obviously could be cited as evidence of this disposition, but my original point is that Twain can be seen as a Calvinist humorist no matter where we plug into his work.

In chapter 6, William Faulkner is the topic, and Faulkner's novels *Light in August, Absalom, Absalom!* and *The Hamlet,* are the primary illustrative texts. Although Faulkner's unillusioned view of life causes Calvinist humor to appear throughout his works,[13] these three, very different novels epitomize his practice of the mode that serves as my topic in this book. As Faulkner's recent biographer Jay Parini observes, *Light in August,* the first of these three novels, concerns "a society driven wild by its dark Calvinism and racism" (206). The same may be said of all his books. Thus, Edmond L. Volpe plausibly concludes in *A Reader's Guide to William Faulkner,* "The concept of racial superiority, with its attendant fear and guilt, molds and controls the individual, just as the Calvinistic-rooted religion, with its emphasis upon sin and punishment, death and damnation, steers him away from life by directing his gaze toward death" (173). Through Faulkner's residual southern Calvinism, we can see in these novels—and other of his novels and short stories—evidence of our common (fallen) human nature as these (often comic) illustrations strike one of America's premiere writers of modernist fiction. To Faulkner, it is a Calvinist truism that we are all susceptible to being fooled as Lena Grove is fooled in *Light in August* and as the horse buyers in *The Hamlet* are fooled. It is equally likely and only to be expected from fallen man that we will be frustrated by circumstance, as characters are in all of Faulkner's works. V. K. Ratliff observes about Ab Snopes's gulling by Pat Stamper, the genius horse trader, in *The Hamlet,* "[I]t was not only right and natural that Ab would have to pass Stamper to get to Jefferson, but it was foreordained and fated that he would have to" (38). That is to say, there is no way for Ab to avoid making a fool of himself, and there is no way for the rest of us either. Thus, although the subject matter in this fiction is admittedly as grim as all the critics claim, there is still a level of Calvinist humor in Faulkner's fiction equal to that evident in the works of the American Puritans or of Mark Twain.

Another saint of American literary modernism is the subject of chapter 7. In Ernest Hemingway's fiction, especially in the collection of stories *In Our Time* and the famous novel *The Sun Also Rises,* we can see a Calvinist sensibility at work even after all forms of Christianity—perhaps even of religion—have disappeared from the writer's life. Calvinist humor still results as characters like Robert Cohn and a drunken bullfighter fail to measure up to the standards that critics have identified as the Hemingway "code," and as such displaced Calvinistic successes as Nick Adams and Jake Barnes succeed in doing so.

There is little religious orthodoxy remaining in the novels of Nathanael West either, and yet the secular/Jewish West shares with the ostensibly Protestant American writers treated earlier a Calvinist understanding of human nature and a humorist's resolve to bring this understanding to our attention even while making us laugh bitterly. West's characters are equally cut off from hope and from dignity. This is perhaps only to be expected because, as Aliki Barnstone, Michael Tomasek Manson, and Carol J. Singley maintain in *The Calvinist Roots of the Modern Era,* "Catholic, Jewish, and African American writers . . . although not in direct lineage from the Puritans, engage Calvinism through their experience as Americans" (xiii).[14] In all of West's novels, the pathetic efforts of his characters to find some sense of value to replace a vanished religious orthodoxy are bitterly frustrated. West's writers, artists, and economic strivers all find that there is nothing to hope for and that this is as good as it's going to get. These characters foolishly continue to believe in some sort of (usually secular) salvation, however, and so they merit West's bitter Calvinist laughter. Therefore, West also merits a chapter—chapter 8.

Probably no American writer deserves the designation *bitter* more truly than Flannery O'Connor, the subject of my last chapter of discussion. Although she drastically differs from Hemingway and West in her professions of religious orthodoxy, O'Connor reveals throughout her career a bleakly humorous form of criticism that either of these earlier writers—or their historical ancestors—might envy. Whether ridiculing the small conceits of Mrs. Freeman and Hulga in "Good Country People" and other characters in her short stories or laughing roundly at the delusions of characters like Hazel Motes in her novel *Wise Blood*, O'Connor seems driven to expose how far her fictional creations depart from any sort of prelapsarian norm and to encourage us to join in her Calvinist laughter at their antics.

What is so funny about all of this and what it all adds up to is the subject of my concluding chapter, "Calvinist Humor Revisited."

As this introductory discussion perhaps shows, the definition of Calvinist humor that I develop throughout this book definitely involves some consideration of situation. Creating or recognizing Calvinist humor involves a position of superiority from which we may recognize what the subject of the humor, the butt of the joke, usually cannot: that this subject is behaving as a fallen human being—however religiously or secularly this fallen nature may be defined—might be expected to behave, all the while without realizing that he or she is doing so. When the viewer is *only* superior to the butt of the joke—as is usually the case in West's work and O'Connor's—the humor is Calvinistic, and it offers little emotional release. When the viewer is simultaneously superior to *and also* aware of being equally involved as a participant in fallen human nature, as so often in the fiction of Twain and Faulkner, then Calvinist humor—despite its intimidating title—can be both pleasurable and liberating. This sustained effort at definition has been the same. Although I can agree with Huck Finn that "if I'd a knowed what a trouble it was to make a [definition] I wouldn't a tackled it and I aint agoing to no more" (366), I am glad that I tried to do so just this once.

2 Calvinist Humor and the American Puritans
"The Just Hand of God"

It is impossible to think about the history of the United States of America without thinking about the Puritans who settled New England in the seventeenth century. The Pilgrim fathers, the first Thanksgiving, John Alden and Miles Standish—all are ineradicable parts of the American imagination. As Samuel E. Morison writes in his preface to William Bradford's *Of Plymouth Plantation* (1630–50), "[T]his story . . . has made the Pilgrim Fathers in a sense the spiritual ancestors of all Americans, all pioneers" (xii). All Americans, that is to say, must trace themselves imaginatively back in some way to the people who have somehow caused Thanksgiving to be celebrated as an autumn harvest festival—complete with pumpkin pie and cranberries—even in sunny places like Phoenix, Arizona, and Los Angeles, California.[1]

At the same time, these Puritans have come down in the imagination of later Americans as decidedly on the side of what Nathaniel Hawthorne calls "gloom" in his story "The May-Pole of Merry Mount," rather than on the side of "jollity," and as the social influence that—according to Henry Adams's autobiography—regards "sex [as] a species of crime."[2] In Hawthorne's tale, the jolly colonists of Merry Mount sing and dance around a phallic maypole to the unbearable annoyance of the gloomy Puritans, "most dismal wretches, who said their prayers before daylight, and then wrought in the forest or the cornfield, till evening made it prayer time again" (365). In Adams's account, Boston is a morally chilly contrast to the nation's capital, with its "intermixture of delicate grace and passionate depravity" (268).[3] For both of these American literary artists, steeped for generations in the influence of Puritanism, the culture of New England epitomizes all that is upright and uptight in American life. Max Weber explains this disposition among the elect in *The Protestant Ethic and the Spirit of Capitalism:* "Combined with the harsh doctrines of the absolute transcendentality of God and the corruption of everything pertaining to the flesh, this inner isolation of the individual contains, on the one hand, the reason for the entirely negative attitude of Puritanism to all sensuous and emotional elements of culture and in religion, because they are of no use toward salvation and promote sentimental illusions and idolatrous superstitions. Thus it provides a basis for a fundamental antagonism to sensuous culture of all kinds" (105). Given all this attention, positive and negative, we might reasonably expect the American Puritans to be included in any history of American Calvinism.

Humor, though, may be a different issue altogether since most of us probably are initially disposed to agree with Constance Rourke, who wrote in her history of humor in America, "As the texture of early Puritan life is examined, sources of Yankee strength become apparent, but not of Yankee humor; for humor is a matter of fantasy, and the fantasies of the Puritan, viewed with the most genial eye, remain sufficiently dark" (9).[4] It may just be, though, that this very darkness is the key to what I am talking about. Hawthorne's tale, although it is admittedly dark, still has its weirdly amusing side, as when Endicott, the leader of the Puritans, says that, after the Puritans have dragged the defeated and captured Merry Mount colonists to civilization, "[F]urther penalties, such as branding and cropping of ears, shall be thought of . . ." (368). This joke—if joke there is—is a grim one indeed, but the excessive severity of the Puritans is somewhat laughable even so. The extremity of Hawthorne's vision is matched in E. A. Robinson's poem "New England," where "the wind is always north, north-east / And children learn to walk on Frozen toes" (ll. 1–2). All of this is just too bad to be true! People who think this way are ludicrous, but—apparently—so is the observer who provides this insight. Adams's excessive irony in *The Education of Henry Adams* also paints the citizens of Boston in too grim a light to be taken with absolute seriousness.[5] As this autobiographer candidly admits, "Henry was in a savage humor on the subject of Boston" (269), and this "savage humor" decidedly colors his treatment of the region and its inhabitants. In this regard, Hawthorne, Robinson, and Adams all engage in Calvinist humor.

As I noted in the previous chapter, there is a similar kind of Calvinist humor at work when William Bradford invites us to chuckle in *Of Plymouth Plantation* at the fate of the 950 stricken Indians who "did rot above ground for want of burial" (270). This Calvinistically humorous effect is somewhat surprising, perhaps, since James D. Hart describes Bradford's history in *The Oxford Companion to American Literature* in terms of its "dignified, sonorous style, deriving from the Geneva Bible." In consequence, Hart says, "The Narrative is naturally grave . . ." (660). As Ian Marshall explains, "Bradford's intention in using [the] tools of humor is rarely to be funny, but humor need not be, and usually is not, devoid of serious purpose" (158). Thus Bradford wants us to see something supernaturally funny about these rotting Indians. Characteristically, Bradford takes no personal responsibility for the potentially humorous aspects of this perception, since the Indians' sickness occurred only because "it pleased God" that it should be so. This combination of dark laughter and freedom from personal moral responsibility often characterizes the Calvinist humor of the Puritans—and of their successors, including Nathanael West and Flannery O'Connor.

Another example from Bradford's account, also based on divine intervention in physical illness, should make this clear. In the earliest days of the Puritan settlement, a great sickness afflicted the Pilgrims while they were still on board their ships so that they "were hasted ashore and made to drink water that the seamen might have the more beer." Even accepting beer as the normal beverage of the day rather than as an aid to "jollity," it must seem clear that the sailors are seeking their own happiness and comfort at the expense of the Saints. Then, when "one [Pilgrim] in his sickness" asked for "but a small can of beer," he was answered by the sailors that "if it were their own father he should have none." Up until this point, the emotional direction of the anecdote is all toward sympathy for the grievously afflicted Puritans. Then, once again, as in the case of the stricken Indians, God intervenes on behalf of the Puritans so that "[t]he disease began to fall amongst [the sailors] also, so as almost half of their company died before they went away, and many of their officers and lustiest men, as the boatswain, gunner, three quartermasters, the cook and others." In the face of such clearly appropriate divine intervention, "the Master was something stricken and sent to the sick ashore and told the Governor he should send for beer for them that had need of it, though he drunk water homeward bound" (78). Bradford is obviously pleased that God showed these sailors who was boss in this way, and he expects us to show our equivalent pleasure by smiling a dry Calvinist smile at the way things turned out.

Moses Coit Tyler, the first real historian of American literature, makes a similar point about the impact of the stories in *Of Plymouth Plantation:* "The prevailing trait of its pages is of course grave; but at times this sedateness is relieved by a quaint and pithy emphasis of phrase that amounts almost to humor. But a writer like Bradford is more likely to condescend to a solemn sort of sarcasm than to humor . . ." (128). Ian Marshall agrees: "Bradford's *Of Plymouth Plantation* is admittedly not the stuff of high comedy, but Bradford frequently can elicit a smile" (158). Although the critical missions of Tyler and Marshall are, admittedly, quite different from mine, it still seems to me that their judgments of Bradford's stylistics apply to the examples I have cited already and to the following case—my favorite joke in Bradford's whole book. On the original journey across the Atlantic, there occurred what Bradford identifies as "a special work of God's providence." "There was a proud and very profane young man," he writes, "one of the seamen, of a lusty, able body, which made him the more haughty." This heathenish sailor "would always be contemning the poor people in their sickness and cursing them daily with grievous execrations; and did not let to tell them that he hoped to help to cast half of them overboard before they came to their journey's end, and to make merry with what they had; and if he were by any gently reproved, he would curse and swear more bitterly." As in the case of the sailors who refused to give any of the Pilgrims even "a small can of beer," the reader's human sympathies are initially engaged by the lamentable situation of these idealistic people who seem merely to be trying to fulfill what they see as a divine mandate. As in the case cited earlier, moreover, the hand of God comes down to balance the scales more favorably to the Puritans: "But it pleased God before they came half seas over, to smite this young man with a grievous disease, of which he died in a desperate manner, and so was himself the first that was thrown overboard." Just in case anyone misses the point of this Calvinist joke, Bradford adds: "Thus his curses light on his own head, and it was an astonishment to all his fellows for they noted it to be the just hand of God upon him" (58).

From a Calvinist perspective, the sailor's fellow crewmen are right on target in their understanding of what has been going on here because, as Calvin writes in *The Institutes of the Christian Religion,* "[I]f every success is God's blessing, and calamity and adversity his curse, no place now remains in human affairs for fortune or chance" (207). If this cursing sailor appropriately died while making things unpleasant for the Puritan Saints, chance is not involved in the case. God was just doing what a faithful Puritan might expect. Throughout *Of Plymouth Plantation,* Bradford develops incidents that he surely intends to be understood as humorous in this sense of Calvinistic appropriateness. The Reverend John Lyford, for example, tried to influence the English supporters of the colony to repudiate Bradford's associates, encouraging partisanship and discord among those who might ideally be expected to live in perfect harmony. The hand of God once again intervenes on the side favored by Bradford, however: "And so these troubles produced a quite contrary effect, in sundry here, than those adversaries hoped for. Which was looked at as a great work of God, to draw on men by unlikely means, and that in reason might rather have set them further off" (164). It is significant, it seems to me, that Bradford attributes none of these happy results to the strength of his own theological position or to his own wisdom in guiding the colony or, conversely, to human flaws in Lyford's strategy. We must recognize, he says, that what happened was "a great work of God" even as we applaud its humorous appropriateness. This is Ian Marshall's point when he writes that "Bradford's black humor . . . results from the satisfactory working-out of a divine plan in which sinners get punished. It is poetic justice, in which the fitting end is comic (though not necessarily funny) because the audience can see it coming, and approves, while the sinners remain foolishly unaware of their inevitable, well-deserved ill fate" (164). The same may be said for the comeuppance that divine providence dished out to John Peirce. Despite all of Peirce's efforts to profit at the Puritans' expense, Bradford says, "I am sorry to write how many here think that the hand of God was justly against him, both the first and the second time of his return" (125). This is just how things work out when you are on the wrong side—that is to say, on the non-Puritan side, the side opposed by "the hand of God."

The story of Isaac Allerton—who, according to a note supplied by Samuel Eliot Morison, "used his fellows even worse than did the merchants [sic] adventures" (184, n. 1)—makes a similarly humorous point. With an eye to personal profit, Allerton always seemed to be pursuing some plan to score a financial coup at the Puritans' expense. In 1628, when things turned out badly for him, he—unsurprisingly—abandoned his associates to save himself, leaving it up to them to look out for their own necks. In Bradford's words, "And to mend the matter, Mr. Allerton doth in a sort wholly desert them; having brought them into the briars, he leaves them to get out as they can." As in so many other cases in which someone else's interests opposed those of the Puritans, however, "God crossed him mightily." In specific economic terms—terms of which Bradford is usually quite fond—"having hired the ship of Mr. Sherley at £ 30 a month, [Allerton] set forth again with a most wicked and drunken crew, and for covetousness' sake did so overlade her, not only filling her hold but so stuffed her between decks as she was walte [unsteady], and could not bear sail. And they had been like to have been cast away at sea, and were forced to put for Milford Haven and new stow her, and put some of their ordnance and more heavy goods in the bottom. Which lost them time and made them come late into the country, lose their season, and made a worse voyage than the year before" (244). As Calvin maintains, "God so attends to the regulation of individual events, and they all so proceed from his set plan, that nothing takes place by chance" (203), including—or, perhaps, especially including—matters of largely financial significance.

But Allerton's bad example can be used to illustrate other comically appropriate Calvinistic points also. Bradford draws this lesson in connection with the "wicked and drunken crew" mentioned in the previous anecdote: "The rest of those he trusted, being loose and drunken fellows, did for the most part but cozen and cheat him of all they got into their hands. [So] that howsoever he did his friends some hurt hereby for the present, yet he gat little good, but went by the loss by God's just hand" (245; Morison's brackets). All events seem to point in the same, providentially validated direction.

Despite his ideological disagreements with Bradford and his associates, even Moses Coit Tyler must concede that Bradford's "history is an orderly, lucid, and most instructive work . . ." (124). Therefore, most modern conservative thinkers, including those of a religious persuasion, might be inclined to second Bradford's final judgment on the plausibility of communal ownership: "The experience that was had in this common course and condition, tried sundry years and that amongst godly and sober men, may well evince the vanity of that conceit of Plato's and other ancients applauded by some of later times; that the taking away of property and bringing in community into a commonwealth would make them happy and flourishing; as if they were wiser than God" (120–21). Bradford might seem equally wise to this audience when he considers the possibility that unrighteousness might spring up even among the godly: "Another reason may be, that it may be in this case as it is with waters when their streams are stopped or damned up. When they get passage they flow with more violence and make more noise and disturbance than when they are suffered to run quietly in their own channels; so wickedness being here more stopped by strict laws, and the same more nearly looked unto so as it cannot run in a common road of liberty as it would and is inclined, it searches everywhere and at last breaks out where it gets vent" (316–17). One such conservative thinker, George M. Marsden, opines that the historical Calvinist should be understood to "hold . . . to a realistic view of human nature" (246–47). That this is the view shared by Hawthorne and Faulkner will appear more clearly later on.

It seems to me that the examples cited so far may have created the impression that Puritan Calvinist humor necessarily partakes of the Pharisaical.[6] To show that this is not necessarily the case, let me recount Bradford's tale of Captain Thomas Cromwell, who put down a riot by a group of raucous sailors by using his sword to kill "a desperate fellow of the company." All of the right-thinking Puritans were pleased by this development, and at first it seemed that God would reward the just in the same way that He punished the wicked: "This Captain Thomas Cromwell set forth another voyage to the West Indies from the Bay of Massachusetts, well manned and victualed, and was out three years, and took sundry prizes and returned rich to Massachusetts." The humorous irony that was the signature of the God of the Puritans was still in effect, however, as Bradford's story goes on to show: "And there [Cromwell] died the same summer, having got a fall from his horse, in which fall he fell on his rapier hilt and so bruised his body as he shortly after died thereof, with some other distempers which brought him into a fever. Some observed that there might be something of the hand of God herein; that as the forenamed man died of the blow he gave him with the rapier hilt, so his own death was occasioned by like means" (346). Bradford does not say whether he was among the "some" who saw the hand of Providence at work in Cromwell's death; each of his readers may decide for him- or herself and probably titter accordingly.

However one decides, it should be clear that the humor of Bradford's grim justice arises from his perception of the mote in others' eyes, irrespective of whether he admits to the beam in his own.[7] As we have seen, H. L. Mencken writes about the Puritanically inclined, in "Puritanism as a Literary Force": "[T]he sinner who excited his highest zeal and passion was not so much himself as his neighbour [sic]; to borrow a term from psychopathology, he was much less the masochist than the sadist" (232). This is the tendency in Calvinism that F. H. Buckley reports on in *The Morality of Laughter* when he notes that, according to the medieval theologian Tertullian, "One of the particular joys of heaven, it seems, will be the ability to peer down from on high and observe the sufferings of sinners in Hell" (8). That this is not an admirable form of amusement is undeniable, but that it is an eternal joy anticipated by many Puritan writers is equally undeniable. In his very sympathetic biography of Jonathan Edwards, for example, Marsden writes, "In one of his more controversial observations, Edwards argued that the saints in heaven would rejoice in knowing of the punishment of the wicked" (536, n. 15).

This amused vindictiveness is readily apparent in Bradford's history and in many other Puritan texts, but it is—surprisingly—less obvious in what Mason I. Lowance, Jr., calls a "special variant . . . of the providential history theme" (76), Mary Rowlandson's justly famous *The Sovereignty and Goodness of God* (1682). Lowance describes Rowlandson's account of her Indian captivity during King Philip's War as part of "a generic subgroup in which the reader not only finds the predictable sense of God's providential guidance in the safe deliverance of his elected saints from the pagan Indians but is also witness to the autobiographer's immersion in a Native American culture quite foreign to his own" (76). As this critical passage attests, twentieth- and twenty-first-century critics intent on discovering multicultural resonances in earlier texts may well find Mrs. Rowlandson's descriptions of her captors anthropologically valuable, but it is clear to most readers that the author's original motives participate much more in the project of Calvinist humor than in any effort to pay suitable homage to "Native American culture."

First of all, Mrs. Rowlandson characterizes her captors as "murtherous wretches" (68), "bloody Heathen" (69), "Wolves," and "hell-hounds" (70), as well as using other highly pejorative terms. Then, she recounts the horrific incident in which she and her mortally wounded daughter, Sarah, fell from a horse and "they like inhumane creatures laught, and rejoiced to see it, though I thought we should have ended our dayes, as overcome with so many difficulties" (73). She is censorious also about the customs of Indian warfare: "But before they came to us, Oh! the outrageous roaring and whooping that there was: They began their din about a mile before they came to us. By their noise and whooping they signified how many they had destroyed (which was at that time twenty three)" (76). Even though dangerous and murderous, these Indians can be appropriately looked down on as childish. Another incident seems at first to follow the same pattern of demonstrating white superiority: "I went with a good load at my back (for they when they went, though but a little way, would carry all their trumpery with them) I told them the skin was off my back . . ." (87). The Indians' involvement in "trumpery" is very much what a superior (civilized) white person like Mrs. Rowlandson—or William Bradford—might expect. When the Indians answer her "that it would be no matter if my head were off too," we begin to see another, more appealing side of the narrative. Mrs. Rowlandson is willing to write about herself in terms of the less censorious form of Calvinist humor, the side that is more willing to see that the speaker is not always right, that she can laugh at herself, that she is just another fallen creature among many.

It is this dimension of *The Sovereignty and Goodness of God* that makes Mrs. Rowlandson's account one of the more appealing instances of Calvinist humor among the American Puritan writers. Typically, Mrs. Rowlandson honestly writes that, before her captivity, she believed "I should chuse rather to be killed by them than be taken alive," but when the event actually occurred, "my mind changed: their glittering weapons so daunted my spirit that I chose rather to go along [as a prisoner]" (70). There is, in other words, a world of difference between what we heroically plan out in the peace and privacy of our rooms and what actually happens in life. How true! we must observe. There is also a vast difference between how we behave in the security of society and how we find ourselves behaving in the wilderness. In testimony to this, we can note Mrs. Rowlandson's reflections on the first Sabbath of her captivity: "I then remembered how careless I had been of Gods holy time: how many Sabbaths I had lost and misspent . . ." (74). Any of us might entertain similar regrets in similar circumstances, and this is one key to Rowlandson's Calvinist humor. As in the case of Twain's maxims in *Pudd'nhead Wilson*, the recognizable truth of the observation will touch most readers. This is also the case when Mrs. Rowlandson realizes that, even though she had done nothing outrageously harmful to any of her Puritan neighbors, "I saw how in my walk with God, I had been a careless creature . . ." (91). In fact, we may even suspect that she is being too hard on herself. We can, though, agree totally with her feelings toward the close of her narrative. Before her captivity, she writes, "I should be sometimes jealous least I have my portion [of trial and suffering] in this life," but after the fact she can see, "Affliction I wanted, and affliction I had, full measure (I thought) pressed down and running over" (112). Who could think otherwise after all the events recorded in this narrative? And yet, we smile even as we nod in agreement.

Another side of Mrs. Rowlandson's narrative style is also likely to win over most readers, and that is her very human foibles. She says regarding the initial Indian attack on her homestead, for example, "We had six stout Dogs belonging to our Garrison, but none of them would stir, though another time, if any Indian had come to the door, they were ready to fly upon him and tear him down" (69). This canine inactivity can be seen in retrospect to be Providential: if the dogs had driven off the Indians, then Mrs. Rowlandson would not have undergone her cleansing trials. Even so, it can easily be seen in the time of immediate crisis as typical doggy behavior: when you don't need their help, dogs are everywhere; when you really need them, they are nowhere to be found. Another detail likely to strike most readers as typical is the usually starving Mrs. Rowlandson's willingness to eat whatever she could get her hands on. By the third week of her captivity, she reports, "[T]hough I could think how formerly my stomach would turn against this or that, and I could starve and die before I could eat such things, yet they were sweet and savory to my taste" (79). In illustration, there is the account later on of an occasion on which Mrs. Rowlandson and a small English child are each given a hunk of horse's hoof to eat. Mrs. Rowlandson immediately scarfs hers down, but "the Child could not bite it, it was so tough and sinewy, but lay sucking, gnawing, chewing and slobbering of it in the mouth and hand." So, Mrs. Rowlandson "took it of the Child, and ate it myself" (96). Even as we are impressed by the honesty of her account, we must recognize how apt we would be to do the same in the same circumstances. The overall rationale for this kind of all-too-human behavior is that exiguous circumstances tend to focus one's attention on oneself. This point is confirmed when Mrs. Rowlandson's son, who is also a captive, tells her that he spends much of his time feeling sorry for his absent father, who must surely lament the capture of his family. Mrs. Rowlandson says that she "wondered at his speech" because "I had enough upon my spirit in reference to my self, to make me mindless of my Husband and every one else: they being safe among their Friends" (89). Under the circumstances, it is probable that most of us would curse our worthless dogs, eagerly eat whatever we could get our hands on, and think about our current woes instead of our safe loved ones.

But, after all, Mrs. Rowlandson writes as an American Puritan, and in this sense she is both like the rest of us and radically different. She accepts, for example, that the worst that can happen to her is no more than she deserves simply for being descended from Adam and Eve.[8] Therefore, she reflects about God's goodness in providing her with so much suffering: "But I knew he laid upon me less than I deserved" (88). This sense of immediate Providential attention individually to her is evident throughout Mrs. Rowlandson's account, especially in the aptness of the Bible verses that she encounters every time she turns to the scriptures for consolation. This is true even when she first opens the Bible that an Indian had recovered in a raid on Medfield and comes across very discouraging news in Deuteronomy 28 about iron yokes and heavenly curses. Fortunately, she reads on until she gets to the highly encouraging thirtieth chapter so that she can conclude: "There was mercy promised again, if we would return to him by repentance, and though we were scattered from one end of the earth to the other, yet the Lord would gather us together, and turn those curses upon our enemies" (77).

This last pious reflection points toward another strain of Calvinist humor in this famous captivity narrative. If we, guided merely by our human intellects, were in charge, there is no question that the (white) settlers would be on top in every way. But, because of the inscrutable designs of divine Providence, the Indians sometimes seem to be winning. Even this is a good thing, however, because it is a sign of God's dissatisfaction with the Puritans, as Mrs. Rowlandson explains: "But now our perverse and evil carriages in the sight of the Lord, have so offended Him, that instead of turning His hand against [the Indians], the Lord feeds and nourishes them up to be a scourge to the whole Land" (106). There can be no other explanation for the apparent success of the settlers' enemies. Luckily, though, the Lord eventually feels that the Puritans have learned their lesson, and so the tide turns against the Indians: "[T]hough they had made a pit, in their own imaginations, as deep as hell for the Christians that Summer, yet the Lord hurll'd themselves into it. And the Lord had not so many wayes before to preserve them, but now he hath as many to destroy them" (107). Not only is Mrs. Rowlandson to be restored to her husband and community, but the war will soon incline generally toward the English settlers. Typically, the Indian who cursed and abused Mrs. Rowlandson's sister during the latter's captivity "was hanged afterward at Boston" (102). Here, Mrs. Rowlandson sounds much more like William Bradford reveling in the misery of other fallen creatures and much less like Mark Twain recognizing their common fallen state.

On one final subject, though, Mary Rowlandson sounds like no one but herself. Throughout the narrative, ransom money is a major concern. The final ransom for Mrs. Rowlandson, for example, is concluded at twenty pounds. In a specially happy and comic turn of events, Mrs. Rowlandson's daughter, Mary, is ransomed totally without cost. Mary and her Indian guide just wandered away from the tribe and ended up in English hands. Mrs. Rowlandson sounds ecstatic in reporting this: "The Indians often said, that I should never have her under twenty pounds: But now the Lord hath brought her in upon free-cost, and given her to me a second time" (110). The triumph of the cash nexus is, as usual, a cause for celebration. Max Weber makes this point about Calvinism in characteristically swollen terminology: "Capitalism was the social counterpart of Calvinist theology" (2). Mrs. Rowlandson makes a similar point in scriptural terms by way of a quotation from Ecclesiastes: "Mony answers all things" (111). I will admit that when I first read this passage years ago, I had doubts about whether this was an actual Bible verse, but sure enough Ecclesiastes 10.19 reads, "A feast is made for laughter, and wine maketh merry, but money answereth all things." Given the circumstances obtaining in Puritan New England, it was probably prudent of Mrs. Rowlandson to downplay the feast and wine parts of this verse, but money has always been a valued part of American culture—and often of Calvinist humor. Whatever the case, I have always found these parts of *The Sovereignty and Goodness of God* very funny.

Oddly enough, the same may be said for Michael Wigglesworth's *The Day of Doom* (1662). According to Kenneth Murdock, this poem "sets forth more vividly [than any other Puritan text] what Calvinism meant for individuals, sects, nations, [so that] for years [it] influenced . . . all the activities of life by its curious hold on the mind of man" (ix). This is not necessarily unmixed praise of the poet and his poem. Roy Harvey Pearce, for example, calls it "the most notorious of Puritan poems" (20), and Moses Coit Tyler argues in a balanced analysis that "[t]his great poem . . . with entire unconsciousness, attributed to the divine Being a character the most execrable and loathsome to be met with, perhaps, in any literature, Christian or pagan . . ." (294). The sticking point for Tyler, it seems to me, is Wigglesworth's willing acceptance of an understanding of life and its inevitable resolution in the Last Judgment that is inflected by Calvinist humor. Up until the Last Judgment, people who cannot be counted among the Saints will often seem to be very much in the saddle as the Indians were in Mrs. Rowlandson's account. However, according to Wigglesworth, things will not always remain that way: "Calm was the season, and carnal reason / thought so 'twould last for ay" (#1, ll. 3–4). Sooner or later, the tables will be turned—by God—and then the first will be last and the last first.[9] This is what the poem says: "The Saints behold with courage bold, / and thankful wonderment, / To see all those that were their foes / thus sent to punishment" (#19, ll. 1–4). This "thankful wonderment" very closely resembles the attitude of someone who sees hostile Indians perishing of plague or an obnoxious Indian ending up on the scaffold in Boston. In Wigglesworth's case, we should recognize the added satisfaction of understanding that this triumph will go on forever-more.[10] The only appropriate response for the Saints is, Ha! Ha!

This is one of the recurring themes of *The Day of Doom,* the unde-niable pleasure of seeing one's enemies "get theirs"—and, delightfully, not at the hands of some puny human agency, but of an almighty God. Later in the poem, Wigglesworth writes about the Saints and the (justly) damned again, this time treating them in reverse order: "Such whom they slighted, and once despighted / must now their Judges be!" (# 50, ll. 3–4). After hearing Bradford's version of Puritan history, and reading even a few lines from Wigglesworth, we can easily anticipate the severe judgments that will be meted out by these "Judges." While some soft-hearted readers might claim such vindictiveness to be inappropriate for true Christians and call instead for mercy, Wigglesworth's Saints see the theological foolishness of such views and say instead, "Now such com-passion is out of fashion, / and wholly laid aside" (# 196, ll. 5–6). Given the premises outlined by the Synod of Dort, there is no reason to feel sorry for anyone condemned to eternal hellfire. The damned had plenty of chances to repent in this life and failed to do so: "You oft were told, and might behold, / that Death no Age doth spare; / Why then did you your time foreslow, / and slight your Souls welfare?" (#112, ll. 5–8). But, suppose someone should object that the human soul is incapable of repentance on its own: "You argue then: But abject men, / whom God resolves to spill, / Cannot repent, nor their hearts rent; ne can they change their will" (#153, ll. 1–4). To Wigglesworth, there is still reason enough to condemn these folks to eternal hellfire—just for being human and fallen. As Norman Foerster writes, *The Day of Doom* is "little more than versified Calvinism" (12).[11] In Calvinist terms, there is no reason to quarrel and quibble about anything that is predicted to happen in the poem. Max Weber summarizes this Calvinist attitude in this way: "For the damned to complain of their lot would be much the same as for animals to bemoan the fact they were not born as men" (103). As a foundation for such thinking, John Calvin writes in *The Institutes*: "[W]hile the wicked on the contrary flourish, are prosperous, obtain repose with dignity and that without punishment—we must straightaway conclude that there will be another life in which iniquity is to have its punishment, and righteousness is to be given its reward" (62–63). Thus, the damned soul's quarreling and quibbling about mercy and forgiveness only increase the naughty pleasure of seeing those who thought they had it made in worldly terms go plummeting down to hell.[12] This effect is consistent with Roy Harvey Pearce's judgment that, "at a time when Puritans were already backsliding," this poem "was intended to renew in them a sense of their obligations as Puritans and of the justness of God's way with both the elect and the damned" (20). This, then, gives the poem and its author a sound theological footing, but it possibly does little toward evoking a chuckle from readers today.

The problem involved in finding *The Day of Doom* a work of Calvinist humor arises with especial force in the poem's treatment of unbaptized babies, who are—in terms of theological consistency—also destined for eternal hellfire. About this aspect of the poem, Kenneth Murdock writes in extenuation, "Repulsive as is the picture of the wretched children in *The Day of Doom,* it is the picture which countless Christians of different sects in many periods must have drawn had they faced, as Wigglesworth did, the task of revealing all the imagined details of the last judgment." He adds that "[a]ny good Calvinist would have found it hard to think of their [the condemned infants'] situation as better than that which Wigglesworth gives them in 'the easiest room in Hell'" (viii). Here Murdock is referring to the passage in the poem in which Wigglesworth softens the harsh inevitability of eternal punishment by having God say to the infants: "But unto you I shall allow / the easiest room in Hell" (# 181, ll. 3–4). Perhaps, as Murdock explains, many "good Calvinists" would endorse Wigglesworth's view, but most contemporary American readers would find it hard to do so—or to find anything funny in the way the whole poem treats these babies. As Moses Coit Tyler writes, "No one holding a different theology from that held by Michael Wigglesworth, can do justice to him as a poet, without exercising the utmost intellectual catholicity; otherwise, disgust and destestation for much of the poet's message, will drown all sense of the picturesqueness, the imaginative vigor, the tremendous realism, of many of the conceptions under which his message was delivered" (284). But Tyler's judgment is, after all, an aesthetic one, and we are interested here primarily in humor.

According to Murdock, Wigglesworth was himself concerned about the dangers of humor: "Let me rather live a melancholy life all my days, than by merriment run into a course of provoking my God" (qtd. in Murdock vi). Few readers are likely to feel that Wigglesworth traveled very far on this dangerous course. Like the Endicott who appears in Hawthorne's tale, he seems far more disposed toward "gloom" than to "jollity." Despite these very likely responses by most readers today, even Murdock must admit that The Day of Doom "is—or seems—comic" (xi). The cause of this perception is the same as that influencing our responses to Hawthorne's tale, Adams's autobiography, and Robinson's poem: excessive gloom of this sort translates in retrospect into a kind of macabre humor. Most of us, too, derive a certain satisfaction in seeing the tables turned on those who think they have it made—especially in worldly terms.

Of the writers considered earlier in the chapter, we should admit that, even apart from his demonstration of any Calvinist sense of humor, William Bradford might surface in many histories of early American settlement. On the other hand, Mary Rowlandson and Michael Wigglesworth are likely to be included only in those anthologies of American writing that aim at total inclusiveness. About Jonathan Edwards, the last writer to be discussed here, most would be likely to concede that he is supremely important to any discussion of the developing American mind. As Alan Heimert writes in the *Columbia Literary History of the United States,* "Of the plenitude of 'religious' writers who filled the American literary landscape in the years between the twilight of Puritanism and the emergence of the ideological struggles of the Revolution, only Jonathan Edwards has held his place in the American literary canon" (113). Edwards was not only a significant writer who deservedly belongs to many American literary traditions, including the tradition of American Calvinist humor; he was also a major theologian, a defining force in the powerful religious revival of the American eighteenth century usually called the Great Awakening, and an ancestor of note.[13] In summary, Heimert goes on to say that "Edwards has . . . come to be recognized as perhaps the finest mind ever to emerge in America . . ." (113). For that very reason, it is only to be expected—or perhaps it is not—that Edwards's most famous work, the sermon "Sinners in the Hands of an Angry God" (1741), would abound in Calvinist humor.

Cleanth Brooks, R. W. B. Lewis, and Robert Penn Warren write in their anthology of American literature that Edwards was "the strictest and most uncompromising Calvinist New England ever produced" (83). And, even Edwards's very sympathetic biographer, George M. Marsden, concedes that "Edwards is not usually thought of as a progenitor of the American party of hope . . ." (337). But, as in the cases of Hawthorne and Adams cited earlier, that is part of the grand Calvinist joke. Isn't it funny in a macabre sense that Edwards chooses to ask those who are sitting in the pews on Sunday morning instead of lolling in bed, "[H]ow many is it likely will remember this discourse in hell? And it would be a wonder, if some that are now present should not be in hell in a very short time, even before this year is out. And it should be no wonder if some persons, that now sit here, in some seats of this meeting-house, in health, quiet and secure, should be there before to-morrow morning" (104). This dire prediction, moreover, is likely to come true despite how "moral and strict, sober and religious, they may otherwise be" (104). The thought of sober, church-going Puritans going straight to hell "to-morrow morning" is surely risible. And, furthermore, this hell is going to be dreadful beyond anyone's expectations, according to Edwards's sermon: "If you cry to God to pity you, he will be so far from pitying you in your doleful case, or showing you the least regard or favour, that instead of that, he will only tread you under foot. And though he will know that you cannot bear the weight of omnipotence treading on you, yet he will not regard that, but he will crush you under his feet without mercy: he will crush out your blood, and make it fly, and it shall be sprinkled on his garments, so as to stain all his raiment" (103). While all of this is going on, the damned will undergo the additional indignity of having the Saints look delightedly down on their suffering, as Michael Wigglesworth earlier promised. As Edwards writes, "[W]hen you shall be in this state of suffering, the glorious in-habitants of heaven shall go forth and look on the awful spectacle, that they may see what the wrath and fierceness of the Almighty is . . ." (103). Whoa, Nelly! No wonder Edwards sagely concludes: "To what a dreadful, inexpressible, inconceivable depth of misery must the poor creature be sunk who shall be the subject of this!" (102).

The Calvinist humor in this sermon surely derives from the elevated perspective from which Edwards views those poor souls who are destined for hell. In this respect, he is—to no one's great surprise—more of Wil-liam Bradford's persuasion than of Mark Twain's. Another light is just as surely shone on these grim jokes from the perfect assurance with which Edwards speaks of the unknown. Although he operates from the theo-logical premise that "God is not altogether such an one as themselves though they [human beings] may imagine him to be so" (99), Edwards still can know just how God thinks about many significant matters. Thus, he says with perfect confidence that "God is a great deal more angry with great numbers that are now on earth: yea, doubtless with many that are now in this congregation, who it may be are at ease, than he is with many of those who are now in the flames of hell" (99). We can't help wondering how Edwards happens to know this, and this wonder leads to at least a mild chuckle.[14]

This is no wonder because Edwards's biblical text for "Sinners in the Hands of an Angry God" almost necessarily leads in some humorous directions. Calling on Deuteronomy 32.35, "To me belongeth vengeance, and recompence; their foot shall slide in due time: for the day of their calamity is at hand, and the things that shall come upon them make haste," Edwards would necessarily have to stress divine punishment and the relatively short time remaining for atonement in his sermon. However, the sliding foot buried in this verse calls out for comic—even burlesque—treatment: somebody is going to have to slip on a banana peel or just fall down gracelessly! Early in the sermon, Edwards stresses these images by referring to "slippery places," "slippery ground," and even "slippery declining ground" (98). These comic possibilities continue when the sermon's imagery shifts from the slippery slope to a precarious board across a bottomless gulf: "Unconverted men walk over the pit of hell on a rotten covering, and there are innumerable places in the covering so weak that they will not bear their weight, and these places are not seen" (99). The imagery seems to come out of a Mack Sennett silent comedy. Buster Keaton is surely going to fall through that "rotten covering" into something very nasty. Some of Edwards's later imagery is, admittedly, more fearsome, as when God holds the human soul "over the pit of hell, much as one holds a spider, or some loathsome insect . . ." (101). Even then, if we are able to see ourselves as the hand rather than the spider, the elevated perspective is that of a Calvinist humorist. This whole line of imagistic sermonizing comes to a peak in a passage combing all of these Calvinistic elements: "Your wickedness makes you as it were heavy as lead, and to tend downwards with great weight and pressure towards hell; and if God should let you go, you would immediately sink and swiftly descend and plunge into the bottomless gulf, and your healthy constitution, and your own care and prudence, and best contrivance, and all your righteousness, would have no more influence to uphold you and keep you out of hell, than a spider's web would have to stop a fallen rock" (101). The metaphor at the end will stand up under any Calvinist theological interrogation. Human efforts to achieve salvation, including a "healthy constitution, and your own care and prudence, and best contrivance, and all your righteousness," are no more likely to succeed in a theological sense than a spider web is to arrest a heavy rock. At the same time, the ludicrous imagery of a rock falling on a spider web is basically comic.

However, the part of "Sinners in the Hands of an Angry God" that has always struck me as the most sublime example of Calvinist humor is Edwards's explanation of the difference between human and divine wisdom. Most Christians, he explains, think that hell is for other people: "They hear indeed that there are but few saved, and that the greater part of men that have died heretofore are gone to hell; but each one imagines that he lays out matters better for his own escape than others have done. He does not intend to come to that place of torment; he says within himself, that he intends to take effectual care, and to order matters so for himself as not to fail" (100). Edwards's verbs—"hear," "imagines," "intend"—imply that there is another (superior) way of looking at what these people think and that from this superior perspective these people can be seen to be mistaken. In fact, Edwards goes on to call on testimony from beyond the grave to support this point:

> The greater part of those who heretofore have lived under the same means of grace, and are now dead, are undoubtedly gone to hell; and it was not because they were not as wise as those who are now alive; it was not because they did not lay out matters as well for themselves as to secure their own escape. If we could speak with them, and inquire of them, one by one, whether they expected, when alive, and when they used to hear about hell, ever to be the subjects of that misery: we doubtless, should hear one and another reply, "No, I never intended to come here: I had laid out matters otherwise in my mind. . . ." (100)

The central issue, it seems to me, should not be Edwards's own religious situation: his positive sincerity or negative self-righteousness. Rather, in terms of Calvinist humor, we should note Edwards's capacity to entertain two perspectives simultaneously—the potentially damned soul's very human confidence in its own integrity and virtue and a supernatural recognition that no human achievement can matter *sub specie aeternitatis*. That the deluded "Christian" in question cannot attain a similar perspective is Edwards's Calvinist joke. As Edwards says, somewhat redundantly, "[H]e flatters himself that he shall escape it; he depends upon himself for his own security; he flatters himself in what he has done, in what he is now doing; or what he intends to do. Every one lays out matters in his own mind how he shall avoid damnation, and flatters himself that he contrives well for himself, and that his schemes will not fail" (100). But Edwards knows that this Christian is deludedly flattering himself, and Calvinist humor doesn't get any better than that!

In an effort to recuperate Puritan thinkers and writers for a postwar American reading audience, Norman Foerster wrote, in his *American Poetry and Prose* (1947): "We have come to realize that our conventional picture of the Puritans as grimly righteous and forbidding is scarcely adequate" (8). The intellectual climate has assuredly changed considerably in the more than half a century since Foerster felt obliged to defend the Puritan sense of humor in this way. Even so, much of the evidence quoted in this chapter might still lead us to focus more on what Nathaniel Ward called the "sobriety, justice, [and] piety" of these early Americans than on their "laughter." That is, unless we are willing to concede that there is a kind of laughter peculiar to Calvinism, and of that kind of laughter, as John Dryden said of Geoffrey Chaucer, "here is God's plenty."[15]

3 Nathaniel Hawthorne

"That Would Be a Jest Indeed"

In her very aptly titled book *Hawthorne: Calvin's Ironic Stepchild,* Agnes McNeill Donohue writes, "In spite of Hawthorne's ambivalence toward the Puritanism of the American past, especially that of his own ancestors, his artistic imagination, creative consciousness, and conscience were conditioned by Calvinism" (ix). In fact, it was Hawthorne's negative disposition toward the fictional characters that he had himself created that first got me thinking that there might just be such a thing as Calvinist humor. Even a few examples should make the case.

Let us consider, for instance, how, in tales published during the mid-1830s, Hawthorne treats two sincere religious believers. In "Young Goodman Brown" (1835), the title character confidently says about his family and community, "We are a people of prayer, and good works, to boot, and abide no such wickedness" (278).[1] On the basis of our readings elsewhere in Hawthorne and in the book of life "to boot," we can conclude either that these folk are truly unique or that Goodman Brown is comically mistaken. Of course, the latter assumption accords more closely with the presuppositions of Calvinism, and this points to one of Hawthorne's Calvinist jokes. Goodman Brown attends a demonic forest ceremony, at which his parents and wife may also be present, and this ruins the whole rest of his life: "And when he had lived long, and was borne to his grave, a hoary corpse, followed by Faith, an aged woman, and children and grand-children, a goodly procession, besides neighbors, not a few, they carved no hopeful verse upon his tomb-stone; for his dying hour was gloom" (289). In "The Man of Adamant" (1837), Richard Digby's claim to exceptionality is more restricted than Brown's, embracing only himself. As the narrator says, Digby's "plan of salvation was so narrow, that, like a plank in a tempestuous sea, it could avail no sinner but himself" (421). In consequence of his self-conviction of righteousness, Digby expects the Almighty to act as Digby would do and smite the supposedly unrighteous. The narrator reports the results:

> But, as the sunshine continued to fall peacefully on the cottages and fields, and the husbandmen labored and children played, and as there were many tokens of present happiness, and nothing ominous of speedy judgment, he turned away, somewhat disappointed. The further he went, however, and the lonelier he felt himself, and the thicker the trees stood along his path, and the darker the shadow overhead, so much the more did Richard Digby exult. . . . So congenial was this mode of life to his disposition, that he often laughed to himself, but was displeased when an echo tossed him back the long, loud roar. (422)

What Digby is actually hearing is the long, loud roar of Calvinist laughter directed at his deluded conviction of religious exceptionality by Hawthorne and his readers.[2] Digby may be correct in assuming that many of his townsmen are sinners, but he is grossly mistaken in believing that he is not a sinner also. He apparently misses the pun through which the title of the tale connects him with the Adam who brought about the fall of all mankind. John Calvin affirms that "the uncleanness of the parents is so transmitted to the children that all without any exception are defiled at their begetting" (248), and this is something that Hawthorne surely knew about. He assumes that we know about it, too, and our mutual laughter therefore results when Brown and Digby reveal that they are not in on the joke. Hawthorne's treatment of fictional characters like Brown and Digby bears out Alfred Kazin's opinion, in God and the American Writer: "In some respects [Hawthorne] was harsher than the Puritans, and left out of his work the love and fellowship that the leaders of puritan society invoked for their own members" (29).

Even when Hawthorne's characters are not especially religious, they are subject to the same sorts of delusions and the same sort of ridicule. Doctor Giocomo Rappaccini's belief that he can protect his daughter, Beatrice, from mortality predictably results in her death. In "Rappaccini's

Daughter" (1844), as Beatrice lies dying, Rappaccini asks, "Wouldst thou, then, have preferred the condition of a weak woman, exposed to all evil, and capable of none?" and Beatrice (correctly) answers, "I would fain have been loved, not feared" (1005). The case is far more touching than Richard Digby's, and yet the cause is similar: someone's mistaken notion that a human being can escape the human condition. We laugh sourly at Digby because the conviction of exceptionality is his own; we sympathize with Beatrice because the conviction was her father's. We probably also feel that we are allotting our emotional responses appropriately and that this allotment is tragically correct. It is a Calvinist humorist, however, who gives the last line of "Rappaccini's Daughter" to the mad scientist's rival, Pietro Baglioni: "Rappaccini! Rappaccini! And is *this* the upshot of your experiment?" (1005). The same emotional balance is struck in "The Birth-mark" (1843). Here the scientist Aylmer believes that he can transcend the limits of nature by removing from his wife's cheek the imperfection named in the title. Aylmer claims to be motivated by love: "Georgiana, you have led me deeper than ever into the heart of science. I feel myself fully competent to render this dear cheek as faultless as its fellow; and then, most beloved, what will be my triumph, when I shall have corrected what Nature left imperfect, in her fairest work!" (768). Aylmer's focus on his own skill and imagined triumph alerts readers to his true motivation, however. Like Rappaccini, he hopes to get the best of nature, totally ignoring the fact that, by Calvinist standards, he is himself a product of fallen human nature. As we might expect, Georgiana dies as soon as the birthmark is removed. Again, an innocent woman falls victim to a male's deluded conviction of exceptionality. Again, a Calvinist laugh anticlimactically follows the victim's death. Here Aylmer's deformed laboratory assistant, Aminadab, has the last (Calvinist) laugh: "Then a hoarse, chuckling laugh was heard again!" (780). Hawthorne's narrator then enunciates the sort of reflection that Hawthorne's idealistic new bride might approve of: "Thus ever does the gross Fatality of Earth exult in its invariable triumph over the immortal essence, which, in this dim sphere of half-development, demands the completeness of a higher state."[3] Despite these sentimental effusions, Georgiana is still dead, and Aminadab is still laughing, and it turns out that nobody is really special after all! This is Hawthorne's favorite kind of Calvinist joke, and he seems to derive such pleasure from repeating it that he merits a leading place in the parade of the Calvinist humorists of American literature.

One sign of Hawthorne's adoption of this role is his frequent use of what narratologists such as Wallace Martin call the "gnomic present" (124), a tense ideally suited to annunciating unquestioned "truths" about life. The practice is epitomized by a passage from "The New Adam and Eve" (1843) in which the title characters contemplate their prospects for ascending directly into heaven from the world in which they have found themselves following The Day of Doom. Hawthorne's narrator explains: "In the energy of new life, it appears no such impracticable feat to climb into the sky! But they have already received a woful lesson, which may finally go far towards reducing them to the level of the departed race, when they acknowledge the necessity of keeping the beaten track of earth" (748–49). This necessary lesson recommended by the narrator is recommended also by the heroine's "gloomy kinsman" in "The Lily's Quest" (1839). In this highly allegorical tale, a young couple named Adam Forrester and Lilias Fay believe that it is their destiny to construct a perfect temple of joy. The young woman's kinsman predicts failure for their idealistic efforts because, as he says, "In one shape or other, every mortal has dreamed your dream" (687). Why should they alone succeed in an activity that everyone else has failed at? A similar reflection occurs to the "immitigable zealot" Endicott at the end of "The May-Pole of Merry Mount" (1836). After the Puritans have demonstrated by force of their superior arms that "gloom" will be more influential than "jollity" in the development of America, their leader is (surprisingly) touched by the plight of two young adherents of jollity: "Yet the deepening twilight could not altogether conceal, that the iron man was softened; he smiled, at the fair spectacle of early love; he almost sighed, for the inevitable blight of early hopes" (370). Since this is John Endicott, "almost" is as close as he comes to sighing over the fact that the world is not different from what he knows it to be. The young lovers in this tale are like the new Adam and Eve in learning early the "woful lesson" that this is so. As a result, they attract smiles rather than the more withering laughter that the author directs toward those who are slower to learn their lessons. As another narrator remarks in "Wakefield" (1835), "Would Time but await the close of our favorite follies, we should be young men, all of us, and till Doom's Day" (297). But, of course, time will not wait, and many are not capable of wisely abandoning their "favorite follies."

This is one of the great truths about human nature popular with Calvinists of all sorts: that people will continue to behave as we have known other people to behave for uncountable centuries. In the "Intelligence Office" (1844), Hawthorne's narrator observes about the book in which human character is detailed, "There was an endless diversity of mode and circumstance, yet withal such a similarity in the real groundwork, that any one page of the volume—whether written in the days before the Flood, or the yesterday that is gone by, or to be written on the morrow that is close at hand, or a thousand ages hence—might serve as a specimen of the whole" (882). "The Great Stone Face" (1850) provides corroboration when a politician named Old Stony Phiz revisits his boyhood home, and the narrator observes, "Of course, he had no other object than to shake hands with his fellow-citizens, and neither thought nor cared about any effect which his progress through the country might have upon the election" (1079). What we all know to be the truth about politicians and their self-serving motives is the basis for this joke, as what we all know to be the truth about young female heirs is the basis of another Calvinist joke in "Mr. Higginbotham's Catastrophe" (1834). In this tale, the plot requires that the niece of the title character show up in time to discredit a story about his hanging and her inconsolable grief over his murder. In an aside irrelevant to this plot, the narrator adds, however, that "some shrewd fellows had doubted, all along, whether a young lady would be quite so desperate at the hanging of a rich old uncle" (195). The actual young lady in question is a loving relative with no apparent designs on her uncle's fortune, and yet our usual assumptions about everyone's unworthy, but very human, motivations allow us to share in a joke about her—or possibly our—"real" feelings in this case. In the same way, we know that when Old Squire Saunders fails to ask the Reverend Mr. Hooper back to his house for his usual Sunday dinner in "The Minister's Black Veil" (1836), he fails to do so not "by an accidental lapse of memory," as the narrator ironically suggests (374), but because he is as terrified and disgusted by the minister's black veil as everyone else is. The joke arises partly from our superior penetration of the squire's motives and partly from our recognition that we would probably not invite Mr. Hooper to dinner either.

Almost any human behavior can be viewed in this way. In "Chippings with a Chisel" (1838), an elderly man accompanied by his fourth wife comes to buy tombstones for the first three "who had once slept by his side [and] were now sleeping in their graves." The narrator reports, "There was even—if I wrong him it is no great matter—a glance side-wise at his living spouse, as if he were inclined to drive a thriftier bargain by bespeaking four grave-stones in a lot" (619–20). "[I]t is no great matter" if the narrator is maligning this man because we all know real people so financially driven that they would try to strike a similar bargain. That is just human nature in one of its varieties. Vanity is often a part of human nature too, as we see in a telling passage from "Peter Goldthwaite's Treasure" (1838). At this point in the tale, the elderly, half-crazed Goldthwaite is as strongly convinced that he is just about to discover a hidden horde of gold as the reader is that Goldthwaite will not. The narrator goes blandly on: "Having lived thus long,—not too long, but just to the right age,—a susceptible bachelor, with warm and tender dreams, he resolved, so soon as the hidden gold should flash to light, to go a wooing, and win the love of the fairest maid in town. What heart could resist him?" (529–30). The narrator adds, "Happy Peter Goldthwaite!" but readers understand that the exclamation is mocking. Goldthwaite's delusions, rather than his happy prospects, are the object of the narrator's—and the reader's—superior and laughing scrutiny. In the same way, readers probably know that it is psychologically impossible for Young Goodman Brown—or for anyone else—to "cling to [his wife's] skirts and follow her to Heaven" after merely "one night" spent in evil debauchery (276), but the Calvinistic humor in the situation derives from Brown's inability to see this. As so often, we are above one of Hawthorne's characters looking down and laughing at the character's delusions, but, again, there is a nagging sense that we are all subject to similar delusions.

One of the most seductive delusions for Hawthorne's characters—and perhaps for all Americans—is a belief in progress. Its political form, during the great nineteenth-century age of reform, is typified by this passage from "Earth's Holocaust" (1844): "And now the drums were beaten and the trumpets brayed all together, as a prelude to the proclamation of universal and eternal peace, and the announcement that glory was no more to be won by blood; but that it would henceforth be the contention of the human race, to work out the greatest mutual good . . ." (894–95). The thematic intention of this tale—as of so many of Hawthorne's works—is to demonstrate the foolishness of such beliefs, here by proposing that all occasions of human misery, including war, might be destroyed in a giant bonfire. That this generation will not see the end of war—as it will not see the end of vanity, avarice, and fear—is a Calvinist certainty. Even some less-illusioned characters in the story know this: "They comforted themselves, however, in the belief that the proposed abolition of war was impracticable, for any length of time together" (894). That anyone might think otherwise is a Calvinist joke. That many—like Margaret Fuller and Ralph Waldo Emerson—were thinking so even as Hawthorne was writing this tale is a joke too good to keep to himself.

Progressive thinking during the nineteenth century would see massive strides taken toward the issues of total abstinence, votes for women, the abolition of slavery, the scourging of sailors, and the abuse of animals. Might not even the strenuous matter of salvation be put on a more progressive track? In "The Celestial Rail-road" (1843), Hawthorne answers with a mordant "No."[4] Searching like the new Adam and Eve for an easy access to heaven, the characters in this tale have constructed a modern railroad to supplant the arduous road to heaven trudged by John Bunyan's character Pilgrim in the "unenlightened" seventeenth century. Hawthorne's narrator ironically observes: "It would have done Bunyan's heart good to see it. Instead of a lonely and ragged man, with a huge burthen on his back, plodding along sorrowfully on foot, while the whole city hooted after him, here were parties of the first gentry and most respected people in the neighborhood, setting forth towards the Celestial City, as cheerfully as if the pilgrimage were merely a summer tour" (809–10). As the narrator and his readers well know, however, the pilgrimage of life must be as demanding as it is significant—and this seems to be true whether or not anyone believes in the existence of an actual Celestial City.

Another source of Calvinist humor is the absolute fixity of human nature not only from generation to generation, but also within individual natures, and this is a joke that Hawthorne shares with Mark Twain. When the pilgrims bound for Canterbury in Hawthorne's tale of that title (1833) discover that the Shaker community is flourishing, the failed business-man immediately begins planning how to invest the colony's financial surplus, and the failed poet begins working on some new poems. Neither man has learned a thing, apparently, from the bitter experiences that have led them to quit the world and seek Shaker asylum in the first place. In "Dr. Heidegger's Experiment" (1837), the scientist of the title offers a potion bringing renewed youth to four friends as damaged by life as the Canterbury pilgrims. Beforehand, however, Dr. Heidegger also offers some advice: "Before you drink, my respectable old friends, . . . it would be well that, with the experience of a life-time to direct you, you should draw up a few general rules for your guidance, in passing a second time through the perils of youth. Think what a sin and shame it would be, if, with your peculiar advantages, you should not become patterns of virtue and wisdom to all the young people of the age!" (474). To the surprise of no Calvinist, the four friends ignore the doctor's sage advice and by the end of the tale are blindly repeating all the errors of their youths.

This predictable development is, of course, ironic, and this kind of irony provides a sizable number of Calvinist laughs in many of Haw-thorne's other tales and sketches. In "The Christmas Banquet" (1844), a character named Mr. Smith has been warned that strenuous laughter might cause the heart attack that will kill him. When "a man of stricken conscience" expresses a wish to cleanse his heart of guilt in Mr. Smith's presence, "[t]his strain of conversation appeared so unintelligibly absurd to good Mr. Smith that he burst into precisely the fit of laughter that his physicians warned him against, as likely to prove fatal. In effect, he fell back in his chair, a corpse with a broad grin upon his face . . ." (860). When something so predictable happens in a story, the true Calvinist laughs at it. The character Oberon in "The Devil in Manuscript" (1835) be-comes the butt of a different form of irony. After trying futilely to catch the attention of his townspeople through his writing, Oberon despairs and burns all of his manuscripts. When sparks from this conflagration fly up the chimney, they set neighboring roofs afire, and the fire quickly spreads. "Huzza! Huzza!" Oberon shouts, "My brain has set the town on fire!" (337). Since this is certainly not the way in which he expected to affect the town, a different form of Calvinist humor develops through an ironic fulfillment. The title character of "The Ambitious Guest" (1835) seems to share Oberon's ironic success or successful irony. The only victim of a famous avalanche who is even interested in worldly fame, he is also the only victim who remains unknown to posterity. Here is "a jest indeed!" (601), as Ralph Cranfield observes in "The Threefold Destiny" (1838). Another jest develops when it turns out that the ambitious guest and the other characters need not have died after all. Because they live in a locale where avalanches are frequent, the family in the story are accustomed to seek shelter behind "a sort of barrier" whenever a rockslide occurs. On the occasion represented in the story, "[j]ust before it reached the house, the stream [of rocks] broke into two branches—shivered not a window there, but overwhelmed the whole vicinity, blocked up the road, and annihilated everything in its dreadful course" (306). Ironically enough, "everything" includes the family and their guest, hiding behind their apparently safe "barrier." Talk about a sick joke! In "The Procession of Life" (1843), the narrator comments gnomically, "The fact is too preposterous for tears, too lugubrious for laughter" (804). The fate of the ambitious guest corresponds to this description in the sense that even though it may not produce laughter, it is still humorous.

The prediction offered by a "yeoman's wife" to a couple of young lovers in "The Canterbury Pilgrims" is not very laughable either, but its tone of grim inevitability resonates with Calvinist humor: "If you and your sweetheart marry, you'll be kind and pleasant to each other for a year or two, and while that's the case, you will never repent; but by-and-by, he'll grow gloomy, rough, and hard to please, and you'll be peevish, and full of little angry fits, and apt to be complaining by the fireside when he comes to rest himself from his troubles out of doors; so your love will wear away by little and little, and leave you miserable at last" (164). There seems to be no happier alternative for this couple—or for the readers. This is probably the sort of reflection that leads Brenda Wineapple to observe in her biography of Hawthorne, "Old time Calvinism, even if on the wane, . . .

helped shape Hawthorne's sense that the world is banked in sorrow" (80). Although it is not part of her critical project to say so, Wineapple might have gone on to connect this dour sense of inevitable doom to what I have been calling Calvinist humor.

More sustained examinations of Hawthorne's works point toward similarly Calvinistic conclusions. "The Minister's Black Veil" (1836), for example, is a wonderful illustration of Calvinist humor. The central character, the Reverend Mr. Hooper, is, first of all, a Calvinist clergyman whose preaching displays "the gentle gloom of Mr. Hooper's temperament" (373). For reasons that are never explicitly stated in the story, Mr. Hooper vows to wear a crape veil over most of his face for the remainder of his life in order to symbolize the secret sins of mankind. As we might expect, the other characters in the story are horrified and frightened by this perhaps praiseworthy decision. One old woman in Mr. Hooper's congregation says that the minister "has changed himself into something awful, only by hiding his face," and Goodman Gray pithily concludes that "[o]ur parson has gone mad" (372). Because these reactions are only to be expected, Hawthorne has the minister adopt "a sad smile" in response (374). More telling, to my view, is the judgment of the village doctor, who concludes, "Something must surely be amiss with Mr. Hooper's intellects" (374). The doctor's analysis does not differ substantially from Goodman Gray's, and yet Hawthorne's formulation of the diagnosis goes beyond the language required to indicate some form of madness.[5] It seems to me that this excessive language points to the author's own amusement at the situation. This is the probable motive also when Hawthorne writes this about the younger townspeople's further responses: "One imitative imp covered his face with an old black handkerchief, thereby so affrighting his playmates, that the panic seized himself, and he well nigh lost his wits by his own waggery" (377). It is, assuredly, very unusual to mix the awful and the humorous in this way, but it is a way that Hawthorne often adopts.

Another problem confronting Hooper is the vulgar curiosity which forces him to abandon his relaxing walks in the cemetery because "when he leaned pensively over the gate, there would always be faces behind the grave-stones, peeping at his black veil" (380). Perhaps it is the word *peeping* that makes this horrible situation so comic; more likely, it is the situation itself. Once again, the awful and the humorous collide in a Calvinist joke. There should be nothing comic about the exchange in which Hooper's fiancée Elizabeth tries to reason with him either, but Hawthorne introduces a bleak Calvinist humor into the scene even so. "Lift the veil but once, and look me in the face," Elizabeth very reasonably asks. "Never! It cannot be!" Hooper replies. Elizabeth responds with only two words: "Then, farewell!" (379). In this scene Elizabeth concedes that she will be willing to put up with Hooper's veil for the rest of their lives if he will make one small gesture of concession. He refuses to do so, but he does promise that the veil will not be an obstacle to their happiness in the afterlife. *Farewell* is a perfectly sensible response to his obstinacy according to any natural standard, but Hooper—and perhaps Hawthorne—insists that a natural standard may not be the most appropriate one to apply in this case. In any event, "Mr. Hooper smiled to think that only a material emblem had separated him from happiness, though the horrors which it shadowed forth, must be drawn darkly between the fondest of lovers" (379–80). That "material emblem" is especially good, I think, and so is Mr. Hooper's smile. As a true Calvinist Hooper knows that most things are unchangeable, but as the creation of Nathaniel Hawthorne he can afford to smile about it.

Hooper even dies with this smile on his face. Before that final development, however, the Reverend Mr. Clark has tried to persuade Hooper to remove his black veil lest it become an occasion of scandal: "[I]s it fitting that a father in the church should leave a shadow on his memory, that may seem to blacken a life so pure?" (383). Despite this perfectly reasonable request, Hooper is, once again, unpersuadable. "Never," he replies, all the while adopting his usual "sad smile" (383). Clark is horrified by Hooper's determination to maintain his "eccentric whim," but Elizabeth—faithfully watching at Hooper's deathbed—is apparently used to such intransigence by now. In fact, she has been standing by faithfully and, according to the narrator, would have "with averted eyes, covered that aged face, which she had last beheld in the comeliness of youth" (382). Therefore, Hooper dies with his veil intact, but not before having indicted the faithful church members gathered around his deathbed for having "on every visage a Black Veil!" (384). In this stinging accusation,

Hooper can be seen to echo Calvin's principle enunciated in his *Institutes of the Christian Religion*: "Thus, from the feeling of our own ignorance, vanity, poverty, infirmity, and—what is more—depravity and corruption, we recognize that the true light of wisdom, sound virtue, full abundance of every good, and purity of righteousness rest in the Lord alone" (36). On the other hand, perhaps Hooper has gone overboard in his indictment of his fellow man, especially of those who have gone to some personal inconvenience to watch with him in his final hours. Calvin also writes, "But godliness, to stand on a firm footing, keeps itself within its proper limits" (117). Hawthorne refuses to say which statement comes closer to describing the "truth" of Mr. Hooper's situation. That is, after all, how Hawthorne usually operates.[6] Whichever way we lean, however, we confront Calvinist humor. Either Hooper is right, and we are all horribly guilty and rightfully condemned despite our human efforts to be good, or Hooper is a badly deluded fool. It's kind of funny either way.

"The Threefold Destiny" is an even more schematic story than "The Minister's Black Veil." As we might expect, therefore, it abounds with Calvinist humor. The central character, Ralph Cranfield, "had imbibed the idea, and held it firmest among his articles of faith, that three marvelous events of his life were to be confirmed to him by three signs" (599). On Hawthorne's Calvinistic behalf, the narrator uses the term *imbibed* to warn careful readers that Cranfield might be mistaken in his understanding of his destiny, but just in case we miss this subtle hint, the narrator adds, about Cranfield's conviction of exceptionality, "[W]e say not whether it were revealed to him by witchcraft, or in a dream of prophecy, or that his brooding fancy had palmed its own dictates upon him as the oracles of a Sybil." In any case, he "had imbibed the idea" that he would somehow rise above the common lot of mankind by finding a treasure, a great love, and a position of "extensive influence and sway over his fellow-creatures" (600). Few experienced readers can expect that Ralph Cranfield will be rewarded for his conviction and, of course, he is not rewarded. On the other hand, he is not severely punished either.

After spending ten years seeking the three signs of his personal excellence in Hindostan, Spain, Arabia, Turkey, and the Arctic, Cranfield returns to his native village, "not with the aspect of a triumphant man"

(600) but with a resolution to rest and regroup so that he can search further for his destiny. Soon he discovers that his childhood sweetheart, Faith Egerton, is the fated love of his life, that his position of "extensive influence and sway over his fellow-creatures" involves becoming master of the local school, and that his greatest treasure is lying right in his own back yard. It is this last discovery that Cranfield describes as "a jest indeed," and he elaborates, "Now a credulous man . . . might suppose that the treasure which I have sought round the world, lies buried, after all, at the very door of my mother's dwelling" (601). A credulous man might think this, that is to say, if he had a sense of Calvinist humor. And, this same Calvinist humorist might be tempted to draw the kind of moral that Hawthorne's tale draws: "Happy they who read the riddle without a weary world-search, or a lifetime spent in vain!" (606). But, Ralph Cranfield eventually reads the riddle correctly, marries Faith Egerton, accepts the job of schoolteacher, and finds his "sphere of duty, of prosperity, and happiness, within those precincts, and in that station where Providence itself has cast [his] lot" (606). That is to say that, from a Calvinistic perspective, he makes out all right in the end and does not spend his whole life in vain. The Calvinist joke is that he doesn't make out all right all along but foolishly wastes ten years looking for this very same happy ending.

"Young Goodman Brown" has no happy ending of any sort and so is probably the ultimate in Calvinist irony.[7] After all, the story concludes with these words: "his dying hour was gloom" (289). Along the way to this bitter conclusion, Hawthorne engages frequently in Calvinist humor. First of all, Brown seriously deludes himself, much as Ralph Cranfield and (perhaps) Mr. Hooper do. Brown's delusion is, as we have seen, that he can participate in a Satanic ritual for just one night and then go back to living the upright life of a New England Puritan. This idea is so foolish that everyone else in the story is allowed to ridicule Goodman Brown. His evil companion—who just may be the Devil—"burst[s] into a fit of irrepressible mirth" (279) when Goodman Brown expresses his trust in "that good old man, our minister." Later, Goody Cloyse refers to Brown as "the silly fellow that now is" (280). Shortly thereafter, the whole forest rings with some sort of uncanny laughter, and then even Goodman Brown joins in the laughter himself.[8] Apparently there is nothing funnier to a Calvinist humorist than an individual's conviction that he or she is exempt from the defects of human nature.

This principal joke is enhanced along the way by frequent humorous asides from Hawthorne's narrator. When Brown promises himself that he will engage in evil for only this one night and practice virtue ever after, the narrator observes, "With this excellent resolve for the future, Goodman Brown felt himself justified in making more haste on his present evil purpose" (276). When Brown decides that he will go no further into the forest with his evil companion, the narrator says, "The young man sat a few moments by the road-side, applauding himself greatly . . ." (281). When the evil journey terminates in some kind of witches' meeting and then Brown suddenly finds himself alone in the forest, the narrator wonders whether Brown may have just dreamed the whole thing. "Be it so, if you will," he observes, "But, alas! it was a dream of evil omen for young Goodman Brown" (288). That is to say, it doesn't matter whether or not anything "really" happened. Goodman Brown's "dying hour was gloom" in any case. Hawthorne's stories seem to question over and over the possibility that things might be different from what they are. Apparently, the answer is No, or perhaps No, in thunder.

Hawthorne's longer works provide similar answers. *The Scarlet Letter* (1850), as nearly everyone knows, focuses on the adulterous relationship between Hester Prynne and the Puritan minister Arthur Dimmesdale. Putting aside several very vexing questions, we must at least notice a discrepancy between Dimmesdale's religious profession and his role as Hester's paramour. Ironic opportunities to contemplate heaven, hell, salvation, and damnation consequently flourish in the book. In *The House of the Seven Gables* (1851), the wild radical Holgrave ends up marrying the domestic goddess, Phoebe, settling down, inheriting a fortune, and turning conservative. The scheming and avaricious Judge Pyncheon, on the other hand, dies without an heir just before he can bring any of his nefarious dynastic schemes to fruition. Nothing works out the way anyone planned it, as should probably be expected from an author whose wife scratched on a glass pane with a diamond, "Man's accidents are God's purposes" (Edwin Haviland Miller 210). In *The Marble Faun* (1860), murder may just be the only avenue to developing a mature conscience in the faunlike Italian, Donatello. The most banal and self-righteous characters in the book, Hilda and Kenyon, ultimately prosper. Once again, no character we care much about gets what he or she wants. Along the way in each book, moreover, Hawthorne's narrators comment gnomically on the plot, the characters, and life in general. Calvinist jokes therefore abound. The longer work by Hawthorne that most clearly resonates with Calvinist humor, however, is *The Blithedale Romance* (1952), which is described in Brenda Wineapple's biography of Hawthorne as "a fantasy of what-might-have-been from the conflicted position of what is" (250).

The disconnection between desire and attainment that Wineapple identifies in *Blithedale* frequently defines the perspective of the Calvinist humorist here and elsewhere. As we have already seen, Hawthorne explores this humorous territory repeatedly, in tales and sketches including "Earth's Holocaust," "The Threefold Destiny," and "The New Adam and Eve." In all of these shorter works, plans for a better life are frustrated. Since the principal setting of *The Blithedale Romance* is an idealistic community devoted to a "scheme for beginning the life of Paradise anew," as Hawthorne's narrator, Miles Coverdale, explains (9), we can only anticipate that things will turn out badly for the communards. Since, as Edwin Haviland Miller comments on the book, "Depression and despair suffuse the atmosphere, and social schemes cannot lift despair" (375), we are safe, by this point, in assuming that these unhappy endings will develop in some Calvinistically comic light.

The basic problem that Hawthorne addresses in this book lies in the very foundation of this prospective new way of life—an assumption that the world can actually be made different from what everyone really knows it to be. As Coverdale accurately observes, "Altogether, by projecting our minds outward, we had imparted a show of novelty to existence, and contemplated it as hopefully as if the soil, beneath our feet, had not been fathom-deep with the dust of deluded generations, on every one of which, as on ourselves, the world had imposed itself as a hitherto unwed bride" (128). One can imagine the "immitigable zealot," Endicott, shaking his head in agreement with this insight, along with Lilias Fay's kinsman, the narrator of "The New Adam and Eve," and John Calvin. The world will apparently continue along the same old tracks, irrespective of anyone's wishes to the contrary.

Behaving otherwise seems to be morally corruptive in or out of this book. Coverdale observes at one point, "[T]he besetting sin of a philanthropist . . . is apt to be a moral obliquity" (132). The desire for change, that is, can blind one to what really matters, especially what really concerns other people. Seeing life through the prism of a black veil, a sense of scientific certainty, or an idealistic philanthropy is very likely to yield a distorted perception. In one way or another, this is what is wrong with the people gathered into the Blithedale community. Everyone has his or her own narrow conviction about how life can be improved to accord more closely with his or her own needs. The centrality of this moral issue is clear in the fact that, even in his preface to the book, Hawthorne reduces his fictional characters to formulations focused on these convictions (2). There he identifies his principal characters as "[t]he self-concentrated Philanthropist" (Hollingsworth), "the high-spirited Woman, bruising herself against the narrow limitations of her sex" (Zenobia), "the weakly Maiden" (Priscilla), and "the Minor Poet" (Coverdale). These formulas reduce each character to a single principle. Having any kind of monomaniacal answer to life's problems is a guarantee that the answer will be false. This is Hawthorne's point when in his penultimate chapter he draws a lesson about the dangers of having a "ruling passion." The whole problem of the ruling passion can be tied to "the most awful truth in Bunyan's book," he says there, namely, that "from the very gate of Heaven, there is a by-way to the pit!" (243). That is to say that even the best of intentions are likely to go astray—as the most famous work of Puritan fiction attests.

Since, as I have previously remarked, Hawthorne is less univocal in his Calvinist humor than John Bunyan is in *Pilgrim's Progress,* it will naturally turn out that his depiction of these issues will be more ambiguous in *The Blithedale Romance.* Lawrence Sargent Hall encapsulates the danger of simplifying Hawthorne's attitudes on the subject when he writes, in *Hawthorne: Critic of Society,* "The very frequency of Hawthorne's references to reform is sufficient to refute the argument that he was indifferent to it, suspicious and skeptical though he may have been" (8). As a result of this authorial ambivalence, Coverdale functions safely within the tradition of Calvinistic irony when he writes about his initial departure for the Blithedale experiment, "The greater, surely, was my heroism, when putting out a final whiff of cigar-smoke, I quitted my cosey pair of bachelor rooms . . . and plunged into the heart of the pitiless snowstorm, in quest of a better life." A nineteenth-century Bunyan might well have written something similar. However, he would probably not have added, as Hawthorne does, "The greatest obstacle to being heroic, is the doubt whether one may not be going to prove one's self a fool; the truest heroism is, to resist the doubt. . . ." Here we see Hawthorne engaging in the famous obscurantism for which he has been excoriated by readers like Yvor Winters.[9] We are safely back within the precincts of Calvinist humor, however, when the passage concludes: ". . . and when [the doubt is] to be obeyed" (10). Hawthorne therefore allows us to harbor some attachment to idealism even as we laugh at its inevitable frustration. With Endicott, moreover, we may "almost" sigh at being forced to laugh at such failure.

One pressing idealistic issue in *The Blithedale Romance* is women's rights, as Hawthorne's introductory schema suggests. As we might expect, the issue of equality between the sexes leads to both humor and ambiguity.[10] As A. N. Kaul writes, "His attitude toward it [equality of the sexes] is ambiguous in the sense that he accords to it the dignity of a serious though not one-sided argument" (63). Thus, about halfway through the book, Zenobia "declaimed with great earnestness and passion, nothing short of anger, on the injustice which the world did to women, and equally to itself, by not allowing them, in freedom and honor, and with the fullest welcome, their natural utterance in public" (120). Later on she says, "Women possess no rights, . . . or, at all events, only little girls and grandmothers would have the force to exercise them" (141). This conviction of sexual discrimination leads to a wonderful exchange between Zenobia and Coverdale, with the former asking the latter, "How can [a woman] be happy, after discovering that fate has assigned her but one single event, which she must contrive to make the substance of her whole life?" When Coverdale fatuously replies that "by constant repetition of her one event, [she] may compensate for the lack of variety," Zenobia economically responds, "Indeed!" (60). Elizabeth's pithy departure from Mr. Hooper in "The Minister's Black Veil" is probably the only passage in Hawthorne's works displaying Calvinist humor with equally concentrated force. Therefore, readers can hardly help being attracted by the energy of Zenobia's feminist ideology. But, as Miller writes about this book, Hawthorne had "little interest in ideas or ideology" (366).

Thus, he has Zenobia fall helplessly in love with Hollingsworth, an idealist bitterly opposed to sexual equality. Even when Hollingsworth rejects her in favor of Priscilla, Zenobia continues to defend him by saying to Coverdale, "Presume not to estimate a man like Hollingsworth! It was my fault all along, and none of his" (225). It would seem that something stronger than ideology actually controls human behavior, even the behavior of attractive fictional characters like Zenobia. Zenobia even makes this point in the book, but she makes it more obviously in the light of Calvinist humor:

> There are no new truths, much as we have prided ourselves on finding some. A moral? Why, this:—that, in the battlefield of life, the downright stroke, that would fall only on a man's steel head-piece, is surely to light on a woman's heart, over which she wears no breastplate, and whose wisdom it is, therefore, to keep out of the conflict. Or this:—that the whole universe, her own sex and yours, and Providence, or Destiny, to boot, make common cause against the woman who swerves one hair's breadth out of the beaten track. Yes; and add (for I may as well own it, now,) that, with that one hair's breadth, she goes all astray, and never sees the world in its true aspect afterwards! (224)

This probably sounds to most readers like "The New Adam and Eve" all over again.

In this case, the Adam that Zenobia prefers could hardly be less suited to her dream of sexual equality. As Hollingsworth explains his beliefs about womanhood, "She is the most admirable handiwork of God, in her true place and character. Her place is at man's side. . . . The heart of true womanhood knows where its own sphere is, and never seeks to stray beyond it" (122–23). In fact, Hollingsworth is actually prepared to take up arms and resist women with brute force if they should attempt to violate these apparently divinely ordained limits. No wonder he reminds Coverdale of "the grim portrait of a Puritan magistrate" (214)! Whatever the case, he is the man of Zenobia's dreams, and when he scorns her, Zenobia sees no way out but suicide. Even so, Hollingsworth hardly lives happily ever after. Having come to Blithedale in order to redirect the commune's money and efforts toward an idealistic plan for the reformation of criminals, Hollingsworth must confess at the end of the story that his grand plan to reform others has failed and that he is instead riddled with personal guilt because of Zenobia's death.

In these ways, *The Blithedale Romance* demonstrates the inefficacy of idealistic schemes to change the world. Coverdale has a glimpse of this truth when he writes, "No sagacious man will long retain his sagacity, if he live exclusively among reformers and progressive people, without periodically returning into the settled system of things, to correct himself by a new observation from that old stand-point" (140–41). The "settled system of things" and the "old stand-point" comprise the philosophical angle from which the Calvinist views plans for change. In this novel, the commune's resident farmer, Silas Foster, often gets to embody the wisdom of this perspective. When all of the idealists are baffled about how to respond to Priscilla when she first comes to Blithedale out of a bitter snowstorm, for example, Foster—whom Arlin Turner calls "the earthy voice of commonsense and skepticism" (15)—says, "Give the girl a hot cup of tea, and a thick slice of this first-rate bacon" (31). When Coverdale, Hollingsworth, and Foster drag the pond for Zenobia's drowned corpse, Foster exclaims, "Heigh-ho!—well!—life and death together make sad work for us all" (232). While we may all assume that there is more to life than coming to terms with physical existence, this book raises serious questions about what this "more" may be. In the course of the book's development, several highly plausible idealistic answers are raised and rejected. And so, the "settled system of things" and the "old stand-point" embodied in the prosaic life of Silas Foster come to seem more sensible by contrast. That there are so many who don't actually see this fact is the Calvinist's joke, and it is a joke that Nathaniel Hawthorne never grew tired of.

The Blithedale Romance is, assuredly, a very complicated book. In addition to the feminism and economic communism that we have already noticed, the book addresses Mesmerism, theatrical showmanship, economic reversals, love, and jealousy. Furthermore, the romance admits several responses to each of these issues. After all, *The Blithedale Romance* was written by Nathaniel Hawthorne! It therefore lends itself to many highly plausible readings. In a typically incisive interpretation, A. N. Kaul writes, "The criticism of the Blithedale community therefore lies not in its hostile relation to the surrounding social system but rather in the absence of the promised bond within itself and in the divergence between its theory of mutual sympathy on the one hand and its reality of fresh antagonisms and mutual suspicions on the other" (68). However, Lawrence Sargent Hall finds any reading of this sort highly problematic because, as he writes, "Throughout *The Blithedale Romance* there runs the deep vein of sarcasm, which, in its most humorless moments, closely resembles the grimmest satire of Swift, for whose writing Hawthorne had a natural taste" (10). Despite his high-church disposition, that is to say, Dean Swift can be seen to have much in common with the New England Calvinist humorist in his doubts that human life will change in any substantial way. Claudia Johnson sees the levels of irony in *Blithedale* as even more intertwined because she believes—as is true of Swift's "A Modest Proposal" (1729)—that we cannot even trust what the narrator tells us: "The narrative of *The Blithedale Romance* is Coverdale's attempt to reorder the world to his own liking, to work situations and relationships for their greatest impact . . ." (93). All of these propositions make sense because, as Arlin Turner writes in his introduction to the Norton paperback edition of the novel, "It was not Hawthorne's habit to write stories or novels about people or places or events, or about social institutions or social philosophies, though these of course were the matter of his fiction and often furnished the starting point in the development of a story in his mind. He wrote about ideas, usually ideas with a moral tincture and with a bearing on human conduct and human character" (14). If Turner had added that these ideas are often inflected toward Calvinist humor, he would thoroughly summarize my feelings on this matter. And so, we are left with most of the pieces still on the table. The only thing we can be sure of is that there are no simple answers to the problems of life or death or society or gender. A never-ending source of Calvinist humor for Hawthorne is the fact that there are people who believe there are easy answers.

Many of Hawthorne's critics have been engaged by the question of the degree to which—or even whether—Hawthorne shared the convictions of the Calvinist religionists who were so prominent in the New England of his youth and manhood. F. O. Matthiessen, for example, simply presumes "[t]he background of Calvinistic thought over which Hawthorne's imagination played" (435) in *American Renaissance* (1941). In this respect, Matthiessen retraces the footsteps of Hawthorne's sister Ebe, who recalled that "there was also much related to the early History of New England, with which I think he become pretty well acquainted, aided, no doubt, by the Puritan instinct that was in him" (qtd. in Wineapple 61). Therefore, in 1993, G. R. Thompson could summarize the conventional thinking on this topic by identifying Hawthorne as the "presumed inheritor of New England Calvinism" (3). More exhaustively, Margaret B. Moore devotes a chapter entitled "Hawthorne's Instinct of Faith" (102–22) to the issue in her *The Salem World of Nathaniel Hawthorne* (1998). In other words, the critical discussion of Hawthorne's probable connection to Calvinism continues. As Agnes McNeill Donohue concludes, however, "Whether Hawthorne read the *Institutes* or not is unimportant; what is significant is that Calvin's major tenets were completely ingrained in him—through his inheritance, his obsession with Puritan history, his eager reading of the lives and sermons of Puritan divines (both English and American), and his childhood churchgoing" (18). This is also the opinion of Marius Bewley, who writes, "In view of the inexorable fate that overtakes the men and women who err in Hawthorne's stories and novels, his inability completely to forgive them, or to mark a termination to their punishment—in view of these things, it is tempting to say that Hawthorne's conception of human nature continued to be corrupted by Calvinism, even though, intellectually, it was unacceptable to him" (172). That is finally to say, whether or not Hawthorne actually embraced any orthodox affiliation with the theological assumptions of John Calvin, he certainly wrote as if they shared a common view of human nature.

4 Herman Melville

"In No World but a Fallen One"

James E. Miller, Jr., claims, in *A Reader's Guide to Herman Melville,* that
"Melville's primary works clearly place him, alongside Hawthorne, in the
Calvinistic tradition of American literature . . ." (20). Melville's membership in this Calvinistic fraternity is thus a matter of record. Lawrance
Thompson explains that "[i]n his youth, Melville inherited the Reformation dogma of John Calvin, in a quite undiluted form" (4). As William Braswell points out, "[t]he Calvinist tradition had been established
on both sides of the family generations before Melville was born" (4).
Andrew Delbanco explains that Melville's mother "not only took her
churchgoing . . . seriously but was warmly committed to the Calvinist
creed to which her family subscribed in its Dutch Reformed version" (22).
Even Nathaniel Hawthorne emphasized Melville's preoccupation with
the Calvinist religious tradition, writing, in his *English Notebooks,* about
Melville's November 1856 visit to Liverpool:

> [W]e took a pretty long walk together, and sat down in a hollow among
> the sand hills (sheltering ourselves from the high, cool wind) and smoked a
> cigar. Melville, as he always does, began to reason of Providence and futurity,
> and of everything else that lies beyond human ken, and informed me that he
> had "pretty much made up his mind to be annihilated"; but still he does not
> seem to rest in the anticipation; and, I think, will never rest until he gets hold
> of a definite belief. It is strange how he persists—and has persisted ever since
> I knew him, and probably long before—in wandering to-and-fro over these
> deserts, as dismal and monotonous as the sand hills amid which we were sit-

ting. He can neither believe, nor be comfortable in his unbelief; and he is too honest and courageous not to try to do one or the other. (432–33)

In other words, Melville's wrestling with the troubling theological issues of free will, predestination, salvation, and damnation that so engaged orthodox Calvinists in earlier centuries was profound enough to serve as something of an irritant to the less interested Hawthorne. Both Melville's obsession and Hawthorne's annoyance are perhaps understandable in light of T. Walter Herbert, Jr.'s assertion in "Calvinist Earthquake: *Moby Dick* and Religious Tradition": "[Oliver Wendell] Holmes was quite right [in "'The Deacon's Masterpiece, or the Wonderful 'One-Hoss Shay'"] in judging that such items of belief, and even the great central issues of providence and original sin, were losing their power over the religious imagination of Americans in the mid-nineteenth century" (109). Herbert is assuredly correct in his assessment of declining nineteenth-century Calvinist orthodoxy. Nevertheless, the very fact that twentieth-century critics have produced works such as *Melville's Religious Thought* by William Braswell (1943), *Melville's Quarrel with God* by Lawrance Thompson (1952), and *"Moby Dick" and Calvinism: A World Dismantled* by T. Walter Herbert, Jr. (1977) demonstrates that Melville's theological obsessions are intellectually engaging even if not altogether typical. The question remaining, then, is whether these Calvinist preoccupations produced any true Calvinist humor.

To help answer that question, we should note at least one reason for the mid-nineteenth-century decline in orthodoxy: the rise of the kind of transcendental thinking usually associated with Ralph Waldo Emerson. Caught up in such enthusiasm, erstwhile Calvinists might very well conclude, in the formula provided by Harry Levin, that "[c]osmic optimism will win out over skeptical irony" (33)—the latter being the Calvinist mode of skepticism regarding human perfectibility practiced by writers like Jonathan Edwards and Nathaniel Hawthorne. Cosmic optimism obviously runs counter to the belief that man is decidedly fallen from his prelapsarian state and is therefore unequipped for much improvement of any sort. To the transcendental contrary of Calvinism, Emerson writes, in "The American Scholar" (1837), "It is a mischievous notion that we are come late into nature; that the world was finished a long time ago. As the world was plastic and fluid in the hands of God, so it is ever to so much of his attributes as we bring to it" (65). Even more shocking to the Calvinistically inclined would be Emerson's confident pronouncement in his "Divinity School Address" (1838): "If a man is at heart just, then in so far is he God . . ." (74). As we might expect of any thinker raised and caught up in the Calvinist tradition, Melville found these Emersonian principles unsuited to his needs even though he clearly knew about them. As F. O. Matthiessen explains in *American Renaissance*, Melville was "[r]esponsive to the shaping forces of his age as only men of passionate imagination are." Even so, "[h]e recognized the inadequacy of transcendentalism on most of the essential problems." Simple rejection of Emersonian optimism was possible for Melville, but rejection provides by itself no acceptable alternative belief. As Matthiessen goes on to explain, "when [Melville] tried to reassert the significance of Original Sin there was no orthodoxy that he could accept" (458). Therefore, we end up with Herman Melville holding onto a Calvinistic view of human nature divorced from a Calvinist belief in predestination. All that is left, it seems, is Calvinist humor.

Miller says about Melville's comic strategies in his 1857 novel *The Confidence Man*, "Certainly we do not cry, and perhaps we don't even laugh, but surely we smile, if a little grimly . . ." (170), and the same may be said about all of Melville's writing. For, example, it is certainly amusing that Bartleby the scrivener, in Melville's story of that title (1853), continues to say, "I would prefer not to," irrespective of what he is asked to do.[1] However, it is not amusing at all to recognize the absolute misery of Bartleby's life or to see him starve himself to death at the story's conclusion. To "smile, if a little grimly" seems to be the most appropriate response to this story. The most effective way to theorize this matter is to recognize further that by this grim smile we recognize that Melville is engaging in Calvinist humor. We may say the same about the other tales and sketches published in Melville's *Piazza Pieces* (1856) and about his novel *The Confidence Man*. As Warner Berthoff has maintained about the first of these books, "A kind of supervisory humor is [Melville's] natural idiom as a writer . . ." (13). The "supervisory" observer in these late works obviously looks down on his fictional characters with all the humorous serenity of a Calvinist sage, despite the decline in orthodox Calvinism of which Holmes took such witty notice.

"Benito Cereno" is a suitable point at which to begin looking at Melville's Calvinist humor as it appears in his later works. In this narrative, an American sea captain named Amasa Delano (with the suggestive initials A. D.) comes to the rescue of a Spanish sea captain named Benito Cereno (with the suggestive initials B. C.) only to discover—after much doubt and confusion—that Cereno's ship has actually been taken over by the mutinous slaves whom he was transporting for his friend Alexandro Aranda. Delano's confusion about who is in charge on the San Dominick is long protracted because he is "a person of a singularly undistrustful good-nature, not liable, except on extraordinary and repeated incentives, and hardly then, to indulge in personal alarms, any way involving the imputation of malign evil in man." As the representative modern, progressive type of man described by Emerson, Delano can hardly be expected to suspect the worst of his fellows. Melville's untranscendental narrator observes, however, "Whether, in view of what humanity is capable, such a trait implies, along with a benevolent heart, more than ordinary quickness and accuracy of intellectual perception, may be left to the wise to determine" (67). At the beginning of the narrative, even the wise might be willing to accord Delano the benefit of the doubt. As the suspicious circumstances mount, however, only someone like Delano, a man of "such native simplicity as to be incapable of irony or satire" (90), could maintain his transcendental optimism. This is apparent in my favorite passage from this darkly humorous tale as Delano struggles to regain his sunny outlook after briefly suspecting that Cereno and his apparent valet, Babo, may have been planning to murder him: "What, I, Amasa Delano—Jack of the Beach, as they called me when a lad—I, Amasa; the same that, duck-satchel in hand, used to paddle along the water-side to the school-house made from an old hulk—I, little Jack of the Beach, that used to go berrying with cousin Nat and the rest; I to be murdered here at the ends of the earth, on board a haunted pirate-ship by a horrible Spaniard? Too nonsensical to think of! Who would murder Amaso Delano? His conscience is clean" (111). Melville shows us how to respond to all of these transcendental and antitranscendental signals by observing that "Captain Delano's nature was not only benign, but familiarly and humorously so" (121).[2] Perhaps we needn't add by this point that the humor involved here is of the Calvinist kind even if Melville does not qualify as a churchgoer.

In a passage that calls up echoes of Jonathan Edwards and his rotten plank,[3] the finally rescued Cereno asks Delano to think about how much danger actually resulted from his "credulous good-nature" (138): "Do but think how you walked this deck, how you sat in this cabin, every inch of ground mined into honeycombs under you" (167). Delano's response shows how little he has learned from his shattering experience: "Besides, those feelings I spoke of enabled me to get the better of momentary distrust, at times when acuteness might have cost me my life, without saving another's" (168). In other words, ignorance has brought Amasa Delano unharmed to bliss. He has stumbled along blindly like Mr. Magoo and come out successfully on the other side with his illusions still intact. One explanation for these comfortable illusions is Delano's unshakable conviction that everything will always work out for the best. While he is trying to convince himself that nothing bad can happen to him because he used to be "Jack of the Beach," for example, he remembers that "[t]here is someone above" (111). This providential reassurance returns when Delano is trying to assuage his lingering suspicions of Cereno and Babo just before returning to his own ship, the *Bachelor's Delight*: "Once again he smiled at the phantoms which had mocked him, and felt something like a twinge of remorse, that, by harbouring them even for a moment, he should, by implication, have betrayed an atheist doubt of the ever-watchful Providence above" (139). When all is said and done and all atheist doubts have been satisfactorily dealt with, Delano can still conclude, "Yes, all is owing to Providence, I know" (168). Thus the original question about whether such a trusting mind can be seen to possess "ordinary quickness and accuracy of intellectual perception" must be answered in the negative. Once this negative answer is given, the grim smile identified by Miller probably follows.

Melville stresses throughout "Benito Cereno" the insufficiency of the optimism that drives Delano's actions. When he first sees the *San Dominick*, for example, this ship that will soon prove to be a nest of depraved and bloody-minded murderers looks to Captain Delano like "nothing less than a ship-load of monks" (68). Later, after he momentarily suspects the motives of the wicked Ashanti warriors who are grimly sharpening hatchets, Delano sees "the whole file, like so many organ-grinders, still stupidly intent on their work, unmindful of everything besides." As a result of this mistaken perception, "he could not but smile at his late fidgety panic" (85).[4] That is to say that even when Delano finally approaches something like an adequate explanation for what is going on, he ends up misjudging the reality of the case. When he finally notices that Benito Cereno is behaving oddly as he is about to leave the latter's ship, "the good sailor," as Melville calls him, explains this behavior away by concluding that it probably arises "from a genuine twinge of conscience" (135) rather than from Cereno's fear that he will be abandoned to the murderous rebels.

Part of the problem, according to Melville, is Delano's ability to transvalue any true Calvinist insight regarding fallen human nature into a corresponding affirmation of optimism. One passage is especially effective in presenting this moral criticism by means of a metaphor: "All this is very queer now, thought Captain Delano, with a qualmish sort of emotion; but, as one feeling incipient sea-sickness, he strove, by ignoring the symptoms, to get rid of the malady" (110). Delano is, of course, successful in denying the proddings of good sense and thus continues to treat the whole mysterious encounter as Jack of the Beach would. That is, he continues to be what Harry Levin calls, in *The Power of Blackness,* "a typically innocent American" (189).[5] To Levin, to Melville, and to the reader, this American innocence must be somehow figured as grimly comic. In fact Melville often sounds amazed at the behavior of his own character, as when he has his narrator say, "Pressed by such enigmas and portents, it would have been almost against nature, had not, even into the least distrustful heart, some ugly misgivings intruded" (97). Misgivings do intrude on Delano's sunny worldview, but they are usually mistaken and are always unheeded, as the narrator reports: "In short, [there was] scarce any suspicion or uneasiness, however apparently reasonable at the time, which was not now, with equal apparent reason, dismissed" (99). These transvaluations are particularly inappropriate because the apparent valet

Babo—who is actually the mastermind behind the whole imposture—is extremely shrewd by any worldly standard. In the words of the court that decides Babo's ultimate fate, this rebellious slave "the better to disguise the truth, devised many expedients, in some of them uniting deceit and defence" (158). The optimistic, Emersonian Captain Delano is no match for such expedients, as the narrator and reader both see with Calvinist amusement.[6]

We are encouraged to see also that one of Delano's especially enfeebling traits is a form of racism that happily combines with his transcendental optimism to make him indifferent to the facts right before his eyes. It never occurs to him, for example, that Babo could be in charge— simply because Babo is black, and blacks are automatically inferior in all ways to whites. As Kenneth S. Lynn explains, Delano views the murderous slaves as "so many amiable Newfoundland dogs" (102). This misprision is evident when Babo, using the Spanish flag as a sheet, runs a sharp razor across Cereno's throat. Ignoring the possibility of bloody murder implied by the scene, Delano merely remarks that "[m]ost Negroes are natural valets and hair-dressers; taking to the comb and brush congenially as to the castanets, and flourishing them apparently with almost equal satisfaction" (120). In his supreme (white) self-confidence, Delano is convinced that what he thinks of as "the [generalized] negro" deservedly has "the repute of making the most pleasing body-servant in the world" (75). As the trial evidence later makes clear, the servant-master relationship aboard the San Dominick is the exact opposite of what Delano assumes, but Jack of the Beach "could not but bethink him of the beauty of that relationship which could present such a spectacle of fidelity on the one hand and confidence on the other" (82) because thinking of this sort accords with his own assumptions in a way that the direct testimony of his eyes will not do. Delano also transvalues the slave women on the ship, concluding about one young mother, "There's naked nature, now; pure tenderness and love" (105). The impression of natural maternal virtue seems highly improbable, given what John Calvin and many others—including Melville's narrator—have observed about human nature, but later developments in the tale make the point insistently.

It comes out in the trial, for example, "that, had the Negroes not restrained them, [the women] would have tortured to death, instead of simply killing, the Spaniards slain by command of the Negro Babo . . ." (163). This is a very bleak discovery about what Delano surely thinks of as the weaker sex, but its bleakness is compounded by the contrast it provides to Delano's fundamental views of race. Perhaps the clearest statement of these views occurs during one of the few moments in which Delano thinks he may be the object of a fatal conspiracy. As is consistent with his usual wrong-headedness, Delano thinks that Cereno and Babo may be planning his death together. Then he blithely dismisses these suspicions: "Besides, who ever heard of a white so far a renegade as to apostatize from his very species almost, by leaguing in against it with negroes?" (108–9). Amasa Delano is not even as shrewd as Hawthorne's Robin Molineux,[7] as all Calvinist humorists would happily agree, but these passages show how much of his basic foolishness is the product of his unquestioned racism—another occasion for Calvinist humor because it assumes a human superiority (based in whiteness) that the doctrine of the universal fall of man denies.

While "Benito Cereno" makes these horrific points about "reality" in terms of unsatisfactory human conduct, another portion of *The Piazza Tales*, "The Encantadas," makes these same Calvinistic jokes in terms of nature. We might, first of all, recall Emerson's encouragement to the reader of his first work, "Nature," to "[b]uild therefore your own world." If the reader will try to do so, Emerson promises, "disagreeable appearances, swine, spiders, snakes, pests, mad-houses, prisons, enemies will vanish" (50). About the part of the world called the Encantadas or Galapagos Islands, Melville's narrator simply says in response, "In no world but a fallen one could such lands exist" (183). A fallen world is just the place to test out the relative merits of optimism and Calvinist realism, and that is just what Melville does in "The Encantadas."

The narrator, first of all, observes about the simple geography of these islands: "Nothing can better suggest the aspect of once living things malignly crumbled from ruddiness to ashes. Apples of Sodom, after touching, seem these isles" (185). In such a decidedly fallen world, nothing very pleasant is likely to occur. Even the tortoises who inhabit the isles fit in with this gloomy assumption: "Lasting sorrow and penal hopelessness are in no animal form so suppliantly expressed as in theirs; while the thought of their wonderful longevity does not fail to enhance the impression" (186). To make matters even worse, the tortoises seem committed to a sort of monomaniacal singleness of purpose, so that they will struggle fruitlessly against any barrier in order to maintain their straight-ahead path. The narrator generalizes that this tendency is "their drudging impulse to straightforwardness in a belittered world" and sadly observes: "That these tortoises are the victims of a penal, or malignant, or perhaps a downright diabolical enchanter, seems in nothing more likely than in that strange infatuation of hopeless toil which so often possesses them" (191). On the positive side, then, we have the tortoises' long lives and their secure sanctuary against most predators. On the negative, we have the inhospitable, manifestly fallen character of this sanctuary and their almost accursed commitment to singleness of purpose. As Levin concedes, the narrator's apparently balanced understanding of the complex of good and bad qualities inherent to the tortoises' situation bespeaks "a mature perception" (199). In metaphoric language, this perception entails the narrator's attention to both the tortoises' dark shells and their bright calipees. It is significant, though, how Melville expresses this balance: "But after you have done this [exposed the calipee], and because you have done this, you should not swear that the tortoise has no dark side. Enjoy the bright, keep it turned up perpetually if you can, but be honest, and don't deny the black" (189). No one who considers the Encantadas as living evidence that the world is fallen is likely to deny the black. It is rhetorically significant, though, that Melville concludes his "mature perception" by noting the dark side. Still, it does not follow that this vision necessarily entails anything very comic.

Melville's consideration of the fish found in these latitudes does point in a comic direction. Because they are so unaccustomed to fishermen, these fish are very easily caught. The narrator's reflection upon what Emerson (19) would call this "natural fact" of the fish assumes a mildly ironic tone: "Poor fish of Rodondo! in your victimized confidence, you are of the number of those who inconsiderately trust, while they do not understand, human nature" (198). There is probably a buried Calvinist joke in the final comment about "human nature," but the humor—though present—must be conceded as slight in any case. More in line with what we have been seeing in other Calvinistically humorous authors, and also in Melville's other work, is the narrator's description of the birds found nesting on Rock Rodondo: "As we ascend from shelf to shelf, we find the tenants of the tower serially disposed in order of their magnitude:—gannets, black and speckled haglets, jays, sea-hens, sperm-whale-birds, gulls of all varieties—thrones, princedoms, powers, dominating one above another in senatorial array; while, sprinkled over all, like an ever-repeated fly in a great white piece of embroidery, the stormy petrel or Mother Carey's chicken sounds his continual challenge and alarm" (197). The sequence "thrones, princedoms, powers" probably involves some sort of satire involving angelic orders, but the decline in tone from "senatorial array" to "Mother Carey's chicken" most certainly qualifies as Calvinist humor by puncturing any tendency to focus too intently on the bright calipee of nature. To call the bird a "stormy petrel," as many might be tempted to do in this case, would be to pass up a chance for Calvinist humor. To think that anyone might be foolish enough to settle for the more elevated term or to expect better testimony than this from nature is to invite a grim smile.

This is the sort of smile we might adopt after understanding the "natural fact" of Rock Rodondo's real and symbolic appearance: "Its bird-lime gleams in the golden rays like the whitewash of a tall lighthouse, or the lofty sails of a cruiser. This moment, doubtless, while we know it to be a dead desert rock, other voyagers are taking oaths it is a glad populous ship" (198). Such Emersonian voyagers would seem to be as mistaken as the congregants in Jonathan Edwards's church who delude themselves about their eternal salvation. Those who have attained the superior position of the Calvinist humorist can only laugh at the foolishness of such optimists. Furthermore, getting to exploit a term like *bird-lime* only deepens the naughty pleasure. Another naughty pleasure involves the narrator's claim that nothing is simple, that positive results can follow on negative causes. This is the lesson taught by the rescue of the only appealing human character in "The Encantadas," that of Hunilla, the Chola Widow. This woman was left totally abandoned three years ago by the drowning deaths of her husband and brother and has been living in isolation and horror ever since. In fact, some of her experience has been so awful that the narrator cannot bring himself to re-create it on the page: "Those two unnamed events which befell Hunilla on this isle, let them abide between her and her God. In nature, as in law, it may be libelous to speak some truths" (229). This history is certainly grim enough to provide no occasion for smiling, and yet the cause of Hunilla's rescue may qualify as an occasion of Calvinist humor. One sailor, being slightly drunk on Peruvian Pisco, happened to look up as the ship was pulling away from the shore just in time to notice the distant widow, who had been unseen by all of the upright sailors, and this sighting simply led to her rescue. The narrator is therefore moved to observe, "Now, certainly, Pisco does a deal of mischief in the world; yet seeing that, in the present case, it was the means, though indirect, of rescuing a human being from the most dreadful fate, must we not also needs admit that sometimes Pisco does a deal of good?" (220). As when the narrator playfully invokes bird lime, the naughty exploitation of Pisco only adds to the pleasure of noticing something that others might prefer to ignore.

At other points in "The Encantadas," Melville's narrator is pushed beyond grim or even naughty laughter all the way to misanthropic pessimism. Reflecting on the fate of the Chola Widow, for example, the narrator first examines her unproductive prayers for deliverance: "Ah, heaven, when man thus keeps his faith, wilt thou be faithless who created the faithful one?" Then the narrator bitterly observes, "But they cannot break faith who never plighted it" (224). This same narrator concludes that "naught else abides on fickle earth but unkept promises of joy" (222). Such bleak assertions are all of a piece with a later metaphorical reflection: "Dire sight is it to see some silken beast long dally with a golden lizard ere she devour. More terrible, to see how feline Fate will sometimes dally with a human soul, and by a nameless magic make it repulse a sane despair with a hope which is but mad" (227). In summary, this disillusioned narrator consistently says, "Events, not books, should be forbid" (226–27). Later on, the voice of Nathanael West will echo this tone.

One is reminded of West too by Melville's somewhat less bitter characterization of the hermit Oberlus, for many years the sole inhabitant of an island composed of "dark pounded black lava, called Black Beach, or Oberlus's Landing. It might fitly have been styled Charon's" (236). Like most of the Encantadas, Oberlus's Landing seems to be a decidedly fallen landscape, but its hermit ruler acts as if this is not the case. First of all, the narrator detects in Oberlus an incomprehensible vanity. As he writes, "[A]ll this must have gradually nourished in him a vast idea of his own importance, together with a pure animal sort of scorn for all the rest of the universe" (239). To balance this unattractive quality somewhat, the narrator also acknowledges in Oberlus "a certain clerkliness . . . [and] the strangest satiric effrontery" (247). This mysterious mixture of human qualities comes into play when the narrator records the most salient story about Oberlus, the one about the letter he left for anyone who might later stumble across his abandoned hermit's lodge. This letter concludes mischievously: "Behind the clinkers, nigh the oven, you will find the old fowl. Do not kill it; be patient; I leave it setting; if it shall have any chicks, I hereby bequeath them to you, whoever you may be. But don't count your chicks before they are hatched." Then the narrator adds: "The fowl proved a starveling rooster, reduced to a sitting posture by sheer debility" (245). Like the Mother Carey's chicken who towers over the other birds at Rock Rodondo, this "starveling rooster" comes as a bitter, Calvinistic, anticlimax to the already bizarre narrative. That Melville intends some such conclusion is evident in the narrator's testimony about this passage: "The letter found in the hut is also somewhat different; for while at the Encantadas [the narrator] was informed that, not only did it evince a certain clerkliness, but was full of the strangest satiric effrontery which does not adequately appear in Porter's version. I accordingly altered it to suit the general character of its author" (247). The letter also suits the narrator's systematic exploitation of the disparity between optimistic expectations and bitterly disappointing results. Once again, a grim Calvinist smile is the only appropriate response.

Optimism frustrated is also the subject of Melville's novel *The Confidence Man*. In fact, this bitter Calvinist conclusion about the futility of hope may be the only subject of the novel because, as John W. Shroeder writes, "Nothing in particular happens in this book" (299). *The Confidence Man* is a novel of ideas if ever there was one,[8] and Melville's chief idea is designed to terminate in bitter Calvinist laughter. What happens in the novel is that the title character—who is probably Satan in disguise—serially tests the spiritual charity and worldly acuteness of a series of representative passengers aboard the riverboat *Fidèle* by asking them to bestow their confidence on him. Levin summarizes this action in *The Power of Blackness:*

> Melville's versatile operator makes his appearance—shortly after a mysterious impostor is reported from the East—as a mute, lamb-like stranger, inscribing a message of charity on a slate. This modest Messiah is quickly succeeded by a Negro cripple, begging for alms and being accused of being "a white masquerading as a black." There is a salesman who offers infernal stock in the Black Rapids Coal Company, but seems equally involved in a land development advertised as New Jerusalem. Patent medicines are peddled, such as the Omni-Balsamic Reinvigorator; then an up-to-date philosophy, which approximates Emersonianism. (193)

As Levin concludes, these incidents represent "all the suspected devices of quackery and chicanery." And as such—we may observe by this point—they provide ample ground for the sort of grim Calvinist smile that we have traced back to Melville's other works.

The "Negro cripple," first of all, is a figure who should provoke sympathetic charity from anyone—Calvinist, Christian, atheist, or just plain human—because he is not only crippled and stigmatized by race but also deaf and dumb. Instead of relieving his physical distress and financial destitution at once, though, the passengers sportively throw coins at his mouth in what they conceive to be a burst of generosity. The narrator reports, "And nearly always he grinned, and only once or twice did he wince, which was when certain coins, tossed by more playful almoners, came inconveniently nigh to his teeth, an accident whose unwelcomeness was not unedged by the circumstance that the pennies thus thrown proved buttons" (8). The (sometimes counterfeit) penny throwers in this scene are clearly objects of satiric scorn for their deluded understanding of generosity, but the more general attitudes of charity givers and receivers are also treated scornfully when the narrator philosophizes further: "To be the subject of alms-giving is trying, and to feel in duty bound to appear cheerfully grateful under the trial, must be more so; but whatever his secret emotions, [the Negro cripple] swallowed them, while still retaining each copper this side of the oesophagus."

This extension of a specific narrative instance to a more general criticism of typical human behavior is often Melville's philosophical strategy in this book, as he shows when a dispute erupts concerning the authenticity of this pathetic Negro's neediness. Chief spokesman for the doubters is a man with a wooden leg whose cynical rejection of the cripple's pleas is only provisionally accepted by the crowd. The "wiser" mode of charity seems to be for the passengers to withdraw into caucus while awaiting further evidence. Again the narrator generalizes the case: "So he with the wooden leg was forced to retire; when the rest, finding themselves left sole judges in the case, could not resist the opportunity of acting the part: not because it is a human weakness to take pleasure in sitting in judgment upon one in a box, as surely this unfortunate Negro now was . . ." (9). But, of course, Melville's point is that it is a very "human weakness" to delight in being "left sole judges in the case." This is also the point that Mark Twain will make over and over again in his *Pudd'nhead Wilson*. Melville is content to make the point only once—at least in this form.

Throughout *The Confidence Man* Melville returns to ideas that have furnished stores of Calvinist humor in other works. In a direct Emersonian denial that man is fallen, for example, the confidence man asks at one point "[W]hat creature but a madman would not rather do good than ill, when it is plain that, good or ill, it must return upon himself?" (34). This is a very grand estimate of human nature, but it is Emerson's not Melville's. As an inveterate reader of Shakespeare, Melville calls on the character Autolycus in *The Winter's Tale* to make a Calvinist point by denying an Emersonian one. The confidence man thus also says about Autolycus, "When disturbed by the character and career of one thus wicked and thus happy, my sole consolation is in the fact that no such creature ever existed, except in the powerful imagination which evoked him" (150). But, of course, many authors—including John Milton—have created characters who are satisfied by their own wickedness. But, the optimist will not have it so.

In the person of a character called the young collegian, Melville attributes this kind of sunny optimism to the familiar belief in an always benevolent Providence: "I say to him, you are happy enough, and you know it; and everybody else is as happy as you, and you know that, too; and we shall all be happy after we are no more, and you know that, too; but no, still you must have your sulk" (41). It may just be, actually, that you or I may not be happy now or later and that we may be mistaken to assume that something will guarantee that we are. As in *The Piazza Tales* a too sunny reliance on an always benevolent Providence is mocked. As in those works, too, Melville oddly recommends an attitude that combines careful distrust of Providence with a firm sense of Calvinistic fate. In *The Confidence Man* the Satanic central character enunciates this complex principle while peddling a bogus "Pain Dissuader": "Oh, Happiness on my right hand, and oh, Security on my left, can ye wisely adore a Providence, and not think it wisdom to provide?—Provide!" (72). Grasping materialism masked by hypocritical piety lurks behind such sayings, and the worldly-wise speaker is mocked along with his credulous hearers. Another signpost pointing forward to Twain appears.

Also Twainian is Melville's repeated revisiting of religious themes for comic effect. One of the confidence man's victims is an "old man . . . a well-to-do farmer, happily dismissed, after a thrifty life of activity, from the fields to the fireside" (206–7). When the confidence man quotes some verses from Ecclesiasticus[9] that unsettle this old man, the devout farmer replies: "Man and boy, I have read the good book this seventy years, and don't remember seeing anything like that. Let me see it" (208). After learning that the book of Ecclesiasticus is only an Apocryphal book of the Bible, the old man says with apparent relief, "The word itself [apocrypha], I've heard from the pulpit, implies something of uncertain credit" (209) and so regains his total confidence in Holy Scripture. Clearly Melville finds this response foolish and laughable and assumes that we will also. Religious doctrinal narrowness and the intolerance that it usually breeds is the subject of another telling passage, in which the narrator introduces the confidence man as the advocate for Seminole widows and orphans: "[I]n the pulpit it has been with much cogency urged, that a merely good man, that is, one good merely by his nature, is so far from thereby being righteous, that nothing short of a total change and conversion can make him so; which is something which no honest mind, well read in the history of righteousness, will care to deny . . ." (31). Melville's excessive language, his indirect syntax, and his obviously ironic employment of the term *righteousness* mark the passage as mockery. That the religiously righteous are the persons mocked is just another one of Melville's jokes, as is his mockery of those who place full trust in the Bible. All of these persons are indirectly indicted as Charlie Noble foolishly exclaims: "And who be Puritans, that I, an Alabamian, must do them reverence? A set of sourly conceited old Malvolios, whom Shakespeare laughs his full at in his comedies" (147). We have seen enough of Puritans by now to seriously doubt Charlie's characterization, and yet the witty invocation of Malvolio carries some weight also. Once again, Melville manages to make fun of two sides of a complex religious issue. Even when he seems to be writing about something else, he can make sly asides about religion. In the famous chapter 33, in which Melville expounds an often-cited theory of prose fiction, he writes, "It is with fiction as with religion: it should present another world, and yet one to which we feel the tie" (158). The observation is hardly withering, and yet it bespeaks a comfortable relation to religion that is far from what Agnes McNeill Donohue calls the "bowel-shattering, awesome vision" of orthodox Calvinism (4–5).

Of course, Calvinist ideas do appear in *The Confidence Man*. It can be deemed a Calvinist sort of Providence as well as an unfortunate fate that brings so much misfortune to poor China Aster in chapter 40 of the novel. That is to say, it could be either John Calvin or Nathanael West writing the following:

> [H]ow it was exactly, there is no telling, but poor China Aster fell to the earth, and, striking his head sharply, was picked up senseless. It was a day in July; such a light and heat as only the midsummer banks of the inland Ohio know. China Aster was taken home on a door; lingered a few days with a wandering mind, and kept wandering on, till at last, at dead of night, when nobody was aware, his spirit wandered away into the other world. (187)

The unbroken streak of bad luck depicted here somehow sounds more like Nathanael West's doing than it does Calvin's, but I detect the true Calvinist spirit at work behind some observations in the novel concerning typical human nature, as in this summary of the action in chapter 36: "In which the cosmopolitan is accosted by a mystic, whereupon ensues pretty much such talk as might be expected" (161). What "might be expected" is a real Calvinist subject, and its unerring regularity is a real Calvinist joke.

Joking—of all sorts—is still another subject that allows Melville to make jokes of just the Calvinist sort we have detected in the writings of other American authors. The confidence man himself, for example, says, "Ah, now . . . irony is so unjust; never could abide irony; something Satanic about irony. God defend me from Irony and Satire, his bosom friend" (119). Obviously, the confidence man is not speaking for the highly ironic and satiric Herman Melville. As Berthoff argues, "Melville's humor is inseparable from the imaginative intelligence supporting his gravest undertakings in fiction" (14). Therefore, it is more probable that Melville means just the opposite of what the confidence man says here, but—according to Lawrance Thompson's book, *Melville's Quarrel with God*—that is Melville's usual stylistic approach: "[T]hese seemingly unintentional emblems and symbols begin to interlock, and as the interlocking is sustained throughout, the narrative gradually achieves an inverted allegorical meaning" (301). So, we should look for Melville's meaning in terms of his inversions. That may mean that the joke is often on us. To avoid being the butt of such jokes, we therefore need to invert the confidence man's assertion: "Man is a noble fellow, and in an age of satirists, I am not displeased to find one who has confidence in him, and bravely stands up for him" (137). Standing up "bravely" for mankind is a ludicrously Emersonian posture, according to this book, but being able to recognize and appreciate humor, irony, and satire is truly virtuous. This is, in fact, what the confidence man directly says at one point: "Humor is, in fact, so blessed a thing, that even in the least virtuous product of the human mind, if there can be found but nine good jokes, some philosophers are clement enough to affirm that those nine good jokes should redeem all the wicked thoughts, though plenty as the populace of Sodom" (141). As we have seen already, there are at least "nine good jokes"—or, perhaps, nine Calvinist jokes—in *The Confidence Man.*

Perhaps we are able to appreciate these jokes because, as T. Walter Herbert, Jr., writes in *"Moby Dick" and Calvinism: A World Dismantled,* Melville's "viewpoints [are] more characteristic of our era than of his own" (ix). Thus, today we may appreciate more easily than his more devout, more easily shocked contemporaries the inverted Calvinist humor that allows Melville to mock the righteous Christians and the biblical literalists. Few readers in the twenty-first century are likely to expect perfection from others—including righteous Christians and biblical literalists—and so few would be shocked to find these others mocked by an author for their only-to-be-expected human imperfections. In fact, contemporary readers may be so "advanced" as to blunt the effect of some of Melville's Calvinist humor. This is a point raised by Hershel Parker in his analysis of Melville's theology of outrage: "The final irony may be that for modern readers able to accept Melville's darkest meanings Christianity is so 'diluted' that they have become insensitive to his satire and, more appallingly, have lost his apprehension that the impracticability of Christianity is tragic" (331). However, even those who never even think about "the impracticability of Christianity" can often relish Melville's insistent skewerings of his fictional characters. Whether we see a reflection of our own foolishness and imperfections in Amasa Delano and the victims of the confidence man or instead see in these characters the pathetic shortcomings of those whom we are oh so happy to find ourselves superior to, we will find ourselves comfortably situated as readers to appreciate Melville's Calvinist humor.

5 Mark Twain

"The Trouble about Special Providences"

Nearly everyone agrees that distinct traces of Calvinist thinking linger in the undeniably humorous writings of Mark Twain (Samuel Langhorne Clemens). H. L. Mencken can speak for many when he observes that "[i]t is, indeed, precisely in the works of such men as Mark Twain that one finds the best proofs of the Puritan influence of American letters, for it is there that it is least expected and hence most significant" (205). George M. Marsden agrees, in his biography of Jonathan Edwards, when he demonstrates the continuing influence of his chosen subject by observing that even in Mark Twain's last fictional works he "was still contending with versions of Edwardsean theology he had first encountered on the Missouri frontier" (500). When critics are pursuing a less theological agenda, they still usually share this view. For example, in introducing a collection of Twain's shorter humorous writing called *The Comic Mark Twain Reader,* Charles Neider readily concedes "Mark Twain's dark side, his pessimism regarding the human condition, his deterministic views of man's fate" (xv), thus nearly providing a profile of the sort of Calvinist humorist that we have glimpsed so far in this book. In *God and the American Writer,* Alfred Kazin makes this connection explicit, noting that Twain "chose to be a satirist, a disturber of convention" largely in reaction to "the early, dutiful, easily terrified Presbyterianism" of his Missouri upbringing (176).

Twain's resemblance to other Calvinist humorists has also attracted attention. James W. Gargano writes, "Like Melville, Twain could quarrel with God about the limits built into creation" (370). Maxwell Geismar draws a similar comparison to Melville but focuses more narrowly on

Twain's 1894 novel *Pudd'nhead Wilson*: "Clemens was deliberately adopting the sardonic and tragic mask which, say, Melville—another innocent native spirit who has felt himself similarly wounded and betrayed by life—used in *The Piazza Tales*" (130). Since we have already seen the Calvinist humor illuminating Melville's *Piazza Tales,* we are perhaps well situated to appreciate the Calvinist humor of *Pudd'nhead Wilson* and of other works by Mark Twain.

F. R. Leavis sets the stage for this appreciation in his 1956 article "Mark Twain's Neglected Classic: The Moral Astringency of *Pudd'nhead Wilson*," when he writes about the residual Calvinism of the author: "There is of course a glance here at the Calvinism of Mark Twain's youth. And it is to be noted that Roxy, while usurping the prerogative of the predestinating Deity, has shown a wholly human compassion, and has invoked a compassionate God in doing so . . ." (241). Although compassion has played a very small part in our discussion to this point, predestination has been a constant concern, and so Leavis's suggestion might be the best place to begin looking at Twain's novel. The slave Roxy's "compassionate" act occurs when she substitutes her own light-skinned son, Valet de Chambre, for her master's white son, Thomas à Becket Driscoll, confident that the two boys look so much alike that her own son, who was born a slave, can take his white master's place in society. The deterministic side of Roxy's act is apparent when she is willing to interrogate divine providence without questioning the finality of its workings: "God was good to you [Thomas]; why warn't He good to him [Valet de Chambre]?" (13). When all is said and done, Roxy accepts the newly defined deterministic explanation for the boys' fates, as everyone else in the town seems inclined to do. In Roxy's case, the stimulus is religious, the sermonizing of "dat ole nigger preacher" who paraphrased John Calvin to this effect: "He said dey ain't nobody kin save his own self—can't do it by faith, can't do it by works, can't do it no way at all. Free grace is de *on'y* way, en dat don't come fum nobody but jis' de Lord; en *He* kin give it to anybody He please, saint or sinner—*He* don't kyer. He do jis' as He's a mineter. He s'lect out anybody dat suit Him, en put another one in his place, en make de fust one happy forever en leave t'other one to burn wid Satan" (15).[1] This speech makes what Henry Nash Smith wrote about the

book even more plausible: "The material drawn up thus into consciousness is not comic, but intensely serious" (174).

And yet, Smith's judgment about the novel's seriousness is not the last
word. In another episode featuring Roxy's religious enthusiasms, the narrator says that "a week or two would limber up her piety, and then she
would be rational again . . ." (11), and Smith observes that "Twain is at his
comic-ironic best in this scene . . ." (178). Apparently, then, this novel is
both serious and comic. If we wonder how this can be so, the explanation
is not far to seek. It lies in recognizing that Twain's humor in the book is
deeply rooted in very serious matters having to do with race, character, and
fate. Robert A. Wiggins explains that "[t]he humor in [*Pudd'nhead Wilson*]
is of a sardonic sort" (255), and Sidney E. Berger, editor of the Norton
Critical edition of the novel, says that Twain's humor here "is not the
guffawing type; it makes one grin and grimace at the same time" (x). In
other words, it is, in the terms that I have been employing to this point,
Calvinist humor. Stanley Brodwin points out that "[f]or Mark Twain,
man was 'damned' in the precise theological sense. He wrote in the mar-
gin of a book by an optimistic evolutionist that man 'was made to suffer
and be damned.' . . . Joseph Twichell chided Mark Twain for being 'too
orthodox on the Doctrine of Total Human Depravity.' . . . Indeed, there
are a great many references in Mark Twain's works to man's sinfulness,
his fall, and the demonic God who punishes him for it" (333, n. 4). This is
clearly the territory staked out by Calvinist humorists, as Gargano makes
clear: "Apparently, humanity is perfectly wrought by the stigmata of its
own nature to bring mischief upon itself, especially when it aspires, as it
is pathologically prone to do, beyond its capabilities" (370). However we
phrase it, the slightly bizarre humor in *Pudd'nhead Wilson* causes us to
"grin and grimace at the same time."

The novel follows the lives of Valet de Chambre, who grows up as the
white Tom Driscoll, and of Thomas à Becket Driscoll, who grows up as
the light-skinned slave called Chambers. There is also some attention to
the title character—who earned his demeaning nickname by making a bad
impression on the townsfolk when he first appeared there—and to a set
of nearly identical twins named Luigi and Angelo. All of this action leads
John C. Gerber to conclude that "like *Catch-22* and *Cat's Cradle*, *Pudd'nhead*

Wilson pictures a bizarre world in which the characters play necessary roles in what can only be called a cruel and on-going joke" (25). In addition to the Calvinist jokes involved in the plot, Twain prefaces each chapter with a bitterly comic epigraph proposed as an entry from Pudd'nhead Wilson's Calendar. The consequent impression is bleak but entertaining. As Gargano concludes, "Though sometimes tempted into sallies of bitterness, Twain generally maintains an ironic balance which views the human spectacle with a wise and lordly amusement" (365). This sort of humorous balance is what we have seen in the works of Melville, Hawthorne, and other Calvinist humorists.

Twain makes some of his Calvinist jokes merely by noting that human nature is consistent from place to place and age to age. This is the motive for the narrator's largely irrelevant observation at one point that "a village fire company does not often get a chance to show off, and so when it does get a chance it makes the most of it" (57). Excessive fire hose use is the burlesque narrative justification for this remark, but our common ability to predict the behavior of any volunteer firemen anywhere is Twain's actual motive for enunciating this maxim. By the same token, Judge Driscoll's inability to believe anything ill of Tom has some influence on the narrative's plot, but the general truth illustrated by this excessive parental trust derives more from the treasury of bitter Calvinist wisdom than from any exigencies of plotting: "One must make allowances for a parental instinct that has been starving for twenty-five or thirty years. It is famished, it is crazed with hunger by that time, and will be entirely satisfied with anything that comes handy; its taste is atrophied, it can't tell a mud-cat from a shad. A devil born to a young couple is measurably recognizable by them as a devil before long, but a devil adopted by an old couple is an angel to them, and remains so, through thick and thin" (92–93). As so often in Twain's work, we are disposed to nod sagely at this observation and grin reluctantly even as we grimace at the apparent truth of what he says.

Even more disturbing is the Calvinist aura surrounding Tom's relations with his actual parent, whom he sells down the river to pay off a gambling debt. Tom assuredly is, as Robert A. Wiggins maintains, "black-hearted by the circumstances of his birth" (256) and thus unlikely to show any redeeming virtues. He is just fated to be evil, irrespective of what the Judge or Roxy do for him. However, Roxy is so desperate to find some redeeming quality in Tom that she misinterprets his anger at her escape from slavery as evidence of his annoyance at her captors: "She was pleased—pleased and grateful; for did not that expression show that her child was capable of grieving for his mother's wrongs and of feeling resentment toward her persecutors?—a thing which she had been doubting" (86). The novel's answer to Roxy's question is a resounding No. Wiggins speaks directly to the point again in saying that "[t]he incident illustrates Twain's Calvinistic-deterministic belief that man is fundamentally evil and incapable of moral goodness" (256). If man is fundamentally evil, as Calvin proposes, then Tom Driscoll easily qualifies for membership in the human race. Tom's unchangingly evil behavior symbolically reinforces one of the novel's narrative devices. Despite his falsely earned nickname, Pudd'nhead Wilson saves the day by discovering Tom's murder of the Judge by means of the newly discovered science of fingerprinting. Wilson assures the townspeople, and Twain's readers, that "[e]very human being carries with him from his cradle to his grave certain physical marks which do not change their character" (108), and this turns out to be true in terms of the novel's plot. Although Wilson does not say so, it is true also of human character. Tom Driscoll is just a bad penny. He always has been one, even in childhood, and he always will be one, no matter what any kind heart expects. Tom is clearly one of the damned.

But Twain's Calvinistic reflections are not always so depressing as this. When the small-town citizens of Dawson's Landing get a chance to wallow in the European celebrity of the twins, for example, Twain's narrator finds their behavior predictable but not necessarily destructive. Thus he can comfortably begin an account of how these townspeople are passing through a receiving line by observing, "Now and then, as happens at all receptions . . ." (29). Twain is confident his readers know that when many people have to pass through a limited space some people are not on their very best behavior. But, after all, they are all fallen human beings, and so who would expect them to act differently? Twain is equally indulgent toward the twins' hostesses, Aunt Patsy Cooper and her daughter Rowena, saying, "There were no idle moments for mother

or daughter. . . . [E]ach recognized that she knew now for the first time
the real meaning of the great word Glory, and perceived the stupendous
value of it, and understood why men in all ages had been willing to throw
away meaner happiness, treasure, life itself, to get a taste of its sublime
and supreme joy. Napoleon and all his kind stood accounted for—and
justified" (29). Aunt Patsy and Rowena's sense of self-importance puts
them on the wrong end of the narrator's irony here, but they are still not
totally worthless, nor are they clearly intended for eternal punishment,
as Tom is.

Twain uses this more forgiving tone when describing the Judge's
behavior toward these distinguished visitors also. Since we have already
recognized the Judge's paternal blindness toward Tom's deep-dyed evil,
we will probably not be surprised to find him foolishly trying to impress
Angelo and Luigi with some very unimpressive sights. The narrator observes: "[T]he twins admired his admiration and paid him back the best
they could, though they could have done better if some fifteen or sixteen
hundred thousand previous experiences of this sort in various countries
had not already rubbed off a considerable part of the novelty of it" (31).
Things are pretty much the same everywhere, as any true Calvinist would
expect, and so the Judge's foolishness and the twins' bored responses are
perfectly understandable. The twins are equally tolerant of the Judge's
feeble attempts at humor. We learn that the Judge mistakenly "told them
a good many humorous anecdotes, and always forgot the nub," and we
are not too surprised to discover that "they were always able to furnish
it, for these yarns were of a pretty early vintage" (31). All of this, in other
words, is pretty much what we would have expected on the basis of our
past encounters with what Twain called "the damned human race."[2]

The damned human race is also the focus of most of the entries from
Pudd'nhead Wilson's Calendar, which serve as epigraphs to the chapters
in Pudd'nhead Wilson. Some of these are just plain jokes aimed at anyone
at all, irrespective of Calvinist sympathies or lack thereof. Thus Twain
prefaces his final chapter with the remark that "[i]t was wonderful to find
America, but it would have been more wonderful to miss it" (113). Twain's
play on the various ways in which the word *find* can be used requires no
bleakness of outlook to appreciate, and yet many of the Calendar entries

are of another, Calvinist sort. In an essay devoted to the subject of the Calendar, Thomas W. Ford writes: "It allows Twain to express certain interests and ideas, which were of major importance to him, without having to weave them into the narrative. He can thus say whatever he pleases, give his thoughts free rein without the fear that they will be out of place in the context of the narrative" (16). Henry Nash Smith agrees that the Calendar entries are "clearly expressing the attitudes of Mark Twain himself" (182), as does Maxwell Geismar, who sees in these sentences "Clemens' own mordant reflections about the bitterness of life, the folly, the tragedy here, much more than any sense of comedy" (136). In other words, Twain's laying off responsibility for these bleak observations on the fictional Pudd'nhead Wilson does not confuse these critics as to their true origin in the author's Calvinist perceptions. Richard Chase articulates this view definitely by writing, "[E]xcept for the ones that are mere easy cynicism we do not believe them to have come from [Pudd'nhead]" (156). Marvin Fisher and Michael Elliott agree: "It is scarcely possible to imagine that . . . Wilson . . . could have produced the penetrating combination of disillusioned wit, cynicism, and iconoclasm in the Calendar" (309). Whatever their views of the entries' source, all of these critics would be inclined to agree with Sidney E. Berger that these "maxims, with their wry humor and satire, make us grimace at how bitter our existence must be, how foolish we all are, how insignificant man is" (xi). That is to say, Pudd'nhead Wilson's Calendar abounds in Calvinist humor, chiefly of the ironic sort favored by Jonathan Swift and Voltaire, among others.

The Calendar is introduced into the novel's principal narrative in this way: "For some years Wilson had been privately at work on a whimsical almanac, for his amusement—a calendar with a little dab of ostensible philosophy, usually in ironical form, appended to each date; and the Judge thought that these quips and fancies of Wilson's were neatly turned and cute; so he carried a handful of them around, one day, and read them to some of the chief citizens. But irony was not for these people . . ." (25). Since the Judge is elsewhere shown to be a true object of Calvinist humor himself, we may be amazed at his sensitivity to the Calendar's irony here, but the Calendar has little direct bearing on the plot of *Pudd'nhead Wilson* in any case. The Calendar's maxims coincide philosophically with the thematic emphases of the novel elsewhere, but their principal purpose seems to be, as Ford explains, to allow Mark Twain to "say whatever he pleases, give his thoughts free rein without the fear that they will be out of place in the context of the narrative."

Some of these maxims resemble Twain's—or Melville's—usual observations about human nature, as when the Calendar observes, before chapter 6 recounts the twins' social success, that "[h]abit is habit, and not to be flung out of the window by any man, but coaxed down-stairs a step at a time" (27). The human race is perhaps not entirely admirable here in its difficulty with giving up bad habits, but neither is it unquestionably damnable. Chapter 9 shows Tom Driscoll in a particularly unflattering light, but the maxim preceding the chapter does not seem especially bitter: "It is easy to find fault, if one has that disposition" (40). The epigraph to chapter 8, on the other hand, resembles Twain's earlier Calendar entry about Adam and the apple in his unillusioned admission that human nature usually follows the lower road: "The holy passion of Friendship is of so sweet and steady and loyal and enduring a nature that it will last through a whole lifetime if not asked to lend money" (33). Apparently this reluctance to help others when it comes down to actual money is intended to be accepted as a universal human trait. In the same way, when Twain generalizes before chapter 11 that "[t]here are three infallible ways of pleasing an author . . ." (47), we are intended to understand that these ways will work with any author anywhere so long as the author is human. This understanding of authorial vanity hardly seems bitter enough for Michael Wigglesworth and other Puritan writers, however. On the other hand, any Calvinist humorist would probably endorse the principle that introduces chapter 16: "If you pick up a starving dog and make him prosperous, he will not bite you. This is the principal difference between a dog and a man" (80). Since this is the chapter in which Tom sells his mother down the river, some sort of philosophical bleakness in the epigraph is probably appropriate, but the black-dog severity of the observation goes beyond the activity of this one fictional character, lending credence to Leslie Fiedler's judgment of the book in his article "'As Free as Any Cretur . . .'":

"[T]here remains beneath the assertion that a man is master of his fate, the melancholy conviction that to be born is to be doomed, a kind of secularized Calvinism" (228).

A "secularized Calvinism" governs much of Twain's plot also, as when the New Orleans bank that Roxy had been counting on to provide for her old age "had gone to smash and carried her four hundred dollars with it" (33). The wicked way things work out in the world is equally evident when Tom continues to disappoint his mother bitterly despite her hopes for his reformation. Thus the narrator remarks, "[I]t took two rebuffs to convince her that her beautiful dream was a fond and foolish vanity, a shabby and pitiful mistake" (37). This is because, as the narrator observes, "Tom imagined that his character had undergone a pretty radical change. But that was because he did not know himself . . . but the main structure of his character was not changed, and could not be changed" (45). In light of such severe predestinatory dicta, there is even some question whether Twain's Calvinism is especially "secularized." Tom is as unquestionably destined for damnation by his very nature as any character that we have encountered so far in this book.

Twain's Calendar entries touch on another Calvinist sore spot, the possibility of special Providences.[3] Before chapter 4, in which Tom reveals his evil disposition even as a child, Pudd'nhead's Calendar wittily observes: "There is this trouble about special providences—namely, there is so often a doubt as to which party was intended to be the beneficiary. In the case of the children, the bears and the prophet, the bears got more real satisfaction out of the episode than the prophet did, because they got the children" (17). The joke is funny enough for anyone, but it should strike Calvinist believers in special Providences with especial force. Alfred Kazin quotes Twain's notebooks to show that the author was not among these believers: "I do not believe in special providences. I believe that the universe is governed by strict and immutable laws. If one man's family is swept away by a pestilence and another man's spared it is only the law working: God is not interfering in that small matter, either against one man or in favor of the other" (qtd. in Kazin 189).[4] Clearly, then, some aspects of John Calvin's thought do not accord smoothly with Twain's own, but Calvin's general disposition toward the damned human race obviously seemed sensible to Twain. And, since Twain was a naturally comic writer, it is only to be expected that he would express his agreement by means of Calvinist humor.

All in all, though, the most distinct instances of Calvinist humor in *Pudd'nhead Wilson* reside in the Calendar. While a Grosset and Dunlap edition of the novel intended for youthful readers claims in its jacket copy that the "story . . . is much more dramatic and complicated in plot" than the rest of Twain's "Mississippi River tales," the tonic acidity of the Calendar maxims probably appeals more strongly than the plot to adult readers, especially to adult readers immersed in the residual Calvinism that characterizes modern American life. Leslie Fielder, for example, opines that "[m]orally, it is one of the most honest books in our literature" (221). The popularity of these dark observations about human nature is not confined to readers of Twain's novel, either at its first publication or upon later critical reflection. In Milton Meltzer's coffee table book *Mark Twain Himself*, for example, two pages are devoted to entries from the Calendar, freely mixing those taken from Twain's 1894 novel with selections from his 1897 travel book, *Following the Equator*, which also prefaced each chapter with an entry from what that book called "Pudd'nhead Wilson's New Calendar."[5]

Many entries from the New Calendar carry on the perceptive but benign judgments enunciated in the earlier book. Thus, in the first volume of *Following the Equator*, the musing voice observes, "Truth is the most valuable thing we have. Let us economize it" (1: 72). This is also the sadder-but-wiser tone characterizing this famous definition, also from the first volume: "'*Classic*.' A book which people praise and don't read" (1: 220). From the second volume comes this insightful but easily dodged barb: "There isn't a Parallel of Latitude but thinks it would have been the Equator if it had had its rights" (2: 366). The form of Calvinist humor that discerns the mote in our neighbor's eye while allowing us to ignore the beam in our own permits us to recognize a truth here without applying it too closely to our own cases. Two other entries from this second volume involve a harsher kind of criticism. After the unthreatening observation prefacing chapter 3, "By trying we can easily learn to endure adversity. Another man's, I mean" (2: 24), comes the parallel but far more critical preface to chapter 4: "Few of us can stand prosperity. Another man's, I mean" (2: 38). Spite, pettiness, and groundless animus seem to be the actuating principles of human nature according to reflections of this sort. In the same way, another entry from the second volume indicts everyone equally: "It takes your enemy and your friend, working together, to hurt you to the heart; the one to slander you and the other to get the news to you" (2: 84). This rationalizes the famous and unsettling judgment that precedes chapter 27 in the first volume: "Man is the Only Animal that Blushes. Or needs to" (1: 238). There is no question whether this is funny. It is, of course. But, it is funny mostly when we accept the fallen nature of human life. Twain's commitment to this sad project is evident in some Calendar entries that seem to go beyond humor—even of the Calvinist sort—into mere misanthropy. Two entries from the first volume epitomize this tone: "Everything human is pathetic. The secret source of Humor itself is not joy but sorrow" (1: 101) and "Pity is for the living, envy is for the dead (1: 167). One entry from the second volume accords especially closely with these sentiments: "The very ink with which all history is written is merely fluid prejudice" (2: 366). Perhaps, as Pudd'nhead Wilson adds, in a conclusion to the first entry above from the first volume of *Following the Equator,* "There is no humor in heaven" (1: 101). There is humor on earth, however, but as these examples show, it is often humor created *sub specie aeternitatis.*

A more earthly form of humor in Twain stems from his reliance on what Mikhail Bakhtin calls "the grotesque body." According to Bakhtin's book *Rabelais and His World,* "The essential principle of grotesque realism is degradation, that is, the lowering of all that is high, spiritual, ideal, abstract; it is a transfer to the material level, to the sphere of earth and body in their indissoluble unity" (19–20). This is probably the literary strategy we see at work in Twain's story "The Notorious Jumping Frog of Calaveras County" when we read about Jim Smiley: "Parson Walker's wife laid very sick once, for a good while, and it seemed as if they warn't going to save her; but one morning he come in, and Smiley up and asked him how she was, and he said she was considerable better—thank the Lord for his inf'nite mercy—and coming on so smart that with the blessing of Prov'dence she'd get well yet; and Smiley, before he thought, says,

'Well, I'll resk two-and-a-half she don't anyway'" (*The Complete Short Stories* 2). The combination of Parson Walker, the Lord's infinite mercy, and the blessings of Providence can stand for the "high, spiritual, ideal, abstract" in this case, and Smiley's irreverence and his automatic rush to bet can represent "the material level." And, Mrs. Walker's physical debility is definitely a bonus. The same ingredients are thus as much present as in Bakhtin's analysis of "grotesque realism." Even so, Twain's writings usually do not produce such a sunny optimism as Bakhtin's.

Bakhtin writes optimistically about the humorous effectiveness of specific physical references:

> The grotesque body, as we have often stressed, is a body in the act of becoming. It is never finished, never completed; it is continually built, created, and builds and creates another body. Moreover, the body swallows the world and is itself swallowed by the world. . . . This is why the essential role belongs to those parts of the grotesque body in which it outgrows its own self, transgressing its own body, in which it conceives a new, second body: the bowels and the phallus. These two areas play the leading role in the grotesque image, and it is precisely for this reason that they are predominantly subject to positive exaggeration, to hyperbolization; they can even detach themselves from the body, as something secondary. (The nose can also in a way detach itself from the body.) Next to the bowels and the genital organs is the mouth, through which enters the world to be swallowed up. And next is the anus. All these convexities and orifices have a common characteristic; it is within them that the confines between bodies and between the body and the world are overcome: there is an exchange and an interorientation. This is why the main events in the life of the grotesque body, the acts of bodily drama, take place in this sphere. Eating, drinking, defecation and other elimination (sweating, blowing the nose, sneezing), as well as copulation, pregnancy, dismemberment, swallowing up by another body—all these acts are performed on the confines of the body and the outer world, or on the confines of the old and new body. In all these events the beginning and end of life are closely linked and interwoven. (317)

Talking about the things that "nice people" don't talk about—or even acknowledge—helps, according to Bakhtin, to bring about a new, highly preferable culture. As Bakhtin hopefully asserts in his book on Rabelais, "[D]egradation digs a bodily grave for a new birth; it has not only a de-

structive, negative aspect, but also a regenerating one" (21). It is noteworthy that Bakhtin holds out these encouraging prospects to us even
after his own grueling Russian experiences with the Czar and with Josef
Stalin.[6] Twain's antagonists are somewhat less dangerous and repugnant
than Bakhtin's, and yet his expectations of ultimate triumph are far more
muted.

The chief enemy for Twain is the genteel tradition, for which his wife
Livy, his dear friend William Dean Howells, and (sometimes) Twain himself were spokespersons. Writing in the *Columbia Literary History of the
United States* about the New England in which Twain spent his mature
years, James M. Cox economically identifies this societal adversary of
Twain's humor: "Having become a world in which body yielded to mind,
life was secondary to learning, nature was superseded by culture, and
passion was dominated by morality, the region was, in a word, genteel"
(769). Under these conditions, it would seem highly improbable that "a
new birth" or "a regenerating" vision might emerge from Twain's comic
renderings of a dog who has had his hind legs cut off by a saw (in "The
Notorious Jumping Frog of Calaveras County") or of a man who fell into
a carpet-making machine (in "The Story of the Old Ram") or of a putre-
fying corpse (in "The Invalid's Story"), and yet Twain wrote about all of
these immediately physical, un-genteel, subjects.[7] His purpose, it seems
to me, is not to trumpet a Bakhtinian glorification of the earthly in order
to bring about a new, better-balanced society, but rather an exploitation
of the undeniably physical in order to insist that all human beings are far
from spiritual perfection, despite their protestations to the contrary, that
they—we—are all fallen from perfect grace.

A brilliant example occurs in chapter 2 of *Adventures of Huckleberry
Finn* when Huck talks about the universal problem of inappropriate
(physical) itches: "There was a place on my ankle that got to itching; but I
dasn't scratch it; and then my ear begun to itch; and next my back, right
between my shoulders. Seemed like I'd die if I couldn't scratch. Well, I've
noticed that thing plenty of times since. If you are with the quality, or at
a funeral, or trying to go to sleep when you ain't sleepy—if you are any-
wheres where it won't do for you to scratch, why you will itch all over in
upwards of a thousand places" (22–23). The passage adds little to Twain's

narrative, but as a reminder to the "quality" that *everyone* feels itchy from time to time, the episode stands as an example of one variety of Twain's Calvinist humor. One of the defining properties of this humor is the author's inclusion of himself and his readers as objects of the joke. He knows what an itch feels like, and he is sure that we do too. When we recall that itchiness plays no part in salvation, we can begin to see Twain's brilliant comic strategy. Many critics have made this observation in a wide variety of ways. Lewis Leary, for example, praises Twain's strategy as an alternative to the less effective strategy of James Fenimore Cooper. According to Leary, Cooper "knew nothing of Mark Twain's secret, that the satirist is safest within the satire, so that it becomes, not what fools *these,* but what fools *we* mortals be" (xxiii). Pascal Covici makes a similar observation when he explains that Twain's humorous "effects do not, ultimately, depend on a detached objectivity that permits the reader to look upon scoundrels and boors as nonhuman beasts of no importance . . ." (13). To Twain, we are all in the same boat, and—unfortunately—this boat is not heading toward the genteel heaven so esteemed by his contemporaries. According to Kenneth S. Lynn, Twain's laughter is thus "more compassionate and humane" than that of most other humorists (167). Another example from the first chapter of *Huckleberry Finn* shows what these critics are talking about. After Miss Watson has persecuted Huck for his very normal physical behavior, she explains how he is probably destined for "the bad place" as a punishment for his very humanity, while she is clearly destined for the genteel heaven to which I have previously referred. Huck says, as any of us might, "Well, I couldn't see no advantage in going where she was going, so I made up my mind I wouldn't try for it." Then, he appeals to our comfortable sense of our own moral excellence by adding, "But I never said so, because it would only make trouble, and wouldn't do no good" (19). Here we are very close to acknowledging the superiority of the physical over the abstractly spiritual, but in Twain's work a mere assertion that the physical actually exists is as far as we are going to get.

Beginning with the case least challenging to a genteel reader intent on denying the physical, we might note what Twain says about Jim Smiley's fighting dog, Andrew Jackson, in "The Notorious Jumping Frog of Calaveras County": "Smiley always come out winner on that pup, till he harnessed a dog once that didn't have no hind legs, because they'd been sawed off in a circular saw, and when the thing had gone on long enough, and the money was all up, and he come to make a snatch for his pet holt, he see [sic] in a moment how he'd been imposed on, and how the other dog had him in the door, so to speak, and he 'peared surprised, and then he looked sorter discouraged-like, and didn't try no more to win the fight, and so he got shucked out bad" (*Complete Short Stories* 3). As simple humor, the incident turns on the age-old device of personification. Andrew Jackson's response to the legless dog is very human and so humorous—especially in the extended sense that any of us might experience a similar surprise in similar circumstances. However, the evidence of Calvinist humor in the incident lies in the dog's very cruel physical condition. Just as Smiley's frog, Daniel Webster, will later be cruelly stuffed with quail shot, this dog has had his rear legs cut off by a circular saw. Because the victims here are animals, however, Twain asks very little recognition of our common humanity from his readers.

In "The Story of the Old Ram" from *Roughing It,* the humorous stakes are somewhat higher. The first challenge might be easily dodged by most genteel readers. Jim Blaine tells us about "a galoot by the name of Filkins—I disremember his first name; but he *was* a stump—come into pra'r-meeting drunk, one night, hooraying for Nixon, because he thought it was a primary" (78). Undermining a prayer meeting and being drunk are physical affronts to propriety in Twain's or Bakhtin's sense of the word, but they can be glossed over here because Filkins is identified as "a galoot," someone clearly below the reader on the social scale. However, in the same tale Miss Jefferson and Miss Wagner seem to have as much social standing as Miss Watson in *Huckleberry Finn.* Even so, they are both missing an eye, and so Miss Jefferson "used to lend [her glass eye] to old Miss Wagner, that hadn't any, to receive company in." Even the missing eyes are not physical enough to puncture aspirations to religio/social excellence, though, because Blaine goes on to explain that "it warn't big enough, and when Miss Wagner warn't noticing, it would get twisted around in the socket, and look up, maybe, or out to one side, and every which way, while t'other one was looking as straight ahead as a spyglass." Because Miss Jefferson is described as a "poor old filly" and Miss

Wagner as "a bashful cretur and easily sot back before company," Twain manages to keep these ladies from becoming mere freaks, even though their physical situations are decidedly grotesque. Just how grotesque Miss Wagner's case is can be seen from the rest of Blaine's account:

> She tried packing it [the glass eye] in raw cotton, but it wouldn't work, somehow—the cotton would get loose and stick out and look so kind of awful that the children couldn't stand it no way. She was always dropping it out, and turning up her old deadlight on the company empty, and making them oncomfortable, becuz *she* never could tell when it hopped out, being blind on that side, you see. So somebody would have to hunch her and say, "Your game eye has fetched loose, Miss Wagner, dear"—and then all of them would have to sit and wait till she jammed it in again—wrong side before, as a general thing, and green as a bird's egg, being a bashful cretur and easily sot back before company. But being wrong side before warn't much difference, anyway, becuz her own eye was sky blue and the glass one was yaller on the front side, so whichever was she turned it it didn't match nohow. (*Complete Short Stories* 78–79)

The incident is grisly—bordering on the macabre—but it is especially relevant to the point I wish to make because Miss Wagner is not a dog or a frog but a human being, a very physical human being.

Maria Martin and her husband are very human also, so much so that they get "et up by the savages" (*Complete Short Stories* 80) in the same tale. In this sense, Twain's physical details reach their ultimate completion—death. Another exemplar of this development is William Wheeler, who "got nipped by the machinery in a carpet factory and went through in less than a quarter of a minute" (*Complete Short Stories* 80). Wheeler's physically revolting mode of death grounds the incident clearly in the physical rather than the genteelly abstract.[8] In case the physical is not comic enough in itself, Twain adds an absurd denouement: "[H]is widder bought the piece of carpet that had his remains wove in, and people come a hundred mile to 'tend the funeral. There was fourteen yards in the piece. She wouldn't let them roll him up, but planted him just so—full length. The church was middling small where they preached the funeral, and they had to let one end of the coffin stick out the window. They didn't bury him—they planted one end, and let him stand up, same as a monument" (*Complete Short Stories* 80). No one can claim exemption from mortality while reading these incidents. We must accept that we will all follow Maria Martin and William Wheeler down that mortal road, even if we travel by means less horrific. In light of this recognition, Twain's narrators insist that physically disturbing incidents like this are merely extreme cases of the ordinary physical condition of fallen human nature.

The tale that brings our common mortality most prominently to the fore, however, is "The Invalid's Story," in which the narrator spends the night traveling in a closely congested railway baggage car with what he assumes to be the body of his deceased friend, John B. Hackett. In fact, as the story establishes early on, he is traveling with a box of rifles and a piece of "peculiarly mature and capable Limburger cheese" (*Complete Short Stories* 188), and so the story consequently turns on the narrator's and the expressman Thompson's assumptions that the odors emanating from the cheese are actually coming from the decomposing body of Hackett. We can easily agree that a comic story can hardly be more explicitly physical than this, but since we know from the first that the smell is actually coming from the cheese, the physical fact of mortal corruption is really absent from the story. This is James D. Wilson's point in his *Guide to the Short Stories of Mark Twain*: "[I]ndeed, if the reader were to believe that the obnoxious odors so vividly rendered actually emanated from a decaying corpse rather than from limburger cheese, he would be less amused than disgusted . . ." (149).[9] Most of us would easily agree with Wilson, and yet Twain's friend William Dean Howells twice convinced Twain to omit the tale from books on the grounds that it was too un-genteel. Frederick Anderson, William M. Gibson, and Henry Nash Smith, editors of some Twain-Howells letters, explain: "Howells's characterization of the story as 'terrible' bespeaks his unusually strong dislike of violent images, especially of such crude organic ones as Mark Twain exploits here" (702). All of the issues surrounding the genteel tradition in America are engaging in their way, and many of them receive Twain's comic attention in this story. Out of all the potential birthplaces for the late Mr. Hackett, for example, Twain chooses Bethlehem, Wisconsin. In the same way, the expressman, Thompson, "went bustling around, here and there and yonder, setting things to rights, and all the time contentedly humming 'Sweet By and By,' in a low tone, and flatting a good deal" (*Complete Short Stories*

188). It is surely part of the joke that Thompson is over-efficient at his job. It may even be a humorous addition that he is usually flat when he hums, but the song he hums is the real slap against the genteel tradition, a hymn called the "Sweet By and By." Despite these historically significant details, though, the arresting point of "The Invalid's Story" is Twain's insistence on the nature of physical decay in all human bodies.

The narrator makes the first statement confirming this melancholy truth: "Presently I began to detect a most evil and searching odor stealing about on the frozen air. This depressed my spirits still more, because of course I attributed it to my poor departed friend" (*Complete Short Stories* 188). The "evil and searching odor" is the sort of thing that Howells—and most upright Americans of the later nineteenth century—might object to. The narrator's embarrassment at his friend's undeniable physicality is the true sign of a Calvinist humorist at work. His exchanges with Thompson only increase this impression. When Thompson asks, "How long has he been dead?" the narrator replies, "Two or three days," because he deems it "judicious to enlarge the facts to fit the probabilities," given the malodorous "facts" of the case. Introducing reason and social discomfort into an inappropriate conversation might seem a good way to sidetrack this discussion. Thompson will not be budged from his conviction that the box of guns represents the way of all flesh:[10] "Two or three *years*, you mean. . . . "Twould 'a' ben a dum sight better, all around, if they'd started him along last summer. . . . I've carried a many a one of 'em—some of 'em considerable overdue, too—but, lordy, he just lays over 'em all!—and does it *easy*. Cap, they was heliotrope to *him*!" (*Complete Short Stories* 189–90). Twain's willingness to laugh at all this is his peculiar genius. His willingness to include us in the joke is what makes him the kind of Calvinist humorist he is.

Twain's inclusion of himself—and his readers—in his negative judgments about human nature are clear throughout his work. In "The Story of the Bad Little Boy," Twain is ridiculing Sunday School texts, but he is also proposing the bad little boy's behavior as recognizably typical: "Once this little bad boy stole the key of the pantry, and slipped in there and helped himself to some jam, and filled up the vessel with tar, so that his mother would never know . . ." (*Complete Short Stories* 6–7).

The same assumptions operate in "The Story of the Good Little Boy," even though they are expressed through a negative rhetoric. The narrator thus says about the good little boy, "He wouldn't play marbles on Sunday, he wouldn't rob birds' nests, he wouldn't give hot pennies to organ-grinders' monkeys; he didn't seem to take any interest in any kind of rational amusement" (*Complete Short Stories* 67). These assumptions about the damned human race appear even when the strictures of Sunday School cant are absent. In the celebrated "What Stumped the Bluejays," for example, Twain has Jim Baker say about this kind of bird: "[O]therwise he is just as much a human as you be. . . . A jay will lie, a jay will steal, a jay will deceive, a jay will betray; and four out of five, a jay will go back on his solemnest promise" (*Complete Short Stories* 160). We are all—man, blue jay, frog, dog—in the same boat, as John Calvin observed long ago.[11] Twain makes an equivalently Calvinistic remark in "The Notorious Jumping Frog of Calaveras County" when he has the stranger say with mild irony, "I don't see no p'ints about that frog that's any better'n any other frog" (*Complete Short Stories* 5). From the perspective of any Calvinist humorist, the same may be said about any human being. Twain's peculiar genius is to include himself in the judgment.

6 William Faulkner

"Waiting for the Part to Begin Which He Would Not Like"

Critics generally concede William Faulkner's involvement in Calvinist habits of mind. Cleanth Brooks, who charted Faulkner's career for many years, identifies "Faulkner's Puritanism" (45) outright in *The Yoknapatawpha Country* (1963). The French critic François Pitavy shows his agreement in *Faulkner's "Light in August"* (1973): "[T]he great importance attached to the theme of femininity and sexuality . . . tend[s] to show that Faulkner did have a puritanical sensibility in the 'American' sense of the term, to use his own words" (107–8). In *God and the American Writer* (1997), Alfred Kazin sees Faulkner as "a Calvinist without religion" (243). Jay Parini, Faulkner's recent (2004) biographer, writes in summary about this whole issue: "We are free, as human beings, to do as we like; the problem is, God determines everything. John Milton couldn't 'justify the ways of God to man' in *Paradise Lost,* nor could Faulkner . . ." (340). Another scholar, Charles Reagan Wilson, goes to some lengths in "William Faulkner and the Southern Religious Culture" (1991) to distinguish theologically among the terms that I have been loosely equating by citing these critics' comments, but he also provides Faulkner's own precedent for such careless theology: "The Southern religious tradition, to be sure, grew out of Calvinism. Faulkner, like others in his era, often used 'Calvinist,' 'Puritan,' and 'puritanical' as synonyms, but they have different historical meanings" (23). Even with Wilson's cogent warning in mind, though, it is hard not to see in Faulkner's works evidence of the disposition that I have previously seen as creating Calvinist humor in the works of other American writers.

Faulkner's story "That Evening Sun" (1931), for example, is, as its title implies, a blues tale full of Calvinist angst. In this story, Nancy Mannigoe is afraid that her lover, Jesus, definitely a bad man "with [a] razor scar on his face like a piece of dirty string" (*Collected Stories* 292), will eventually kill her by cutting her throat with his "razor on that string down his back" (*Collected Stories* 295) because of her promiscuous sexual conduct with white men, including Mr. Stovall, the Baptist deacon. At the story's end, it seems that Jesus will probably do just what Nancy fears.[1] As a true Calvinist, Nancy feels that there is nothing she can do to ward off this tragedy. Thus she tells Mr. Compson, "I can't do nothing. Just put it off. And that don't do no good. I reckon it belong to me. I reckon what I going to get ain't no more than mine" (*Collected Stories* 307). Nancy's situation is, as the current Calvinist cliché goes, "as serious as a heart attack," and it is only worsened by her dependence on the Compsons, the family whose profound inadequacies are recorded in *The Sound and the Fury* (1929), the novel that takes up the Compson family's history at a later date—at which Mr. Compson drinks himself to death,[2] Mrs. Compson becomes a stereotypical self-pitying and demanding faded belle,[3] and all of the children fail miserably in their own ways. However, in the midst of all the misery recorded in "That Evening Sun" and assumed from *The Sound and the Fury*, Faulkner still finds room for some Calvinist humor. When Mr. Compson offers to walk Nancy home on the assumption that Jesus will not kill her in front of a white man, Mrs. Compson is, of course, unsupportive of her husband's good intentions. Quentin, the narrator, says that his mother is speaking "[l]ike she believed that all day father had been trying to think of doing the thing she wouldn't like the most, and that she knew all the time that after a while he would think of it" (*Collected Stories* 294). Faulkner's biographers variously report the artist's own marital discomforts,[4] but there is more to the case than that. Even if we ignore any possible biographical source, we cannot fail to recognize Quentin's characterization of his parents' conflicts as consistent with what we laughingly know about how human beings, male and female, get along with each other when living in close quarters. That is to say, we cannot fail to recognize the passage as an example of the kind of Calvinist humor that includes us all among the imperfect.

Another grisly context for Calvinist humor is provided by Faulkner's famous story "A Rose for Emily" (1931). Once again, the overriding content of the story is bleak enough for anyone. Emily Grierson secretly murders her lover Homer Barron with poison when he decides that he wants to leave her, then keeps his corpse in her Gothic mansion, and defiantly continues to sleep with this corpse for many years. Emily's intransigence—clearly illustrated by all of these actions—also provides Faulkner with surprising opportunities for Calvinist humor. When the good women of the town become scandalized by Emily's flagrant affair with Barron, they coerce the local Baptist minister into visiting the public sinner even though "Miss Emily's people were Episcopal" (*Collected Stories* 126). Faulkner doesn't describe the well-intentioned clergyman's visit, but writes that the minister "would never divulge what happened during the interview, but he refused to go back again" (*Collected Stories* 126). One is reminded—at least I am reminded—of the incident in Hawthorne's story "The Minister's Black Veil" in which a "deputation of the church" comes to remonstrate with the impossible Mr. Hooper about his veil. He refuses to help them broach the subject, and the narrator observes, "The topic, it might be supposed, was obvious enough." Even so, the members of this delegation "sat a considerable time, speechless, confused, and shrinking uneasily from Mr. Hooper's eye, which they felt to be fixed upon them with an invisible glance" (377). This kind of silent refusal—by Hooper and by Emily Grierson—is infuriating on a practical level, but few of us have the initiative to bring matters to a head. Somehow, this is funny. The same thing happens when Emily goes to her local pharmacist to get the poison with which she plans to kill Homer Barron. The druggist says, "[T]he law requires you to tell what you are going to use it for," but "Miss Emily just stared at him, her head tilted back in order to look him eye for eye, until he looked away and went and got the arsenic and wrapped it up" (*Collected Stories* 126). Of course, Faulkner believes—and wants us to believe—that flagrant fornication and poisoning are wrong, but he uses Miss Emily's outrageous sense of herself and her position to induce a melancholy laugh, just as Hawthorne does when he allows Mr. Hooper to remain silent in the face of his concerned congregants.

Faulkner also exploits the humorous possibilities of frustration in *The Sound and the Fury*, another grim report on the state of fallen man, as I have already suggested. In that book, Jason Compson, whom Faulkner ironically calls "[t]he first sane Compson since before Culloden" (*The Portable Faulkner* 716), is wildly pursuing his niece, Quentin, who has inadvertently re-stolen from him the $7,000 that he has cheated her and her absent mother, Caddy, out of for eighteen years. Jason is a moral monster as well as a thief. In addition to stealing the money from Caddy and Quentin, he calls his retarded brother Benjy the "star freshman" of the state asylum (230) and "the Great American Gelding" (263). He also destroys a free ticket to the circus rather than give it to Luster (255), and he refuses to allow Caddy more than a passing glimpse of her daughter even though she has dearly paid for the privilege (205). And yet, Faulkner can still use Jason as the source of Calvinist humor. During his frustrating chase after Quentin and her lover, for example, Jason observes: "I had gotten beggar lice and ticks and stuff all over me, inside my clothes and shoes and all, and then I happened to look around and I had my hand right on a bunch of poison oak. The only thing I couldn't understand was why it was just poison oak and not a snake or something" (241). As Edmond Volpe explains in *A Reader's Guide to William Faulkner*, Jason is "[o]ne of the most despicable characters Faulkner ever created" (119), and yet, as this passage shows, Jason can also be funny. However wrong he may be in his original motivation, Jason's frustration while chasing Quentin is recognizably human even if Jason is outrageous.

Faulkner's character Granny Millard in *The Unvanquished* (1938) is just as outrageous, but in a different way. In the section of *The Unvanquished* called "Riposte in Tertio," Granny has been stealing mules and horses from the Yankees during the Civil War through a legal misunderstanding. As is so often the case when illegality is involved, Granny must deal with criminals, here Ab Snopes and the scary man named Major Grumby who will eventually kill her. Despite the rigors of war, suffering, murder, and vendettas depicted in this novel—or collection of stories— Faulkner still finds room for Calvinist humor. The principal opportunity occurs when Granny enters a rural church to pray in "Riposte in Tertio":

I have sinned. I have stolen and I have borne false witness against my neighbor, though that neighbor was an enemy of my country. . . . But I did not sin for gain or for greed. . . . I did not sin for revenge. I defy You or anyone to say I did. I sinned first for justice. And after that first time, I sinned for more than justice: I sinned for the sake of clothes for Your own creatures who could not help themselves; for children who had given their fathers, for wives who had given their husbands, for old people who had given their sons, to a holy cause, even though You have seen fit to make it a lost cause. What I gained, I shared with them. It is true that I kept some of it back, but I am the best judge of that because I, too, have dependents who may be orphans, too, at this moment for all I know. And if this be sin in your sight, I take this on my conscience too. Amen. (147)

Jonathan Edwards assured his congregants that "God is not altogether such an one as themselves though [human beings] may imagine him to be so" (99), and when a fictional character operates as if this is not so, Calvinist humor results. Faulkner indicates Granny's Christian piety through his use of capital letters to designate any pronouns referring to Granny's creator, and yet he also indicates her outrageousness through her defiant challenges to this same all-powerful God. Granny is willing to "defy" this omnipotent being and to claim that—human though she may be—she is "the best judge" of the morality or immorality of her own actions. This is religious humor raised to a very high pitch indeed!

To see Faulkner's creation of Calvinist humor on a broader canvas than these excerpts reveal, we should turn first to his novel *Light in August* (1932). Faulkner's most respected biographer, Joseph Blotner, finds the focus of this novel to be "the impact of harsh Calvinistic religiosity upon the psyche" (761), and Edmond L. Volpe carefully connects the novel's characters Joanna Burden (161), her ancestors (169),[5] and Simon McEachern (162) to the Calvinist tradition. According to Jay Parini, "Even Joe Christmas [the victimized pivotal character] seems to have swallowed his dose of Calvinist doctrine, seeing the world in terms of crime and punishment, with evil confronting good on a bleak battlefield" (180–81). And Parini concludes more generally, "*Light in August* is a searing novel that meditates on racial hatred in the South and the moral depravity caused by Calvinist obsessions" (178). In light of this critical consensus, we might expect to encounter various forms of Calvinism in the novel, including Calvinist humor, and we would not be disappointed.

The novel tells three interrelated stories. One recounts the optimistic search of the pregnant Lena Grove for Lucas Burch, the man who has impregnated her and then fled. This story connects Lena with Byron Bunch, who falls in love with her and eventually goes off with her and her baby, supposedly in pursuit of Burch. The second story involves Gail Hightower, a failed Presbyterian minister who is obsessed with his heroic Civil War grandfather instead of with his congregation and his increasingly frustrated wife. Then there is the story of the bastard Joe Christmas, who is put in an orphanage by his racially and religiously obsessed grandfather and eventually grows into a violent, misanthropic criminal who enters into a twisted sexual relationship with Joanna Burden, which ends up in her murder and his death and castration. All of the stories carry potentially disturbing narrative possibilities for Calvinistic horror, and all of the stories also offer the possibility for Calvinist humor.

There is, first of all, the mild Calvinist joke entailed in the perception that everyone is pretty much like everyone else, no matter how much they wish to believe otherwise. This is the narrator's point when he observes about Byron Bunch: "Man knows so little about his fellows. In his eyes all men or women act upon what he believes would motivate him if he were mad enough to do what the other man or woman is doing" (47–48). Byron thinks along similar lines: "Byron listened quietly, thinking to himself how people everywhere are about the same . . ." (71). When he feels inclined to expand these perceptions in a more rural, folkloric, direction, Faulkner has his character Will Varner observe: "I reckon that even a fool gal don't have to come as far as Mississippi to find out that whatever place she run from aint going to be a whole lot different or worse than the place she is at" (26). Such remarks provide the foundation for the kind of Faulknerian Calvinist humor in which we can all see ourselves as variants of the fictional characters Faulkner writes about. This is especially the case when Lena Grove, the "fool gal" that Varner was talking about, starts to think about her pregnant and abandoned condition. The narrator helps her toward one gentle Calvinistic discovery: "During this time Lena did all the housework and took care of the other children. Later she told her-self, 'I reckon that's why I got one so quick myself'" (5). Lena comes to her funniest conclusion all by herself, though, as she struggles to sneak through the window to escape from her censorious brother's house: "If it had been this hard to do before, I reckon I would not be doing it now" (6). We feel with a mild chuckle that this insight is economically stated, and perhaps we wish that we might grunt something along the same lines as evidence of our shared humanity.

Byron Bunch's conviction that everyone is pretty much like everyone else is prompted by another economically stated reflection on the part of his co-workers at the sawmill: "I reckon Byron'll quit too, today.... With a free fire to watch" (49). These laboring men know that they are all ir-resistibly drawn to a fire, and so they assume—probably correctly—that everyone else is too. This is what the narrator notices later on when the whole town gathers to watch Joanna Burden's house burn down: "So they looked at the fire, with that same dull and static amaze which they had brought down from the old fetid caves where knowing began, as though, like death, they had never seen fire before" (288). There is no harm done by any of this, as there is no harm done by Lena's cross-country pursuit of the faithless and cowardly Lucas Birch, now known as Brown. Like Jason Compson, the reprehensible Brown is a poor excuse for a human being; he is, though, also funny in a Calvinist way—perhaps for these very reasons. Like Jason, Brown is a victim of frustration, in his case frustration at the chances to do the right thing that keep getting thrown his way: "He seems to muse now upon a sort of timeless and beautiful infallibility in his unpredictable frustrations. As though somehow the very fact that he should be so consistently supplied with them elevates him somehow above the petty hopes and desires which they abrogate and negative" (435). Brown is certain that he has acquired some sort of frus-trated majesty because fate seems determined to keep making him avail-able to marry Lena: "It seemed to him now that they were all shapes like chessmen ... unpredictable and without reason moved here and there by an Opponent who could read his moves before he made them and who created spontaneous rules which he and not the Opponent must follow" (437–38). No one is expected to identify with Brown—he is too low for that—but his perception that things tend to run counter to his desires is one that most of us have shared.

Not all of Faulkner's Calvinist jokes are so mild-mannered, however. In *The American Novel and Its Tradition,* Richard Chase notes that Faulkner "alternate[s] violent melodramatic actions with comic interludes . . ." (210), and the novel abounds in grisly examples of the latter. After Joe Christmas has killed Joanna Burden by practically decapitating her, one witness draws a very grim but very comic conclusion: "Because the cover fell open and she was laying on her side, facing one way, and her head was turned clean around like she was looking behind her. And he said how if she could just have done that when she was alive, she might not have been doing it now" (92). Admittedly, this is a pretty awful thing to say—or even to think of saying—and yet it is undeniably true.[6] It is also awful that Doc Hines gets away with preaching hysterically racist sermons to rural black congregations, but the narrator's comment on the congregation's response is both awful and Calvinistically humorous: "Perhaps they took him to be God Himself, since God to them was a white man too and His doings also a little inexplicable" (344). This goes to show, then, that William Faulkner makes disturbing Calvinist jokes as well as genial ones.

The novel's unquestioning misogyny is one aspect of this disturbing dimension.[7] Varner's immediate diagnosis that Lena Grove is merely a "fool gal" may be a sign of this disposition, but Varner is best understood as a simple rustic wit. By the same token, it is merely funny in the "people say the darnedest things" sense when Henry Armstid provides this thumbnail description of feminism: "[R]ight then and there is where she secedes from the woman race and species and spends the balance of her life trying to get joined up with the man race. That's why they dip snuff and smoke and want to vote" (15). Varner and Armstid are merely fictional rubes, it should be remembered, and so the author need take no personal responsibility for what they say about women. Perhaps a very sympathetic reader might attach the following commentary to another fictional character, Gail Hightower, but a less sympathetic reader might see the ideas as Faulkner's: "[S]ince the town believed that good women don't forget things easily, good or bad, lest the taste and savor of forgiveness die from the palate of conscience. Because the town believed that the ladies knew the truth, since it believed that bad women can be fooled by badness, since they have to spend some of their time not being suspicious. But that no good woman can be fooled by it because, by being good herself, she doesn't have to worry anymore about hers or anybody else's goodness; hence she has plenty to time to smell out sin" (66). Some of the comic energy that Faulkner expends on Mrs. Compson seasons such remarks, but there is also the clear implication that the *everybody* whose ideas are being reflected here is male and male only. When these ideas reach hyperbolic levels with Doc Hines, they take on a comic form of excess, as when Hines laments "the sluttishness of weak human man" (204), or when he continually interrupts Gail Hightower's rational inquiry with screams like "Bitchery and abomination!" (370) and "It's God's abomination of womanflesh" (373). Hines is so far gone in his obsessions that he easily becomes a kind of misogynistic clown. Elsewhere, though, notice of the corruptible (female) body is obviously intended to take on fictional plausibility, as when a very young Joe Christmas and his friends first come up against the fact of menstruation: "It moved them: the temporary and abject helplessness of that which tantalized and frustrated desire; the smooth and superior shape in which volition dwelled doomed to be at stated and inescapable intervals victims of periodical filth" (185). Richard Chase sees such passages as evidence of larger, Calvinistic patterns of thought: "[T]he dark or Satanic principle of the universe decrees that [men] are the weaker sex and are doomed to be frustrated and ephemeral" (212).[8] Nearly cutting off Joanna Burden's head is one way to cope with this gendered frustration, but most readers will likely consider it a rather extreme solution.

Richard H. King traces the ideas in this novel to their religious origins: "Though the Scotch-Irish provenance of some versions of Southern Calvinism is clear, Southern Protestantism was less theologically Calvinist than it was ethically puritanical. What most people mean when they refer to Calvinism and Puritanism in the Southern context is less a theology than a deep suspicion of worldly pleasure, that is, sex, drinking, and dancing . . ." (71–72). This is also Pitavy's view: "Nurtured on the Old Testament and Christian myths, Faulkner retains the Puritan's image of

Woman as the serpent and Man as the eternal Adam, striving in vain to resist the temptation of the proffered apple and to turn away from the eternal Eve" (107). Much of the responsibility for enunciating these views is borne by Hightower, the failed Presbyterian minister.[9] Hightower is, of course, caught up in the novel's insistent misogyny, primarily through his sexually unsatisfied wife's promiscuity, but he is able to generalize about the fallen human condition even so, first of all through his interpretation of Protestant church music: "It was as though they who accepted it and raised voices to praise it within praise, being made what they were by that which the music praised and symbolized, they took revenge upon that which made them so by means of the praise itself" (367). Clearly, such music hardly means raising a joyful shout in the Presbyterian church, and Hightower soon extends his jaundiced analysis to the South in general: "Listening, he seems to hear within it the apotheosis of his own history, his own land, his own environed blood: that people from which he sprang and among whom he lives who can never take either pleasure or catastrophe or escape from either, without brawling over it. Pleasure, ecstasy, they cannot seem to bear: their escape from it is in violence, in drinking and fighting and praying; catastrophe too, the violence identical and apparently inescapable" (367–68).[10] These dire behavioral developments are—not coincidentally—the engines of Faulkner's novel, and they are as grim as anyone might wish. Richard Chase translates these religious matters to the literary realm when he observes that "like many modern novelists, [Faulkner] takes a rather darkly naturalistic view of things" (213). After so many examples, however, we might feel equally justified in saying that Faulkner takes "a rather darkly" Calvinistic view of things and that this view does not totally preclude humor. In this respect Faulkner resembles his own character, Joe Christmas, who at one point in *Light in August* is characteristically "waiting for the part to begin which he would not like" (167).

Faulkner's novel *Absalom, Absalom!* (1936) more than satisfies such grim expectations. Although the critical consensus usually ends up in accordance with Jay Parini's judgment that this novel "remains at the center of Faulkner's achievement, a strangely magnificent and unforgettable work that helps to explain the others" (203), there are also clear grounds for describing the book through John T. Irwin's disturbing title, *Doubling and Incest / Repetition and Revenge* (1975). There would, then, seem to be little likelihood that *Absalom, Absalom!* would abound in humor of any sort. As one of Faulkner's questioners observed in *Faulkner in the University*, "I don't suppose there's any comedy in *Absalom* anywhere, and there's a great deal of course in *The Hamlet* and *The Town*" (97). Even so and despite such reasonable expectations, it may be unsurprising at this point to discover that the book does, in fact, contain Calvinist humor, despite—and sometimes because of—its gruesome subject matter.

The first grand Calvinist joke stands right at the heart of the novel's plot. Thomas Sutpen, like many heroes of American fiction including Horatio Alger's Ragged Dick and F. Scott Fitzgerald's Jay Gatsby, gave his life over to the pursuit of the American Dream. In Sutpen's case, the quest began with a class-based insult at a Tidewater plantation when, just a ragged child, he was sent around to the backdoor of the mansion. This experience led to his discovery that "[y]ou got to have land and niggers and a fine house" (297) if you want to amount to anything in life. Following Sutpen's first attempt to bring this vision to life in Haiti, he discovered that his wife had a slight tint of Negro blood and so realized "that she was not and never could be, through no fault of her own, adjunctive or incremental to the design which I had in mind." And so he "provided for her and put her [and her infant son] aside" (300). On his second opportunity—in Mississippi—Sutpen first secured a hundred square miles of land, then built a magnificent plantation and married a totally white woman who bore him two children, Henry and Judith. Eventually, Sutpen's son from his first marriage, Charles Bon, reappeared, became intimately involved with Henry and Judith, and finally provoked Henry into shooting him dead, thus ruining Sutpen's chances for any permanent fulfillment of his dream. Usually, it is Sutpen's callousness toward others—his first wife and child, his second wife, his children, his faithful retainer Wash Jones, his slaves—that attracts critical commentary.[11] At the University of Virginia, Faulkner took this line himself: "[Sutpen] was going to take what he wanted because he was big enough and strong enough, and I think that people like that are destroyed sooner or later, because one has to belong to the human family, and to take a responsible part in the human family"

(*Faulkner in the University* 81). Unquestionably Sutpen is insensitive—even demonic—in his personal relations, and yet from the perspective of Calvinist humor the problem is not merely how Sutpen goes about realizing his dream but simply that he thinks he—and not the almighty God—can control his own fate.[12] As John Lewis Longley, Jr., points out, "Sutpen's dream of magnificence is typical of the United States as a whole, is indeed an example of the greatest American myth of all and thus is symptomatic of one national cultural failure" (113). An appreciator of Calvinist humor could hardly imagine that anyone would believe that he could fulfill his own "design" when everyone knows that the human condition, including the American human condition, is abjectly fallen.

From a Calvinist perspective, this misguided foolishness is not even an especially American shortcoming. This is evident when Edmund Volpe investigates Faulkner's highly allusive title: "Like King David in the Biblical story from which Faulkner derived the title of his novel, Thomas Sutpen rises through his own power to high station among men, breaks the moral law and brings suffering upon his children. In both the house of David and the house of Sutpen, retribution takes the form of violent crimes by the children—revolt, incest, fratricide. The parallels in the stories are not extensive, but sufficient to indicate a continuity in the human condition through centuries of time" (205). Wash Jones, who eventually slays Sutpen with a rusty scythe, comes to a similar conclusion in the novel when he decides not to flee the posse that will surely come to get him: "[I]f he ran he would be fleeing merely one set of bragging and evil shadows for another, since [men] were all of a kind throughout all of earth . . ." (361). As in *Light in August,* it is a humorous Calvinist observation that people are pretty much equally imperfect all over the world and—according to Volpe—all through history. Since, from Calvin's perspective, all men are, and always have been, fallen from a higher state, we should not be surprised to find them remarkably alike—but we can still smile at the fact.

Faulkner recognizes common humanity by supplying the sort of fictional details and commentary that also appealed to Mark Twain. Thus the men in Jefferson think that Sutpen is ideally situated during the period when he has completed but not furnished his plantation and is camping out there without domestic ties of any sort. According to Mr. Compson, an expert on the male perspective: "[F]or the next three years he led what must have been to them a perfect existence" (44–45). Here we can almost hear Huck and Jim, Natty Bumppo and Chingachgook, Butch and Sundance, Willy and Waylon, and the boys—all shouting amen to that![13] Whatever we hear, we should recognize a very common human attitude. The same narrator strikes another Twainian note when he recounts how the good citizens of Jefferson finally let their irritation with Sutpen's success erupt into an attempt to imprison him. "So at last civic virtue came to a boil" (51), he says mordantly. Mr. Compson is, of course, filled with "detachment and irony," as Edmund Volpe points out (196), but because other characters share this aloof perception of fallen human nature, we might be advised to trace the source back to the author and not simply to the fictional character. In other words, Faulkner is the one making these Calvinist jokes. Faulkner also makes Charles Bon mock the puritanical sexual code of Henry Sutpen and his fellow southerners as "the principles of honor, decorum and gentleness applied to perfectly normal human instinct which you Anglo-Saxons insist upon calling lust and in whose service you revert in sabbaticals to the primordial caverns, the fall from what you call grace fogged and clouded by Heaven-defying words of extenuation and explanation, the return to grace heralded by Heaven-placating cries of satiated abasement and flagellation, in neither of which—the defiance or the placation—can Heaven find interest or even, after the first two or three times, diversion" (143). Some of the bitterness of Pudd'nhead Wilson's Calendar echoes in Bon's indictment, but we should also be able to sort out the Calvinistic view of fallen human nature that animates both and that asks us to smile ruefully in the process.

This view particularly governs Faulkner's treatment of Goodhue Coldfield, the seemingly respectable father of Sutpen's second wife, Ellen. Heretofore Coldfield has been distinguished in the community primarily by his close but upright business practices, so much so, according to Mr. Compson, that "as your grandfather said, a man who, in a country such as Mississippi was then, would restrict dishonesty to the selling of straw hats and hame strings and salt meat would have been already locked up by his own family as a kleptomaniac" (100). Simple praise of Mr. Coldfield's

honesty would have served the same purpose of fictional characterization as this speech in terms of plot development, but—as Hawthorne
embroiders his language when describing Mr. Hooper's eccentricity—so
Faulkner exceeds what is stylistically required to make a Calvinist joke
about Coldfield through exaggeration. Everyone in Jefferson seems surprised when the devious Sutpen chooses for a father-in-law "a man who
obviously could do nothing under the sun for him save give him credit at a
little cross-roads store or cast a vote in his favor if he should ever seek ordination as a Methodist minister" (48). Because Sutpen is so egregiously
far from ever seeking ordination as any sort of minister,[14] the conclusion
of this passage can be seen only as some sort of grim Calvinist analysis
of human behavior. The same must be said of the passage in which Mr.
Compson recounts Coldfield's choice of the Methodist church as the site
of his daughter and Sutpen's wedding: "He seems to have intended to use
the church into which he had invested a certain amount of sacrifice and
doubtless self-denial and certainly actual labor and money for the sake
of what might be called a demand balance of spiritual solvency, exactly
as he would have used a cotton gin in which he considered himself to
have incurred either interest or responsibility, for the ginning of any cotton which he or any member of his family, by blood or by marriage, had
raised—that, and no more" (58). Goodhue Coldfield contributes little to
the disturbing plot of *Absalom, Absalom!* but Faulkner's treatment of this
character develops an indisputable aura of Calvinist humor around him
even so.

Although Sutpen is unarguably more important to the novel, he also
becomes the subject of Calvinist humor. As Mr. Compson recounts: "He
was like John L. Sullivan having taught himself painfully and tediously
to do the schottische, having drilled himself and drilled himself in secret
until he now believed it no longer necessary to count the music's beat,
say. He may have believed that your grandfather or Judge Benbow might
have done it more effortlessly than he, but he would not have believed
that anyone could have beat him in knowing when to do it and how"
(52–53). Even after death, Sutpen can serve as the source of humor, in
this case humor rooted in the corruptible human body. After Wash Jones
has beheaded Sutpen, Judith decides to take the body into Jefferson so

that his funeral service can be conducted in the same Methodist church that he entered so seldom while alive. The ensuing developments are burlesque, showing that former Confederate colonels are just as much parts of fallen human nature as the commonest peasant: "[S]o he rode fast toward church as far as he went, in his homemade coffin, in his regimentals and sabre and embroidered gauntlets, until the young mules bolted and turned the wagon over and tumbled him, sabre plumes and all, into a ditch from which his daughter extricated him and fetched him back to the cedar grove and read the service herself" (233). One would think that this would be enough, that ending up as a dead piece of meat in a ditch would put "paid" to Sutpen's spiritual account, but Faulkner has one more indignity in store. Years later, when Quentin Compson is hunting with his father, he comes across the graves of Ellen and Thomas Sutpen and notices "vanishing into the hole where the brick coping of one vault had fallen in . . . a smooth faint path worn by some small animal—possum probably—by generations of some small animal since there could have been nothing to eat in the grave for a long time" (236). Perhaps we feel at this point that the author has followed Sutpen too far, that he has exceeded in grisliness what is required by a very grisly plot, but then we need to recall the outrageousness of Sutpen's "design," his conviction that he could invent a life for himself and his posterity free from the taint of universal human imperfection.

As I have observed above concerning *Light in August*, the unillusioned eye that looks upon human behavior in Faulkner's fiction with Calvinist amusement is "male and male only." Mr. Compson is often spokesman for this view, as when he explains to Quentin: "[Y]ou will notice that most divorces occur with women who were married by tobacco-chewing j.p.'s in country courthouses or by ministers waked after midnight, with their suspenders showing beneath their coattails and no collar on and a wife or spinster sister in curl papers for witness" (57). We may nod sagely in amused agreement, but we need to wonder how the divorced women in question would feel while reading Mr. Compson's witticism. When Quentin recounts his father's "insights" into (female) human nature, he uses similar terms: "Father said that a man who could believe that a scorned and outraged and angry woman could be bought off with formal logic would believe that she could be placated with money too, and it didn't work" (335). In other words, you know how women are! This is the disposition of Quentin's roommate, Shreve MacCannon, too, as when Shreve seems to mimic Mr. Compson: "They live beautiful lives—women. Lives not only divorced from, but irrevocably excommunicated from, all reality" (240). Quentin observes that Shreve "sounds just like Father" (227), and no wonder. As Albert J. Guerard has demonstrated, Faulkner's misogyny controls the speech and behavior of most of his characters. According to Guerard, Faulkner's misogyny "is unrepressed and even undisguised." At the same time, it "is often comically and extravagantly explicit" (109)—a point that we need to keep in mind while tracking Faulkner's Calvinist humor. This would seem to be the case when Mr. Compson tells Quentin the following anecdote:

> You had an aunt once . . . who was faced with a serious operation which she became convinced she would not survive, at a time when her nearest female kin was a woman between whom and herself there had existed for years one of those inexplicable (to the man mind) amicable enmities which occur between women of the same blood, whose sole worry about departing this world was to get rid of a certain brown dress which she owned and knew that the kinswoman knew she had never liked, which must be burned, not given away but burned in the back yard beneath the window where, by being held up (and suffering excruciating pain) she could see it burned with her own eyes, because she was convinced that after she died the kinswoman, the logical one to take charge, would bury her in it. (240–41)

While the little story is not complimentary to Quentin's aunt, neither is it a stinging indictment of the gender that many Calvinists blamed for the fall of man.[15] The anecdote is just a good Calvinist joke about the way some people behave some of the time.

And, there are other examples of this kind of Calvinist humor in the novel. When the highly sophisticated Charles Bon is being sold on the newly founded University of Mississippi as the site of his future education, the corrupt lawyer who was bilking Bon and his mother observes that at Ole Miss "in a sense, wisdom herself would be a virgin or at least not very second hand" (388–89). This is a funny thing to say about any college anywhere. Sutpen's first exposure to gracious living falls under the same heading. As a boy he notices that the owner of the plantation on which his father is sharecropping "had living human men to perform the endless repetitive personal offices such as pouring the very whiskey from the jug and putting the glass into his hand or pulling off his boots for him to go to bed that all men have had to do for themselves since time began and would have to do until they died and which no man ever has or ever will like to do but which no man that he knew had anymore thought of evading than he had thought of evading the effort of chewing and swallowing and breathing" (277). As with the descriptions of a newly founded college and of a person obsessed with her own funeral, the perception is so accurate that it becomes funny. That is to say that, although *Absalom, Absalom!* is filled with violence, cruel inhumanity, racism, and possible incest, it is also filled with Calvinist humor.

We may recall that one of Faulkner's questioners in *Faulkner in the University* claimed that there isn't "any comedy in *Absalom* anywhere" but was confident that "there's a great deal of course in *The Hamlet . . .*" (97). Our inquiry into *Absalom, Absalom!* suggests that the inquirer was mistaken about the Calvinist humor in that book, but in the second case, the questioner was assuredly correct. *The Hamlet* (1940) abounds in all sorts of humor, including the burlesque Old Southwestern humor of the various animal stories, the mock pastoral of Ike Snopes's romance with a cow, the picaresque humor of various tricksters trying to outmaneuver one another, and the mildly salacious humor of Eula Varner's sexuality. Through it all, however, there abides Faulkner's Calvinist perception of human nature.

I. O. Snopes exemplifies this perception in a largely comic context when the narrator observes his "air of merry and incorrigible and unflagging conviction of the inherent constant active dishonesty of all men, including himself" (177).[16] Mankind is decidedly fallen in I. O.'s eyes, and the plot developments in this novel suggest that the author has similar views. This is apparent, for example, when the narrator observes about Ike, the idiot Snopes who is in love with a cow, that he "is learning fast now, who has learned success and then precaution and secrecy and how to steal and even providence; who has only lust and greed and bloodthirst and a moral conscience to keep him awake at night, yet to acquire" (202).

This jaundiced indictment of human nature is decidedly grim, and yet it is not far from what Mark Twain often wrote in Pudd'nhead Wilson's Calendar. Twain might also endorse V. K. Ratliff's observation about his partners' avarice while they are attempting to swindle Flem Snopes out of some buried treasure: "Just look at what even the money a man aint got yet will do to him" (380).

Not all of Faulkner's observations about the predictability of human behavior are so biting, however. When Will Varner generalizes about how most men are likely to behave on a pleasant country night, his judgment is not very complimentary, but neither is it bitter. According to Varner, "And a night like this one, when a man aint old enough yet to lay still and sleep, and yet he aint young enough anymore to be tomcatting in and out of other folks' back windows, something like this is good for him" (340). Varner's son Jody is something of a rustic philosopher also. Even after he has been frightened into taking Flem Snopes on as a clerk to prevent Flem's father from resorting to barn burning, Jody can still say to his horse, "Come up! . . . "You hang around here very long standing still and you'll be afire too" (21). Jody can direct an equally unillusioned comment toward his sister Eula as well. Noting that Eula seldom moves unless she is forced to, Jody remarks, "At the rate she's going at it, there aint a acorn that will fall in the next fifty years that wont grow up and rot down and be burnt for firewood before she'll ever climb it" (107). This is perhaps not very kind thinking on a brother's part, but it is funny even so. It is also funny when Jody and Eula's mother decides that her son has meddled too much in her and her daughter's business. "I raised eight other daughters," Mrs. Varner says. "I thought they turned out pretty well. But I am willing to agree that maybe a twenty-seven-year-old bachelor knows more about them than I do" (110).

It would seem that everyone in Frenchman's Bend, Mississippi, is something of a caustic wit. This is apparent when V. K. Ratliff returns from a hospitalization to resume his position as Calvinist sage. "What was it that Memphis fellow cut outen you anyway?" one of his associates asks him. "My pocket book," Ratliff replies. "I reckon that's why he put me to sleep first." Ratliff doesn't get the last word in this exchange, because his interlocutor answers, "He put you to sleep first to keep you from selling him a sewing machine or a bushel of harrow teeth before he could get his knife open" (76). Even so, Ratliff still gets the best line. Furthermore, his prominent position in the community is underlined by the joke about his slickness as a salesman and general economic trickster. Thus Ratliff seems entirely on the mark when he tells Will Varner early in the book, "[T]here aint but two men I know can risk fooling with them folks [the Snopses]. And just one of them is named Varner and his front name aint Jody" (30). This is the sort of rural wisdom that controls Ratliff's explanation of goat farming: "If a fellow in this country was to set up a goat-ranch, he would do it purely and simply because he had too many goats already. He would just declare his front porch or his parlor or wherever it was he couldn't keep the goats out of a goat-ranch and let it go at that" (88). Even those among us who can claim no expertise when it comes to goats must acknowledge the apparent soundness of Ratliff's analysis. That's actually the way things are, we conclude.

Another Calvinist belief assumed in this book—as in so much American writing—is the irresistible force of fate. Ratliff plays with this belief comically as part of his story about Ab Snopes's gulling by Pat Stamper, the genius horse trader. "[I]t was not only right and natural that Ab would have to pass Stamper to get to Jefferson," Ratliff recalls, "but it was foreordained and fated that he would have to" (38). That the schoolteacher Labove is fated hopelessly to pursue Eula Varner is probably less comic than the fact that Ab is "a fool about a horse" (48), but both unavoidable destinies are situated within larger comic structures of Calvinist inevitability. We read about Labove that "[h]e must return, drawn back into the radius of an eleven-year-old girl . . . sitting with veiled eyes against the sun on the schoolhouse steps and eating a cold potato," thus confirming Labove's powerlessness in the face of his fated destiny, but we also read that this eleven-year-old girl "postulated that ungirdled quality of the very goddesses in his Homer and Thucydides" (125), thus confirming the exaggerated comedy surrounding Labove's obsession. When we read later that Eula was "not even doomed: just damned" (338), we might take the isolated comment as a serious thematic statement, but in the context of Faulkner's earlier exaggerated treatments of fate, we can glimpse the Calvinist humor echoing in the background.

Another Calvinist echo, familiar from the texts discussed already, arises from Faulkner's depictions of human outrage. Labove, for example, wonders "at times in his raging helplessness how buttocks so constantly subject to the impact of that much steadily increasing weight could in the mere act of walking seem actually to shout aloud that rich mind- and will-sapping fluid softness . . ." (112–13) as Eula Varner's buttocks do. Eula's brother is also nearly driven to distraction by his helplessness in the face of Eula's undeniable ripeness. Jody is at one point "still seething and grimly outraged and fanatically convinced of what he believed he was battling against . . ." (143), thereby coming to resemble Jason Compson in pursuit of his niece or Lucas Burch in flight from doing the right thing. Eventually the fatality surrounding Eula's fecundity comes to a head with the discovery of her pregnancy. Jody continues to writhe in the grip of fate when he learns the news: "For a moment, a minute almost, Jody appeared to be beyond speech. He glared at Varner [his father]. He looked as though only a supreme effort of will kept him from bursting where he stood" (158). Even Mrs. Varner seems caught up in the scandal: "She went out; she seemed to have been sucked violently out of the door by her own irate effrontment" (159). Will Varner gets the last laugh by accepting rather than resisting the force of Calvinist fate: "What did you expect—that she would spend the rest of her life just running water through it?" (160).

Love and outrage at the force of fate seem to go hand in hand in this novel. When Ike Snopes steals the cow with whom he is in love from Jack Houston, Houston is driven nearly mad while pursuing them: "[H]e was boiling with that helpless rage at abstract circumstance which feeds on its own impotence, had no object to retaliate upon; it seemed to him that once more he had been the victim of a useless and practical joke at the hand of the prime maniacal Risbility, the sole purpose of which had been to leave him with a mile's walk in darkness" (208). The farmer from whom Ike steals feed fares no better: "[H]e experienced a shocking bewilderment followed by a furious and blazing wrath like that of a man who, leaping for safety from in front of a runaway, slips on a banana skin" (211). Faulkner's characters are laughable in this way because they seem to forget Calvin's maxim that "true religion ought to be conformed to God's will as to a universal rule; that God ever remains like himself, and is not a specter or phantasm to be transformed according to anyone's whim" (49). Their frustration when things go contrary to their wishes is therefore a continuing source of Calvinist humor.[17] Mink Snopes is another character seemingly caught in the trammels of a fated love, but his romantic obsessions are not relevant here; he enters into Faulkner's comic economy mostly after he has murdered Jack Houston and been frustrated in his efforts to dispose of the corpse. Mink's behavior in this macabre crisis seems to the narrator "as if his body were living on the incorrigible singleness of his will like so much fatty tissue" (251). Mink cannot dispose of the body, and so he is ultimately caught, tried, and sentenced to Parchman Prison Farm, from which he will eventually emerge to slay his kinsman, Flem.

Mink's inability to dispose of Houston's dead body points to another Calvinist dimension of this book, Faulkner's commitment to describing the corruptible human body.[18] For example, after Mink has decided to conceal the body in a hollow tree, he is frustrated to discover that it has gotten stuck, wedged only part-way down. Faulkner's narrator treats the matter in a straightforward manner tinged with dark humor, even while accepting the desperate urgency of Mink's desire: "So he tied one end of the rope about the stub of a limb just below his foot and took a turn of the rope about his wrist and stood up on the wedged shoulders and began to jump up and down, whereupon without warning the body fled suddenly beneath him, leaving him dangling on the rope" (250). This is all pretty awful stuff, but it is also pretty funny in an odd way. Less odd, perhaps, is Faulkner's hyperbolic insistence on the purely physical nature of Eula Varner.

Labove's first sight of Eula sets the tone: "Then one morning he turned from the crude blackboard and saw a face of eight years old and a body of fourteen with the female shape of twenty, which on the instant of crossing the threshold brought into the bleak, ill-lighted, poorly-heated room dedicated to the harsh functioning of Protestant primary education a moist blast of spring's liquorish corruption, a pagan triumphal prostration before the supreme primal uterus" (126). Connecting an eight-year-old girl and "the supreme primal uterus" can only be seen as an act of comedy by any well-regulated mind. Faulkner continues to mine this vein with even greater exaggeration, as when he reaches for literary allusion to express the same swollen conception of Eula's body: "On the contrary, her entire appearance suggested some symbology out of old Dionysic times—honey in sunlight and bursting grapes, the writhen bleeding of the crushed fecundated vine beneath the hard rapacious trampling goat hoof" (105). The very excess of Faulkner's language here is comic. Most of the narrator's descriptions of Eula in *The Hamlet* insist in this way merely on her undeniable physicality, but Faulkner's irrepressible comic genius occasionally intrudes in other ways, as in the following passage devoted to Eula's activities when in the company of her mother and a servant: "The three of them would be seen passing along the road—Mrs Varner in her Sunday dress and shawl, followed by the Negro man staggering slightly beneath his long, dangling, already indisputably female burden like a bizarre and chaperoned Sabine rape" (106). This "Sabine rape" may come from the same literary almanac as the "old Dionysic times" and the "trampling goat hoof" of the earlier passage, but the absurd situation creates comedy of a higher sort in the later passage. Even so, it is the undeniable presence of the human body that enables the humor in the first place.

This focus on the body also serves the narrator well when writing about the potentially disturbing subject of Ike's romance with the cow. At one point, "lying beneath the struggling and bellowing cow, [Ike] received the violent relaxing of her fear-constricted bowels" (192) all over his body and overalls. This is to depict the corruptible body with a vengeance, but Faulkner mitigates the physical directness slightly by having Ike speak to her, "trying to tell her how this violent violation of her maiden's delicacy is no shame, since such is the very iron perishable warp of the fabric of love. But she would not hear" (192). Only an idiot could treat an animal in this way but, then, that is part of Faulkner's joke. As Faulkner explained to his agent about this situation: "Maybe it is funny, as I thought myself" (qtd. in Blotner 1225). However, Faulkner's ultimate joke on this score is accidentally articulated by the overly articulate I. O. Snopes: "Flesh is weak, and it wants but little here below. Because sin's in the eye of the beholder; cast the beam outen your neighbors' eyes and sight is out of mind. A man cant have his good name drug in the alleys. The Snopes name has done held its head up too long in this country to have no such reproaches against it like stock-diddling" (222). The term *stock-diddling* is one of Faulkner's major comic achievements; placing it in the context of I. O.'s wildly mixed language usage raises the purely physical to another level of humor, but let us recall even so that it is Ike's romance with the cow that makes all this possible.

Animals have their share in Faulkner's Calvinistic emphasis on the physical in various ways. Linda Welshimer Wagner assures us that it "is now common knowledge [that] Faulkner was trying to incorporate the typically Southwestern humor stories into *The Hamlet*" (220). Examples are not far to seek. When one of Flem Snopes's wild horses has escaped and encountered Vernon Tull and his family on a narrow bridge, the ensuing events could have come right out of a Sut Lovingood tale:

> [T]he horse now apparently scrambling along the wagon-tongue itself like a mad squirrel and scrabbling at the end-gate of the wagon as if it intended to climb into the wagon while Tull shouted at it and struck at its face with his whip. . . . Then the front end of the wagon rose, flinging Tull, the reins now wrapped several times about his wrist, backward into the wagon bed among the overturned chairs and the exposed stockings and undergarments of his women. . . . He [Tull] struck the bridge on his face and was dragged for several feet before the wrist-wrapped reins broke." (336)

This encounter is pretty rough on the horse, on the Tulls, and especially on Vernon, but the wild disorder of the scene provides both the humor and the Calvinist antidote for any sympathy we might feel for any of those involved.

We are also insulated from sympathy for Eck Snopes's horse when he and his son Wallstreet Panic[19] chase the wild animal into an alley and then tie a rope at the entrance to seal off its escape. A witness reports: "[W]hen it hit that rope, it looked just like one of these here great big Christmas pinwheels" (353). In another episode, after Pat Stamper has pawned off two unsatisfactory mules on Ab Snopes, the mules become exhausted after a very brief trip to town. Then, Ratliff recalls about the tightly hitched animals: "[N]ow they looked exactly like two fellows that had done hung themselves in one of these here suicide packs, with their heads snubbed up together and pointing straight up and their tongues sticking out and their eyes popping and their necks stretched about four foot and their legs doubled back under them like shot rabbits . . ." (43). Admittedly, the physical suffering of horses and mules is not an unacceptable topic of humor in contemporary America, but, as Kenneth Lynn explains in a passage quoted earlier, the Old Southwesterner and his literary scribes "could not be bound by traditional niceties in his humor, because life itself was neither traditional nor nice" (27), and Faulkner is following in the footsteps of these writers in *The Hamlet*. In further extenuation, we might note that the both jokes depend on absurd comparisons: of the horse to a Christmas pinwheel and the mules to the participants in a suicide pact. In neither case is the primary attention directed to the animals' physical discomfort. This is true also when Flem Snopes's partner in the horse swap, the Texan, deals so directly with one of the wild Texas ponies: "Then the beast rushed at him in a sort of fatal and hopeless desperation and he struck it between the eyes with the pistol-butt and felled it and leaped onto its prone head" (318). Surely this would not be the way of dealing with an overwrought horse recommended today on Animal Planet, but Faulkner is as interested in the Texan's comic demeanor in this episode as in the horse's. In the same way, Faulkner is focused primarily on Mrs. Littlejohn when she routs out of her house the wild horse that has run into Ratliff's bedroom. "Get out of here, you son of a bitch," she says to the horse. Then, the narrator reports, "She struck it with the washboard . . ." (335). The final point probably should be that Mrs. Littlejohn's approach here works just fine—and, furthermore, that it is also comical. At the same time, we should recognize that Flem has still hornswoggled a large portion of the adult male population of Frenchman's Creek. As Gary Lee Stonum sadly reports, "[B]ecause of Flem's willingness to exploit Ike's idiocy, Ratliff is unable to keep the trade within the ceremonial forms of humor. Even though his plan otherwise succeeds, Ratliff emerges from the deal emotionally devastated" (178). Less defenseless is Mrs. Littlejohn, who has nothing that Flem Snopes wants and who wants nothing that he has.

Thus Mrs. Littlejohn often stands at the center of Faulkner's Calvinist jokes, especially of those dealing with gender. When the men of

Frenchman's Bend get so caught up in the horse swap that Henry Armstid ends up breaking his leg, Mrs. Littlejohn says to the shamefaced males gathered around the victim: "Go outside. See if you cant find something else to play with that will kill some more of you" (337). She would never buy such a dangerous horse, obviously, as we can see while she steadily continues to do her laundry outdoors all during the sale (316–31). It is no wonder, then, that she is frustrated by Mrs. Armstid's lack of backbone in doubting whether she can get a refund from Flem Snopes. Ratliff reports Mrs. Littlejohn's annoyance without directly identifying it. Instead, he says, "Mrs Littlejohn was washing the dishes now, washing them like a man would, like they was made out of iron" (347); and later, "[I]t sounded just like Mrs Littlejohn taken up the dishes and pans and all and throwed the whole business at the cook stove" (348). At one point, Mrs. Littlejohn exclaims, "You men" (337), but this episode shows that she could just as easily say, "you women!" Cora Tull is less evenhanded in matters of gender. After their wagon has been wrecked and her husband has been dragged along the bridge by Eck's wild horse, Mrs. Tull is in no mood to forgive anyone for anything: "Mrs Tull, [was] a strong, full-bosomed though slightly dumpy woman with an expression of grim and seething outrage which the elapsed four weeks had apparently neither increased nor diminished but had merely set, an outrage which curiously and almost at once began to give the impression of being directed not at any Snopes or at any other man in particular but at all men, all males . . ." (357). Gender is a definite source of Calvinist humor in *The Hamlet,* and in contrast to some of Faulkner's earlier work, this novel displays much greater sympathy for and identification with female characters.

The Pat Stamper–Ab Snopes horse swap story seems to end in a mere understatement even though Vynie Snopes's carefully contrived plan to buy a milk separator gets lost in the deal. Though Vynie now has to borrow milk to separate because her husband has frittered away her own cow, he still gets the last word in this narrative: "It looks like she is fixing to get a heap of pleasure and satisfaction outen it" (52). The fate of Mrs. Armstid is less predictable on the basis of Faulkner's earlier work, however. Her husband Henry is clearly incapable of dealing with a man like Flem Snopes—or even with the Texan—and yet he continues to exercise total male authority over his wife. First he takes her carefully saved five dollars—as Ab Snopes takes his wife's milk separator money—and then he treats his wife like an animal. Even the Texan cannot stand by and bilk Henry and his wife after "the husband turned and struck her with the coiled rope" (326). The Texan says that Flem will return the five dollars to Mrs. Armstid, but instead Flem gives her merely five cents worth of candy: "A little sweetening for the chaps" (350). In other contexts, Flem's outrageous, conscienceless behavior might win some sort of grim Calvinist chuckle, but we must side with Mrs. Armstid here when she is presented so pitifully. At a trial designed to restore order to the community, for example, Mrs. Armstid testifies: "I earned that money a little at a time and I would know it when I saw it because I would take the can outen the chimney and count it now and then while it was making up enough to buy my chaps some shoes for next winter" (360). No wonder that Mrs. Littlejohn is so outraged at Mrs. Armstid's passivity! And yet, Faulkner would have us understand that there are people as corrupt as Flem Snopes. That's what the Fall of Man really means, but it isn't always funny.

Faulkner thus juggles serious and comic elements in *The Hamlet* as he does in his other work. This is apparent in his use of comic characterizations rooted in Calvinist perceptions. We learn in a brief Calvinist characterization of Flem Snopes early in his career that "it was as though the original nose had been left off by the original designer or craftsman and the unfinished job taken over by someone of a radically different school or perhaps by some maliciously maniacal humorist or perhaps by one who had only time to clap into the center of the face a frantic and desperate warning" (57). This warning is necessary, as everything in this novel makes clear, and as this wry judgment of a typical citizen of Frenchman's Bend makes Calvinistically explicit: "Flem Snopes don't even tell himself what he is up to. Not if he was laying in bed with himself in an empty house in the dark of the moon" (309). About his favorite character, Ratliff, on the other hand, Faulkner suggests "that hearty celibacy as of a lay brother in a twelfth-century monastery" (47). While we are not necessarily inclined to disagree with this judgment, neither are we encouraged to take an opposing view or to discover that Ratliff is to be condemned. The same may be said when we read this account: "Ratliff talked, murmurous,

not about gold, money, but anecdotal, humorous, his invisible face quiz-
zical, bemused, impenetrable" (398). The final adjectives might, in fact,
be applied to the author.[20]

Linda Welshimer Wagner claims that "Faulkner's truly mature characters find comedy (and joy) in many unexpected places" (137), and *The
Hamlet* certainly supports her claim. In fact, Faulkner's works generally
encourage us as readers to "find comedy (and joy)" even amidst the darkest Calvinist reflections upon human nature, both mature and immature.
In this respect, as in so many others, Cleanth Brooks seems especially
acute when he observes, in *The Yoknapatawpha Country,* that "Faulkner
tends to take the long view in which the human enterprise in all its basically vital manifestations is seen from far off and with great detachment"
(72). That this is the view that produces Calvinist humor is a point made
repeatedly throughout this book.

7 Ernest Hemingway

"Isn't It Pretty to Think So?"

Even though he is usually assumed to embrace no orthodox religious affiliation, Ernest Hemingway definitely belongs to the fraternity of Calvinist humorists. Hemingway's biographer, James Mellow, says simply that "[a] routine piety prevailed in the Hall-Hemingway household" (12) in which Ernest spent his formative years. Julanne Isabelle adds—more in line with my thesis—that "Oak Park [Illinois, Hemingway's birthplace] exhibited many of the traits typical of village life. The village was predominantly Protestant middle class, and extremely provincial" (22–23). What this might mean in terms of the Calvinist tradition should by now be clear. The influence of these typically Protestant forces may be evident in a 1918 letter from Hemingway to his mother in which he tries to reassure her that he still holds to the old-time values despite the disturbing rumors of his recent "modern" behavior: "Don't worry or cry or fret about my not being a good Christian. I am just as much as ever and pray every night and believe just as hard so cheer up!" (qtd. in Mellow 46–47). As with his predecessors, moreover, Hemingway's absorption into the Calvinist tradition results usually in literature that is as likely to depress as to amuse the reader. As Philip Young explains, "Commencing with our first Puritan writers, and coursing down through Poe, Hawthorne and Melville, say, and spreading widely in our own time, this literature often testifies for gloom indeed, and often for sickness, failure and misery" (*Ernest Hemingway,* 250). As with these earlier writers, too, we may be moved to ask, what's so funny about all of this?

As is the case with his more orthodox literary ancestors, the humor in Hemingway's work usually involves some measure of irony as an assessing eye measures the distance from some imaginary condition to the actual state at hand. Thus Jake Barnes, the narrator of *The Sun Also Rises,* says about Robert Cohn, who is almost the antihero of the novel, "As he had been thinking for months about leaving his wife and had not done it because it would be too cruel to deprive her of himself, her departure was a very healthful shock" (4). Later on in the same book, Mike Campbell tells a story about some authentic military medals that he had drunkenly lost: "Seems some chap had left them to be cleaned. Frightfully military cove. Set hell's own store by them" (136). Cohn surely suffered from his wife's departure, and the actual owner of the medals was probably sincerely distressed to lose them, but Hemingway expects us to share the more humorous perspectives of Jake and Mike so that we will laugh rather than cry at the way things turn out. In the same way, it is probable that the Christian Scientist wife in "The Doctor and the Doctor's Wife,"[1] from Hemingway's *In Our Time,* was truly under the weather in that story, but the story's Calvinist humor depends on our willingness to share the husband's perspective rather than hers, as when "[t]he doctor went out on the porch. The screen door slammed behind him. He heard his wife catch her breath when the door slammed" (26).

Even in the later story "The Gambler, the Nun, and the Radio" (1933), which is so often mined for evidence of Hemingway's deepest beliefs, Calvinist humor prevails. Mr. Fraser, who may stand in for the author, reflects on another character's malapropism:

> Religion is the opium of the people. . . . Yes, and music is the opium of the people. . . . And now economics is the opium of the people; along with patriotism the opium of the people in Italy and Germany. What about sexual intercourse; was that an opium of the people? Of some of the people. Of some of the best of the people. But drink was a sovereign opium of the people, oh, an excellent opium. Although some prefer the radio, another opium of the people, a cheap one he had been using. Along with these went gambling, an opium of the people if there ever was one, one of the oldest. Ambition was another, an opium of the people, along with a belief in any new form of government. (53)

As in the work of Mark Twain and Herman Melville, truths like this may be bitter, but they are probably true nevertheless, and for that reason, they are humorous to the Calvinist mind.

As his pathetic letter to his mother actually demonstrates, however, Hemingway's involvement in any Calvinist worldview differs substantially from that shared by the more predictably orthodox. Julanne Isabelle—who is inexplicably concerned about Hemingway's "religious experience"—finds it "obvious that Hemingway continues to place the blame on individuals and avoids the concept of original sin" (30). This repudiation of original sin might seem to disqualify Hemingway from fellowship with the Calvinists, humorous or otherwise. As it turns out, though, changed times call for changed membership rules in the Calvinist club. Because of the traumatic arrival of modern life, especially the horrific rigors of World War I, one might well see life as dark and grim even without raising the possibility of the Fall of Man. As Paul Rosenfeld explains in a review of *In Our Time,* Hemingway "shares his epoch's feeling of a harsh impersonal force in the universe, permanent, not to be changed, taking both destruction and construction up into itself and set in motion by their dialectic" (69). Thus Hemingway is likely to view actual lives—his own and those of his characters—to be just as fallen from some putative better state as the lives of Jonathan Edwards's parishioners. Philip Young maintains along these lines that "[t]he story of the adventures of Huck Finn and the Hemingway hero is . . . a myth, which relates once more the Fall of Man, the loss of Paradise" (258). Even though Hemingway's characters are "robbed of two fond old enormities," in the words of E. A. Robinson's "The Man against the Sky" (502), they can still measure the distance between what they have and what they would like to have, and this is the gap in which Calvinist humor flourishes. As Deb Wylder observes in her review of Hemingway's *Across the River and into the Trees* (1951), "Hemingway, himself, seemed to be looking for a new set of personal rules by which to live" (396). In other words, this author who was made a Calvinist by his childhood environment sought in his mature years to find a secular substitute for what was irretrievably lost. According to the indefatigable Julanne Isabelle, "His code of ethics is as rigid as any found in religion" (31). In that case, we might expect to see

Hemingway's accounts of his characters' failures to live up to this "code of ethics" dripping with Calvinist humor. Most pertinently to the thesis that I have been pursuing, the fictional works by Hemingway that are most imbued with Calvinist humor are his early collection of stories, *In Our Time* (1925), and his first novel, *The Sun Also Rises* (1926), although the disposition remains with him throughout his writing career.

The very first sentence of the very brief first story in Hemingway's first collection forewarns the reader that mostly bad news will follow: "The strange thing was, he said, how they screamed every night at midnight" (11). Screaming every night is unlikely to bring on the warm feeling that everything is going to happen for the best. In the last fully developed story in this collection, "Big Two-Hearted River," things have gotten very little better—if the experience of Nick Adams's trout-bait grasshoppers is taken as symbolic of the human condition:

> The first grasshopper gave a jump in the neck of the bottle and went out into the water. He was sucked under in the whirl by Nick's right leg and came to the surface a little way down stream. He floated rapidly, kicking. In a quick circle, breaking the smooth surface of the water, he disappeared. A trout had taken him. Another hopper poked his face out of the bottle. His antennae wavered. He was getting his front legs out of the bottle to jump. Nick took him by the head and held him while he threaded the slim hook under his chin, down through his thorax and into the last segments of his abdomen. (148)

The grasshopper that escapes dies; the one that does not escape is threaded on a hook and used as bait. No wonder some people scream at night! As Linda Welshimer Wagner claims about *In Our Time*, "The book [is] unified, finally, by its organ base of tone—a mood of unrelieved somberness, if not outright horror" (57). Michael Wigglesworth could hardly paint a drearier picture.

And yet, in Hemingway's system some can escape this miserable condition, at least temporarily. In his 1961 obituary for Hemingway, John Wain explains this process of escape: "He [Hemingway] sees life as essentially a losing battle, but instead of reasoning from this that nothing matters much he takes the attitude that is, in fact, normal among lofty tragic writers: that a defeat, if it is faced with courage and endured without loss of one's self-respect, counts as a victory" (427–28). This temporary escape from secular damnation is usually figured in terms of the famous Hemingway "code," which is defined in bullfighting terms in *The Sun Also Rises* as "the holding of his purity of line through the maximum of exposure" (168).[2] In the story "My Old Man," from *In Our Time,* the jockey after whom the story is entitled explains the code in this way: "If a jock's riding for somebody too, he can't go boozing around because the trainer always has an eye on him if he's a kid and if he ain't a kid he's always got an eye on himself" (120). More explicitly, Nick Adams enacts the principles of the code during the story in which the grasshoppers meet their doom: "He took the ax out of the pack and chopped out two projecting roots. That leveled a piece of ground large enough to sleep on. He smoothed out the sandy soil with his hand and pulled all the sweet fern bushes by their roots. His hands smelled good from the sweet fern. He smoothed the uprooted earth. He did not want anything making lumps under the blankets. When he had the ground smooth, he spread his three blankets" (138). Making camp in this way involves considerable effort, as does keeping in good enough health to ride horses successfully or to fight bulls effectively, but the characters in Hemingway's works who are willing to make this effort can achieve the temporary secular salvation that is as much satisfaction as is available in his world, and those who will not make the effort fulfill the roles of the secularly damned.

According to Philip Young, who is usually credited with articulating this concept most clearly in critical terms,[3] this code is both secular and rigorous: "It is made of the controls of honor and courage which in a life of tension and pain make a man a man and distinguish him from the people who follow random impulses, let down their hair, and are generally messy, perhaps cowardly, and without inviolable rules for how to live holding tight" (63). According to Young, furthermore, the code needs to be applied constantly: "Hemingway's world is one in which things do not grow and bear fruit, but explode, break, decompose, or are eaten away" (245). In the story "The Doctor and the Doctor's Wife," for example, the doctor of the title becomes "very uncomfortable" (24) when Dick Boulton suggests that the logs the doctor wants cut up into firewood are stolen. Immediately, the doctor begins to behave badly, saying to Bolton, "If you call me Doc once again, I'll knock your eye teeth down your throat." Even if we do not automatically condemn such violent posturing, we can tell that the doctor is in the wrong from the way things turn out. "Oh, no, you won't Doc," Bolton answers. Then, according to the narrator, "he looked at the doctor. Dick was a big man. He knew how big a man he was. He liked to get into fights. . . . The doctor chewed the beard on his lower lip and looked at Dick Boulton. Then he turned away and walked up the hill to the cottage" (25). Clearly, the doctor is in the wrong; he is not living his life according to the secular code of conduct that Hemingway recommends. The Calvinist humor implicit in the situation lies not in this exchange, however, but in the doctor's consequent dealings with his wife, who says to him, "I hope you didn't lose your temper, Henry. . . . Remember, that he who ruleth his temper is greater than he who taketh a city." As if this is not enough to provoke a smile at the wife's expense—and perhaps at the doctor's—the narrator adds, "She was a Christian Scientist. Her Bible, her copy of *Science and Health* and her *Quarterly* were on a table beside her bed in the darkened room" (25–26). When the doctor tries to save face by claiming that Boulton sought to provoke a quarrel to avoid paying a medical bill, the doctor's wife interjects naively, "Dear, I don't think, I really don't think that any one would really do a thing like that" (26). No one is in the right here. Boulton is wrong to try to provoke a pointless argument. The doctor is wrong to allow his discomfort to turn into empty posturing. The doctor's wife is wrong to misjudge everything—and probably for being sick in the first place! Seeing so many people doing the wrong thing when they could so easily do the right thing is an opportunity for the superior form of Calvinist laughter—even though it is probable that no one is actually going to hell.

We can easily conclude how far Hemingway has drifted from the religious orthodoxy of his literary ancestors by considering just a few passages from *In Our Time*. In the highly ironic "A Very Short Story," which concludes with the protagonist "contract[ing] gonorrhea from a sales girl in a loop department store while riding in a taxicab through Lincoln Park" (66), this protagonist and his nurse/lover Luz believe in romantic rather than sacramental union: "They felt as though they were married, but they wanted every one to know about it, and to make it so they could not lose it" (65). As the conclusion clearly demonstrates, this union does not last. Even more significant for my purposes is their repudiation of traditional religious views of marriage. Traditional religion is also repudiated in the following short story, in which the nameless protagonist comes to fear death by military bombardment. As we might expect from earlier tales of this sort, the protagonist turns to prayer in his distress: "Dear jesus please get me out. Christ please please please christ. If you'll only keep me from getting killed I'll do anything you say. I believe in you and I'll tell every one in the world that you are the only one that matters. Please please please dear jesus" (67). As the manic language implies, this prayer springs from desperation rather than conviction, and so this story ends ironically: "The next night back at Maestre he did not tell the girl he went upstairs with at the Villa Rossa about Jesus. And he never told anybody" (67). In such cases, orthodox belief becomes the target of Calvinist laughter rather than being the unassailable position from which such laughter is launched. Therefore, Mrs. Krebs, the mother in "Soldier's Home," becomes the object of wry laughter when she says to her jobless son who has recently returned from the First World War, "There can be no idle hands in His Kingdom." Because the reader probably shares Hemingway's sense that times have changed since the days of Jonathan Edwards, this reader will more than likely endorse Krebs's reply, "I'm not in His Kingdom" (75). Thus, when Krebs's mother says, "Now, you pray, Harold," we probably applaud Krebs's answer: "I can't" (76). What all this goes to show is that Hemingway's readers are often laughing at different things than Hawthorne's or Melville's readers are, but they are still laughing.

As with those earlier writers, there are also occasions on which the reader is encouraged to embrace the character's positive action as well as to applaud his negative rejections. In this way, Krebs is proposed as an admirable code adherent when on "times so long back [in the war] . . . he had done the one thing, the only thing for a man to do, easily and naturally, when he might have done something else" (69–70). Even more admirable is Nick Adams, who is amply rewarded for his assiduous attention to camping detail in "Big Two-Hearted River": "Nick was happy as he crawled inside the tent. He had not been unhappy all day. This was different though. Now things were done. There had been this to do. Now it was done. It had been a hard trip. He was very tired. That was done. He had made his camp. He was settled. Nothing could touch him. It was a good place to camp. He was there, in the good place. He was in his home where he had made it" (139). In Hemingway's world, it doesn't get any better than this.[4]

Then, again, there seems to be very little to laugh at in this story unless we adopt the deliberately contrarian position that Hemingway is making too much out of nothing in detailing Nick's behavior at such length. Delmore Schwartz—as we might perhaps expect—adopts a position close to this in arguing that "the code is relevant, and only relevant, to a definite period of time and to a special region of society" (246). That Hemingway's ideological posture is open to questioning cannot be denied. As Schwartz continues: "Consider, for example, how irrelevant the morality [of the code] would be when the subject matter was family life" (250). On the other hand, and within clearly established parameters, Hemingway's code is unassailable. There is no doubt, for example, that the drunken bullfighter in the brief interchapter XIII is laughably in violation of the code: "When they stopped the music for the crouch he hunched down in the street with them and when they started it again he jumped up and went dancing down the street with them. He was drunk all right" (113)—and so he is the object of our opprobrium and laughter. Where Hemingway most radically departs from his predecessors, however, is in the ultimate working out of his design. Maera, the controlled, professional bullfighter who looks in scorn at his drunken associate, is killed in the very next brief interchapter: "Maera lay still, his head on his arms" (131). As Edmund Wilson cogently observes, "Despite his preoccupation with physical contests, [Hemingway's] heroes are almost always defeated physically, nervously, practically: their victories are moral ones" (*Shores of Light*, 313). Death—especially the death of heroes—is, of course, not an appropriate subject of Calvinist humor. Real or fictional people's failure to attain heroic stature is.

The jockey father in "My Old Man" has already been identified as a code hero by his willingness to take responsibility for his own physical conditioning. He also shows his willingness to endure when he tells his son, "You got to take a lot of things in this world, Joe" (118). Even so, he ends up dead and disgraced, so that his son can only conclude, "Seems like when they get started they don't leave a guy nothing" (129). At the opposite end of the moral pole is the Turkish officer who complains about an enlisted man in the collection's first story. Like the father in "My Old Man," the narrator/officer to whom the complaint is made knows that "[y]ou got to take a lot of things in this world," and so he merely pretends to act on the Turkish officer's protest: "Then I told the Turk the man was being sent on board ship and would be most severely dealt with. Oh most vigorously. He felt topping about it" (11). Dealing with a wrong-doer "most severely" is what the Calvinist tradition has long been about. By Hemingway's time, though, everything seems to have been inverted, and yet the Calvinist tendency to laugh at the failings of others still remains.

This tendency underlies even the more positive descriptions in Hemingway's catalog. This is evident, for example, in Hemingway's development of what Mellow calls "the numbing detail" of "Big Two-Hearted River." While looking for the grasshoppers who will play such a symbolic role in the adventure, Nick "had rolled the log back and knew he could get grasshoppers there every morning" (146). This sort of careful behavior will guarantee good fishing in the future. With equal attention to detail, "Nick had wet the pads at the water cooler on the train up to St. Ignace. In the damp pads the gut leaders had softened and Nick unrolled one and tied it by a loop at the end to a heavy fly line" (147). Thus, when it finally comes time to fish, the leaders are ready to use. The climax, though, is Nick's care in handling a fish that he intends to return to the water: "He had wet his hand before he touched the trout, so he would not disturb the delicate mucus that covered him. If a trout was touched with a dry hand, a white fungus attacked the unprotected spot. Years before when he had fished crowded streams, with fly fishermen ahead of him and behind him, Nick had again and again come on dead trout, furry with white fungus, drifted against a rock, or floating belly up in some pool" (149). What all this goes to show is that Nick is definitely a code master. In terms of Calvinist humor what it goes to show is that the reader would probably fail to perform some—or all—of these necessary acts. Realizing that we would probably run out of grasshoppers, try to attach a fly to a dry, stiff leader, or damage a delicate trout casts most of us into the role of the butt. As soon as we realize how far we are from the secular sainthood that Hemingway depicts, we begin to understand the ironic gap in which Calvinist humor can exist. Admittedly, Hemingway's form of salvation is much attenuated from the eternal bliss assumed to lie in store for the blessed by Calvin and his more immediate successors. As Robert W. Lewis reports, in Hemingway's universe, "[t]he rule book replaces the Golden Rule and is considerably more workable" (191). This is, though, the only form of salvation available in Hemingway's wildly displaced Calvinistic world.

Whether or not this analysis is seen as satisfactory depends to a large degree on how seriously we are willing to take it. To Philip Young, "This is his [Hemingway's] equivalent for what, if he wrote philosophy, would be a system of ideas" (242). Edmund Wilson explains further that Hemingway "is not, of course, a moralist staging a melodrama, but an artist exhibiting situations the values of which are not simple" (344). The perceptiveness of both critics is borne out by the passage in "The Battler" in which Nick Adams reflects on his experience of being beaten and thrown off a freight train as the result of a brakeman's deception: "Oh, well, it was only a black eye. That was all he had gotten out of it. Cheap at the price" (53). Life, in other words, comes at us in segments that can be swallowed and digested in order to extract their fruit of knowledge—as Nick has here learned not to be fooled by the same trick again. Prolonged mastery of such lessons equips one spiritually to face other trials. That this is a lesson also endorsed by the American transcendentalists is only one of the many ironies attending Hemingway's system of ideas. In chapter 1 of *Walden,* for example, Thoreau writes, "[T]he cost of a thing is the amount of what I will call life which is required to be exchanged for it, immediately or in the long run" (21). Despite the fact that, according to Young, Hemingway announced that he "can't read" (187) Thoreau, we find these two quintessential American writers sharing a sense of moral "economy." In keeping with Loris Mirella's claim that "Calvinism is more than a set of religious values; it is also, crucially, a complex structure of beliefs and attitudes that, operating systematically, functions as an intellectual framework for articulating certain attitudes and emotions" (21), perhaps this agreement should come as no surprise. In this story, Nick exchanges a black eye for a certain kind of practical wisdom. The Battler has allowed other fighters to "bust their hands on [him]" (56), and as a result he has attained a pathetic form of triumph. Bugs, the Battler's keeper, has overcome jail, racism, and continual vagabondage to reach his current state of equanimity. People who fail to master these lessons in the other stories of *In Our Time*—Krebs's mother, the drunken bullfighter, fishermen who forget to wet down their leaders or who touch trout with a dry hand—are the ones to be laughed at. They are the objects of Calvinist humor, and Hemingway's lifelong involvement in the project of Calvinist humor is therefore established. As Linda Welshimer Wagner proposes about Hemingway's earliest work, in *Hemingway and Faulkner: Inventors/Masters*, "Thematically, all the later Hemingway writing is here in embryo—the fruitless if still polite marriages, the understated agony of war (both military and personal), veneration for the old but unbeaten, censure for the uncaring and unjust, and the fascination with the way man meets death" (55).[5]

In *The Sun Also Rises* both the Calvinistic modes of thought and the Calvinist humor are more obvious than in *In Our Time,* probably because of the novel's narrator, Jake Barnes. For example, Jake muses, as Nick Adams does, about what it all adds up to, but Jake's conclusions drip with ironic tension: "That was morality; things that made you disgusted afterward. No, that must be immorality. That was a large statement. What a lot of bilge I could think up at night" (149). The last sentence especially shows that nothing is off limits for Calvinist mockery in *The Sun Also Rises*. Jake thus says about Robert Cohn's boxing skills, "He was so good that Spider promptly overmatched him and got his nose permanently flattened" (3). Cohn is even more exposed to mockery when Jake says that "'The Purple Land' is a very sinister book if read too late in life" (9) and "I wondered where Cohn got that incapacity to enjoy Paris. Possibly from Mencken. Mencken hates Paris, I believe. So many young men get their likes and dislikes from Mencken" (42). In the second passage, Cohn comes out sounding foolish for following faddish trends, but H. L. Mencken, a usually sacred cultural cow, is ridiculed too. There are people, apparently, who are willing to follow Mencken's lead even if it means not enjoying Paris, and this willingness is amusing in itself. Also amusing is Robert

Cohn's extreme romanticism. After meeting Brett Ashley once, Cohn is ready to say, "There's a certain quality about her, a certain fineness. She seems absolutely fine and straight . . . I shouldn't wonder if I were in love with her." Jake, who has known Brett much longer, and who isn't susceptible to sudden crushes in any case, cynically explains, "She's a drunk. . . . She's in love with Mike Campbell, and she's going to marry him. He's going to be rich as hell some day" (38). Cohn is, comically, undeterred.

Public posturing, political, military, or otherwise, also comes in for its share of Calvinist abuse. Thus, Jake says about a French statue, "I stopped and read the inscription: from the Bonapartist Groups, some date; I forget. He looked very fine, Marshal Ney in his top-boots, gesturing with his sword among the new horse-chestnut leaves" (29). Public statuary is usually comic in some sense, as Mikhail Bakhtin has explained.[6] Public speaking (speaking in public), especially the kind intended to impress others with what we know, is also comic. Jake is a newspaperman, and so he must attend press briefings. Fairly early in the novel, he plausibly says about one, "Several people asked questions to hear themselves talk and there were a couple of questions asked by news service men who wanted to know the answers" (36). None of these answers have anything to do with the plot of *The Sun Also Rises,* and so they enter the book merely to mock the people who "asked questions to hear themselves talk." The statue of Marshal Ney is not terribly pertinent either, but it can be remotely connected to Jake because of his war wound. Like many of the characters in *In Our Time,* Jake has had to learn to "take a lot of things in this world"; in his case *a lot of things* includes the war wound that has rendered him sexually impotent. Even this horrific development can furnish material for Calvinist humor, however, as in Jake's account of his stay in the military hospital: "That was where the liaison colonel came to visit me. That was funny. That was about the first funny thing. I was all bandaged up. But they had told him about it. Then he made that wonderful speech: 'You, a foreigner, an Englishman' (any foreigner was an Englishman) 'have given more than your life.' What a speech! I would like to have it illuminated to hang in the office. He never laughed. He was putting himself in my place, I guess" (31). True empathy is defined, of course, as putting oneself in another's place, but here the empathetic behavior of the Italian colonel is merely another occasion for humor—even though Jake is himself the initial occasion for that humor.

As in *In Our Time,* there are also moments of secular salvation here, mostly connected to—no surprise!—a fishing trip to Burguete. Jake recalls about the accommodations, "It was a nice hotel, and the people at the desk were very cheerful, and we each had a good small room" (89). More along the lines set down by Nick Adams, Jake says,

> We stayed five days at Burguete and had good fishing. The nights were cold and the days were hot, and there was always a breeze even in the heat of the day. It was hot enough so that it felt good to wade in a cold stream, and the sun dried you when you came out and sat on the bank. We found a stream with a pool deep enough to swim in. In the evenings we played three-handed bridge with an Englishman named Harris, who had walked over from Saint Jean Pied a Port and was stopping at the inn for the fishing. He was very pleasant and went with us twice to the Irati River. There was no word from Robert Cohn nor from Brett and Mike. (125)

Most like Nick's experience is Jake's report of some successful fishing: "I took the trout ashore, washed them in the cold, smoothly heavy water above the dam, and then picked some ferns and packed them all in the bag, three trout on a layer of ferns, then another layer of ferns, then three more trout, and then covered them with ferns. They looked nice in the ferns, and now the bag was bulky, and I put it in the shade of the tree" (119–20). Here, Jake, Bill, and the Englishman are all in what Nick calls "the good place" and what some earlier American writers might have called heaven.

As I have suggested earlier, Jake is usually in charge not only of the salvific moments but also of most of the Calvinist jokes. It is thus Jake who says, "I mistrust all frank and simple people, especially when their stories hold together . . ." (4). The worldly-wise tone of the remark might have appeared in the work of any of the writers discussed earlier in this book, but there is a note of severe disillusionment present that we might think of as altogether typical of Hemingway's own modernist views. This tone is even clearer when Jake says, about the prostitute with whom he is having dinner, "We would probably have gone on and discussed the war and agreed that it was in reality a calamity for civilization, and perhaps would have been better avoided. I was bored enough" (17). The war *was* a calamity and it should have been avoided, but laughing at these indisputable truths sets this book apart from what we might expect from Hawthorne or Melville. Mark Twain was usually amused by foreign languages too, but he probably would not have one of his characters say, "Frances Clyne called, speaking French very rapidly and not seeming so proud and astonished as Mrs. Braddocks at its coming out really French" (18). Little is gained or lost in terms of plot through such remarks, and yet the overall tone of *The Sun Also Rises* is intimately involved in such.

Less successful, in my view, is the humor associated with Bill Gorton. Bill is as assuredly what Lady Brett Ashley calls "one of us" (60), as Jake Barnes is. This is clear when Bill remarks about Brett's affair with Cohn, "What bloody-fool things people do" (102). Even so, Bill's jokes usually leave me flat, even when they involve ridicule of the usually risible status quo. At times, Bill's attitude toward the conventional resembles Groucho Marx's, as when he says, "The saloon must go, and I will take it with me" (123). Not all of his sallies are so effective, however. He starts out well enough on one occasion by saying to Jake, "You know what you are? You're an expatriate. Why don't you live in New York? Then you'd know these things" (115). Many conventional pieties are deservedly mocked in this remark. On the other hand, it is harder to keep laughing when Bill continues, "Listen. You're a hell of a good guy, and I'm fonder of you than anybody on earth. I couldn't tell you that in New York. It'd mean I was a faggot" (116). While what Bill says contains a measure of accurate social criticism toward hysterical definitions of gender, there is also a decided sense of adolescent bravado in the speech. After all, he uses the word *faggot,* usually forbidden by righteous folks like Krebs's mother, but it sounds as if he—like the author—is too pleased with himself for having done so. This self-approval is also evident when Bill mocks William Jennings Bryan's fundamentalist repudiation of evolution: "I reverse the order. For Bryan's sake. As a tribute to the Great Commoner. First the chicken; then the egg" (121). Bill saves the humorous day somewhat when he concludes this rant by saying parodically, "We should not question. Our stay on earth is not for long. Let us rejoice and believe and give thanks" (121). This mixed level of humorous achievement is also present during the same conversation when Bill begins, "Let no man be ashamed to kneel here in the great out-of-doors. Remember the woods were god's first temples," but concludes, "Let us kneel and say: 'Don't eat that, Lady—that's Mencken'" (122). Some of these jokes are just too easy, and the author has awarded Bill no permanent scar to excuse his attitude.

Hemingway's most successful humorous sallies in this book are associated with Robert Cohn. Delmore Schwartz says that Cohn "is a prime example of one character who violates the code again and again" (246). More simply, Jake says, "He's behaved very badly" (181). That is to say, Cohn has failed to follow the Hemingway code when he could have done so, and so he has become a figure of Calvinist fun. He consistently shows himself to be a comic prisoner of outmoded values, as when he says threateningly to Jake early in the book, "You've got to take that back." Jake, who is too thoroughly initiated into the code to be so foolish, says, "Oh, cut out the prep-school stuff. . . . Sure. Anything. I never heard of Brett Ashley. How's that?" When Jake is fully in control of himself, nothing is important enough to get into a foolish fight about. Cohn, though, is operating on a different scale of values, as is evident when he explains, "No. Not that. About me going to hell" (39). A character on Melville's *Fidèle* might find himself in Cohn's situation, but he would not necessarily be held up as a figure of fun in consequence. And yet, this is what happens to Cohn—over and over. After he has beaten a drunken Jake and a sober Pedro Romero, Cohn says to Jake, "You'll shake hands, won't you?" Shaking hands means something to Cohn, as simply being told to "go to hell" does, but neither social convention matters to Jake, and so he answers, "Sure. Why not?" The comic significance attached to the scene is evident in Jake's final comments: "We shook hands. In the dark I could not see his face very well" (195). Cohn gets what he thinks he needs. Jake doesn't care. We all laugh at Cohn for being on the wrong side. The final act of the farce, after Cohn has beaten Romero to a pulp, is recounted by Mike Campbell: "Brett wasn't having any shaking hands, and Cohn was crying and telling her how much he loved her, and she was telling him not to be a ruddy ass. Then Cohn leaned down to shake hands with the bull-fighter fellow. No hard feelings, you know. All for forgiveness. And the bull-fighter chap hit him in the face again" (202). Cohn might as well be a sinner in the hands of an angry God.

Just how far Cohn—and others we could mention—is from being in the situation depicted by Jonathan Edwards can be clarified with just a few passages from *The Sun Also Rises*. Jake sets the tone when he fails to pray in the cathedral at Pamplona. Afterwards he says, "I was a little ashamed, and regretted that I was such a rotten Catholic, but realized there was nothing I could do about it, at least for a while, and maybe never, but that anyway it was a grand religion, and I only wished I felt religious and maybe I would the next time; and then I was out in the hot sun on the steps of the cathedral, and the forefingers and thumb of my right hand were still damp, and I felt them dry in the sun" (97). To Jake—and his fellow expatriates—sacred water is just water. It dries in the sun as the water from a fishing stream would dry. The barrenness of traditional religion is also apparent a little later when Wilson-Harris, the man with whom Jake and Bill Gorton have established a fishing pact, proposes a visit to the monastery at Roncevalles: "Harris was there and the three of us walked up to Roncevalles. We went through the monastery." The monastery is merely a tourist site, however, and as Bill says, "[I]t isn't the same as fishing, though, is it?' Wilson-Harris agrees: "I say not" (128). Even putting aside any potential taint of anti-Romishness, both passages show a disdain for things sacred that would be totally alien to the founders of orthodox Calvinism. How far Hemingway's characters have departed from the traditional path is evident after Brett has finally behaved well by sending her bullfighter away before he is "ruined." "It's sort of what we have instead of God" (245), she says, eliminating any normal equation between what these characters do and what is done by orthodox Christians.

Brett reflects about her decision, "You know it makes one feel rather good deciding not to be a bitch" (245), and many critics have echoed her sentiments. Mark Schorer, for example, writes, in a review of *For Whom the Bell Tolls*, "Brett feels 'rather damned good' because she has behaved according to the tenets of that negative morality, that emphasis on the 'performance en route,' the manner of living, which the group has substituted for belief" (338). And yet, Brett is only marginally saved. Unlike Jake, she tends to backslide into the ridiculous. As she herself explains, "It's my fault, Jake. It's the way I'm made" (55). Therefore, at the novel's end, after she has sent away her bullfighter, Brett says to Jake, "Oh, Jake, . . . we could have had such a damned good time together." Jake, who has learned to "take" the problems associated with his sexual impotence can only reply, "Yes, . . . Isn't it pretty to think so" (247). This last remark might have been contemplated by any of the writers considered earlier, but Hemingway's peculiar disposition gives this closing line its individual slant.

In an effort to bring his story more traditional resonance,[7] Hemingway chose an epigraph that also rationalized his title: "One generation passeth away, and another generation cometh; but the earth abideth forever. . . . The sun also ariseth, and the sun goeth down, and hasteth to the place where he arose. . . . The wind goeth toward the south, and turneth about unto the north; it whirleth about continually, and the wind returneth again according to his circuits. . . . All the rivers run into the sea; yet the sea is not full; unto the place from whence the rivers come, thither they return again." Despite this quotation from Ecclesiastes, nothing about Hemingway's novel is orthodox. Even so, Hemingway's own working out of his characters' destiny in this novel and his other books demonstrates his Calvinist sympathies.

8 Nathanael West

"Gloriously Funny"

In Nathanael West's play *Good Hunting,* Brigadier General Hargreaves
says to Captain Stuart Steward Kilbrecht, the Laird of Ladore, "You carry
your Calvinism too far, really" (502),[1] thereby testifying at least to the
author's familiarity with the subject I have been discussing in this book.
Admittedly, it is surprising that a writer born with the name Nathaniel
von Wallenstein Weinstein should be proposed as an advocate of the literary mode that I have been calling Calvinist humor. However, as we have
seen, Aliki Barnstone, Michael Tomasek Manson, and Carol F. Singley
maintain in *The Calvinist Roots of the Modern Era* that "Catholic, Jewish,
and African American writers . . . although not in direct lineage from
the Puritans, engage Calvinism through their experience as Americans"
(xiii).[2] In this view, the writer who eventually became Nathanael West is
as likely to share a Calvinist perspective on human experience as a writer
raised in an environment drenched in Presbyterian orthodoxy—just because both grew up in America. Surely, this perception is accurate. As an
American of his time and place, West would be in the position of understanding the Genesis story on which Calvin's philosophy is based simply
by joining the narrative toward its traditional close. To West, it doesn't
really matter how human beings got into the position of being fallen; all
that matters is that they seem decidedly to be fallen from some putatively superior state. West's secular Calvinism is evident, for example, in
John M. Brand's sour reflection that for West "[f]allen history is so repetitive that the experience of Adam, Cain and Babel recurs in the select
society, that very society summoned to counter the effects of the Fall by

reenacting the original obedience and dominion of Adam" (61). In Brand's view—and in the view of most of West's critics—no religious affiliation is required on West's part to find most people's experience pathetic and laughable most of the time.

Just as Hawthorne and Melville were moved to Calvinist humor by their transcendental contemporaries' assumptions that life could be different from what it "undeniably" was, so West was driven to Calvinist humor by his dissent from his own contemporaries' comparable assumptions about life in America during the 1930s. With thinkers ranging from those who believed—with Horatio Alger—that life could be converted through positive thinking and acting into an unbroken string of material successes,[3] to those who believed—with the American Marxists—that an economic conspiracy was preventing the average Joe from attaining material comfort, West's America was rife with believers of all sorts. Since West was not himself a believer of any sort, the assumptions of these Americans about economics, sex, the movies, and other popular topics seemed to him as wrongheaded and laughable as the actions of Melville's fools and Faulkner's southerners.[4] West's fictional characters, that is to say, became the targets of his Calvinist humor.

"There is," as Jonathan Veitch argues, "no Heavenly City in West's fiction unless one counts the thwarted, utopian aspirations that lie buried in the cheap artifacts of mass culture . . ." (xiv). At the same time that all supernatural answers must be rejected according to West's sense of secular rationality, there apparently remains on the part of many Americans a decided longing for some sort of universal solution, even if it cannot be exactly figured as a "Heavenly City." Veitch also maintains that West's character Miss Lonelyhearts "can do little but mourn this [secular] state of affairs and hanker after a now bygone Puritan 'Age of Faith'" (82). It would finally seem that Miss Lonelyhearts resembles his artistic creator in this respect. As Leslie Fiedler explains, in *Love and Death in the American Novel*, West is like Franz Kafka in the sense that their fictions are "as uncompromisingly secular as they are profoundly religious" (486–87). When reading West's work, we are therefore in the anomalous situation of watching a devoutly secular writer make Calvinist jokes about characters who are often as secular as he is.

West's path to this aggressive irreligion is easily tracked, but the consequences remain puzzling. As T. R. Steiner explains, West "began early to drift away from what little ethnic heritage he had . . . because of the religious indifference of his father and the nominalist conception of Judaism by his mother" (165). This is also Jay Martin's belief, when he asserts that West "found no absolute standards of value in the beliefs of his parents or family. . . . Nor did he find sources of value in the rituals or traditions of Judaism. His parents left their religion in Russia" (50). However, while leaving orthodox religion behind, West still continued to write as if his characters were somehow fallen from some imaginably superior condition. Thus James H. Bowden is moved to write, "Is he a prophet? . . . A Jeremiah, more likely, except one expects a prophet to speak for a God and there doesn't seem to be any in West's work" (284). As Fiedler observes, West is simultaneously secular and religious, and yet he refuses to endorse either position with heartfelt enthusiasm. In John M. Brand's view, "[A]s he repudiates the Jewish heritage which he expresses in his works, it is not so he can affirm his new Western or American heritage" (59). There is therefore in West's works, "No Promised Land" as well as "No Redeemer"—to vary the formula first articulated by Randall Reid.[5] Even so, many in West's lifetime continued to act as if these unattainable goals actually existed, and to West—as to the differently disposed Hawthorne and Faulkner—this perseverance is humorous.

As a result of this disposition to see the emperor completely naked, West "tended," according to Rita Barnard's *The Great Depression and the Culture of Abundance*, "to be secretive, jokey, and evasive . . ." (144) in his fiction. Needless to say, this is not a formula for popular success, especially the "jokey" part. As West wrote in a letter to F. Scott Fitzgerald (April 5, 1939), the more famous writer's approbation of West's work helped balance literary objections to "what one critic called 'private and unfunny jokes.'" As West continues, "Your preface made me feel that they weren't completely private and maybe not even entirely jokes" (792). But, of course, they are "jokes"—at least from a Calvinist perspective. In a letter to Malcolm Cowley (May 11, 1939), West wrote, "But I'm a comic writer and it seems impossible for me to handle any of the 'big things' without seeming to laugh or at least smile" (794). Most sensitive readers in later times seem to agree with this claim, all the while uncomfortably enjoying some sort of laugh. While reading West, according to Warwick Wadlington, "we teeter precariously between apocalyptic outrage and terrible laughter" (310). Kingsley Widmer recognizes in West's work "the bitterly wry laugh at the ornately grotesque and sardonically pitiful" (181).[6] That these are formulas used by earlier American writers to create Calvinist humor hardly needs to be emphasized at this point. In fact Wadlington also asserts,"[N]ow that an existential failure of confidence cuts at the very quick of our experience, we have discovered the Melville of *The Confidence Man,* the Twain of *The Mysterious Stranger,* and the novels of Nathanael West" (299). Despite his ethnicity, in other words, West is securely in the heart of the heart of Calvinist humorists.

West's subject matter is disturbing in any case. His first novel, *The Dream Life of Balso Snell* (1931), recounts an untalented writer's search through the alimentary canal of the Trojan horse for aesthetic and philosophical answers. The narrative is revealed at the end to be merely the protagonist's wet dream. In *Miss Lonelyhearts* (1933) a male writer produces an advice-to-the-lovelorn column while pretending to be the female authority of the title. In the end he is shot to death by one of his disappointed clients. Lemuel Pitkin, the foolish hero of *A Cool Million,* is progressively deprived of his physical parts while he pursues the American dream of wealth and happiness popularized by Horatio Alger. In the end, he is assassinated. *The Day of the Locust* accelerates West's denunciation of life in America first by puncturing the "dream dump" of Hollywood films and then by terminating in an apocalyptic riot. Homer Simpson, who may be the novel's pathetic hero, is destroyed by the rioting mob. Tod Hackett, the other candidate for hero, probably ends up insane. As West famously said, "There is nothing to root for in my work . . ." (qtd. in Reid 11). Most readers would agree.

Most ludicrous of all to West is the belief of many that there is a single answer to all the questions that life might throw at a person. West's earliest fictional encounter with such undying beliefs on the part of his contemporaries maintains a decidedly philosophical slant notably absent from most of his later works. *The Dream Life of Balso Snell* contains mocking pronouncements such as the following: "[I]f everything is one, and has neither ends nor beginnings, then everything is a circle" (9). The book also proposes to ridicule "the eternal wrangle between the advocates of the Singular and those of the Plural" (9). But, even supposing this humorous critique to be spot on, what is thereby accomplished? Nearly anyone who is not a professional philosopher can spoof the language and preoccupations of that discipline in the same way that amateurs can idly mock the concerns of bakers and garage mechanics. Much more similar to West's later Calvinist humor is this speech made in the novel by the comically named Beagle Darwin: "The clown is dead; the curtain is down. And when I say clown, I mean you [Janey Davenport]. After all, aren't we all . . . aren't we all clowns? Of course, I know it's old stuff; but what difference does that make? Life *is* a stage; and *we* are clowns" (45). The mildly paradoxical term *secular Calvinism* comes to mind in reading this passage. Another brilliantly named character, John Raskolnikov Gilson, introduces a different but equally characteristic piece of Calvinist humor in this novel when he reports Saniette's pathetically optimistic claim: "I won't die! I am getting better and better. I won't die! The will is master o'er the flesh. I won't die!" As we might expect—and as is usually the case in West's best work—Death replies, "Oh, yes you will" (24).[7] The Coué-like confidence of many optimists like Saniette is punctured by what seems to be the inexorable force of circumstance. That's the problem with easy answers, according to West. In fact, that's the problem with all answers!

In *American Superrealism: Nathanael West and the Politics of Representation in the 1930s,* Jonathan Veitch writes about another single answer, the power of positive thinking, "Among other things, Mind Cure begins by transforming social problems into individual ones and then insists that there is no personal problem that the mind cannot cure given the appropriate maxim and sufficient resolve" (71). *A Cool Million* and *The Day of the Locust* clearly illustrate Veitch's point. West's character Miss Lonelyhearts encounters a similar case of univocal thinking in West's second novel when he says to his girlfriend Betty, "What a kind bitch you are. As soon as anyone acts viciously, you say he's sick. Wife-torturers, rapers of small children, according to you they're all sick. No morality, only medicine" (72). West would surely allow us to add to Miss Lonelyhearts's diatribe, "no problems, only opportunities." But, as in the case of Balso

Snell's philosophical critique, positive thinking may turn out to be too easy a target to end up proving much more than its own foolishness. Elsewhere, West also takes on the more problematic issue of health faddism as a simple answer, as when he has Maybelle Loomis, the indefatigable stage mother, ask in *The Day of the Locust*, "Who do you follow . . . in the Search for Health, along the Road of Life?" (334). (Mrs. Loomis herself follows Dr. Pierce along the path of raw foodism.) Perhaps less materialistic, but surely just as foolish, are the reporters in *Miss Lonelyhearts* about whom we read, "At college, and perhaps for a year afterwards, they had believed in literature, had believed in Beauty and personal expression as an absolute end. When they lost this belief, they lost everything" (74–75). What is left when these idealistic alternatives are shattered?

All of West's writing seems devoted to answering that there is nothing left, that—in Calvinist terms—the Fall is absolute and irreversible. In *Miss Lonelyhearts,* West's character Shrike says that "[t]he Susan Chesters, the Beatrice Fairfaxes and the Miss Lonelyhearts are the priests of twentieth-century America" (62). Even if we are willing to accept Shrike's substitution for an apparently vanished orthodoxy, no solace results. In fact, Miss Lonelyhearts makes this point himself: "A man is hired to give advice to the readers of a newspaper. The job is a circulation stunt and the whole staff considers it a joke. He welcomes the job, for it might lead to a gossip column, and anyway he's tired of being a leg man. He too considers the job a joke, but after several months at it, the joke begins to escape him. He sees that the majority of the letters are profoundly humble pleas for moral and spiritual advice, that they are inarticulate expressions of genuine suffering. He also discovers that his correspondents take him seriously. For the first time in his life, he is forced to examine the values by which he lives. The examination shows him that he is the victim of the joke and not the perpetrator" (94). However genuine the correspondents' suffering and however eager Miss Lonelyhearts is to help them, the overall situation is hopeless—and to West this is some kind of joke. It is this disposition, according to Kingsley Widmer, that makes West a significant influence on the "'black humor' in his [literary] descendants" (181).

Economic solutions seem equally simple and equally futile. In *A Cool Million,* Shagpoke Whipple, former president of the United States and current president of the Rat River National Bank, explains that Henry Ford "was dead broke at forty and borrowed a thousand dollars from James Couzens; when he paid him back it had become thirty-eight million dollars." Whipple goes on to say to the novel's "hero": "You're only seventeen and say you're a failure. Lem Pitkin, I'm surprised at you" (200). Pitkin's heroic stature must be called into question by quotation marks because of his incurable foolishness. In West's mocking description, Lem has all the attributes of a true Horatio Alger hero: "Due to his strong physique . . . and a constitution that had never been undermined by the use of either tobacco or alcohol, Lem succeeded in passing the crisis of the dread pulmonary disease" (158). Even so, the simplistic ideology that accompanies this sterling physique turns out to be wrongheaded. After receiving a small tip for collaborating in a devious act of economic exploitation, Lem is suitably encouraged to extrapolate in an optimistic direction: "At this rate of pay, he calculated, he would earn ninety-six dollars for an eight-hour day or five hundred and seventy-six dollars for a six-day week. If he could keep it up, he would have a million dollars in no time" (165). In other words, Lem believes that he might follow in the footsteps of Ragged Dick, Henry Ford, and Shagpoke Whipple down the road to fame and fortune. Instead, he ends up a sacrificial victim to the cause of American fascism.[8]

If all this failure seems illogical to anyone, a suitable villain must be found to explain why the usual plan for economic success does not operate in the usual fashion. In *A Cool Million,* two likely, but logically incompatible, nemeses are identified—both believable as evil influences in the American 1930s. West's narrator seems to adopt the seemingly contradictory conspiracy theories of Shagpoke Whipple when he blames "Wall Street and the Communists" (159), "Jewish international bankers and the Bolshevik labor unions" (173), and "the forces of both the international Jewish bankers and the Communists" (176) for everything that goes wrong in Lem's attempt to climb from poverty to economic success. Of course, we know in our hearts that these complacently equated forces are actually antagonistic and incapable of joint conspiracy. That incapacity is, in fact, how West ridicules the simplistic thinking of the right-wing man on the street. In this novel, however, this insane explanation turns out to be accurate, as we learn when a mysterious secret agent leaves this telephone message, "Operative 6384XM, working out of the Bourse, Paris, France. Middle class organizers functioning on unemployed front, corner of Houston and Bleeker Streets" (175); followed by this one: "Comrade R, this is Comrade Z speaking. Gay Pay Oo, Moscow, Russia. Middle class organizers recruiting on the corner of Houston and Bleeker Streets" (176). This conspiracy could never actually occur, as we know, and yet West's point is that equally incongruous explanations are regularly accepted by supposedly rational people.[9] That is, they are accepted as long as they are simple and total.

In *Miss Lonelyhearts,* the simple answer of popular narratives is exposed: "He saw a man who appeared to be on the verge of death stagger into a movie theater that was showing a picture called *Blonde Beauty.* He saw a ragged woman with an enormous goiter pick a love story magazine out of a garbage can and seem very excited by her find" (103). In *A Cool Million,* Shagpoke Whipple draws on the simple answer of irrational regional piety: "I love the South. . . . I love her because her women are beautiful and chaste, her men brave and gallant, and her fields warm and fruitful" (227). In *The Day of the Locust,* Faye Greener buys into the simple dream of celebrity; "I'm going to be a star some day. . . . It's my life. It's the only thing in the whole world that I want" (286).[10] In that same novel, Mrs. Loomis enunciates a simple climatological answer when she says about Southern California, "Why, it's a paradise on earth" (333). Later in the book, Mrs. Loomis's sunny view is explicitly cancelled by the experience of the people who have come to California to die: "Once there, they discover that sunshine isn't enough" (380). Throughout West's novels, simple answers are exposed in this way as unsatisfactory.

Even as he exposes all simple answers as specious, West engages in stylistic practices that might leave some readers uneasy, especially when he insists on affirming the corruptible human body and the physical imperfection that this implies. Jay Martin says that West "showed . . . a striking preoccupation with the human body, particularly with its odors, its orifices, its corruptibility and diseases, with parasites that feed on the human body" (32). A reader needn't go very far to find corroborative evidence for Martin's claim. In *The Dream Life of Balso Snell,* West calls the flea who lived in the armpit of Christ "Saint Puce, a great martyred member of the vermin family" (11), and he has John Raskolnikov Gilson theorize that "[t]he white paper acts as a laxative. A diarrhoea of words is the result. The richness of the flow is unnatural; it cannot be sustained" (15). To paraphrase Hawthorne's physician in "The Minister's Black Veil," "Something must surely be amiss with Mr. [West's] intellects."[11] Jay Martin says something of this sort in the passage quoted above. And so, West has Gilson also say, "I have a sty in my eye, a cold sore on my lip, a pimple where the edge of my collar touches my neck, another pimple in the corner of my mouth, and a drop of salt snot on the end of my nose. Because I rub them constantly my nostrils are inflamed, sore and angry" (26). This physical misery continues in *Miss Lonelyhearts* when we read, "Flowers would then spring up, flowers that smelled of feet" (63); in that same novel Shrike intones more abstractly, "You are plunging into a world of misery and suffering, peopled by creatures who are strangers to everything but disease and policemen" (119–20). Likewise, *A Cool Million* is subtitled "The Dismantling of Lemuel Pitkin" because the title character progressively loses his teeth in prison, his eye to a runaway horse, his thumb in an auto wreck, his leg in a bear trap, and his scalp to an avenging Indian. The only job available to him in his pitiful physical condition is stooge in the savagely comic vaudeville act of Riley and Robbins:

> The turn lasted about fifteen minutes and during this time Riley and Robbins told some twenty jokes, beating Lem ruthlessly at the end of each one. For a final curtain, they brought out an enormous wooden mallet labeled "The Works" and with it completely demolished our hero. His toupee flew off, his [glass] eye and [false] teeth popped out, and his wooden leg was knocked into the audience.
>
> At the sight of the wooden leg, the presence of which they had not even suspected, the spectators were convulsed with joy. They laughed heartily until the curtain came down, and for some time afterwards. (233)

The narrator concedes: "To be perfectly just, from a certain point of view, not a very civilized one it must be admitted, there was much to laugh at in our hero's appearance" (231). This pattern continues in *The Day of the Locust*. As Harry Greener lies on his deathbed, Tod Hackett notices, "The few beads of sweat that glistened on his forehead and temples carried no promise of relief. It might rot, like rain that comes too late to a field, but could never refresh" (312). Later, Tod notices that after Harry has died and been embalmed, "He looked like the interlocutor in a minstrel show" (318). In light of these passages, perhaps we cannot help but feel that West focuses excessively on the corruptible, that he is half in love with the truly grotesque, but we cannot for that reason declare that he is somehow not Calvinistic enough. After all, John Calvin proposes this in *The Institutes:* "Now suppose that in man's nature there is nothing but flesh: extract something good from it if you can" (289). Since this is in fact what West supposes, then it is no surprise that he can extract nothing good from it.[12] We must be willing to settle for the satisfaction of finding that what he "extracts" is sometimes funny.

An extreme case of the corruptible body in West's work is his treatment of sexuality. Balso Snell's sexual tastes are markedly eccentric, tending toward women whom everyday society would consider physically deformed: "He likened their disarranged hips, their short legs, their humps, their splay feet, their wall-eyes, to ornament. Their strange shortenings, hanging heads, bulging spinesacks were a delight, for he had ever preferred the imperfect, knowing well the plainness, the niceness of perfection" (34). One sexual occasion arising in *A Cool Million* requires Lem Pitkin to prostitute himself to the Maharajah of Kanurani. Putting aside for a moment the potentially inverted character of the encounter, we can still connect Lem's physical infirmity to his sexual victimization: "Then another lucky accident occurred. When Lem bent awkwardly to pick up his teeth, the glass eye that Mr. Hainey had given him popped from his head and smashed to smithereens on the floor" (193). The Maharajah is disgusted, and so Lem is temporarily "saved." While Miss Lonelyhearts does not choose Faye Doyle as his sexual partner either, neither is he forced into the encounter as Lem is. Nevertheless, he still responds bizarrely: "Some fifteen minutes later, he crawled out of bed like an exhausted swimmer leaving the surf, and dropped down into a large armchair near the window" (90). Tod Hackett thinks about Faye Greener in an equally twisted way: "Her invitation wasn't to pleasure, but to struggle, hard and sharp, closer to murder than to love. If you threw yourself on her, it would be like throwing yourself from the parapet of a skyscraper. You would do it with a scream. You couldn't expect to rise again. Your teeth would be driven back into your skull like nails into a pine board and your back would be broken. You wouldn't even have time to sweat or close your eyes" (251). Even though Faye can bring out the worst in Tod, he is still able to come up with a disgusting fantasy in which she plays the part of the victim. Figuring Faye as a cork adrift upon the sea of life, Tod imagines that she has been "set down on a strange shore where a savage with pork-sausage fingers and a pimpled butt picked it up and hugged it to his sagging belly" (376). There is nothing romantic or renewing in any of this sexuality or in Claude Estee's elaboration of a chance remark of Tod's into a simple—albeit disturbing—theory of sex: "Love is like a vending machine, eh? Not bad. You insert a coin and press home the lever. There's some mechanical activity inside the bowels of the device. You receive a small sweet, frown at yourself in the dirty mirror, adjust your hat, take a firm grip on your umbrella and walk away, trying to look as though nothing had happened. It's good, but it's not for pictures" (255–56). In the riot that concludes this novel, a woman who is being sexually molested merely objects, "I ain't no pillow" (386).

As these passages attest, West's "modern" characters may have escaped the Victorian repressions of their ancestors, but they are still in thrall to the flesh. Malcolm Cowley even develops an elaborate comparison in which Freudianism is viewed as analogous to Christianity:

> The picture of human life presented by many analysts can easily be trans-
> lated into terms of Christian theology. First comes the Garden of Eden, or the
> womb, and then the Fall of Man, which is variously interpreted by different
> analysts: sometimes it is the birth trauma, sometimes (as in [Dr. Edmund]
> Bergler) it is masochistic dependence on the mother, and sometimes it is the
> Oedipus complex. Afterward man lives in a state of Total Depravity (or neuro-
> sis) unless he achieves Salvation (or "sublimation," or "adjustment") by an act
> of Charity (which is called "transference"), or else is snatched from the jaws of
> hell by Divine Grace. This last takes the shape of intervention by the analyst,
> whose insight is another word for the Divine. (150; Cowley's parentheses)

This is something that John Calvin would immediately understand. Though secularized by modernist disbelief, the totalizing answer of Freudian sexu-

alism fills the same space for many twentieth-century Americans as orthodox Christianity did for Calvin's contemporaries and their successors. To
West, however, this total answer is as unsatisfactory as earlier ones, with
the disastrous and violent results that his works of fiction make clear.

According to Randall Reid, "West does not invite the reader to see
himself as a sensitive soul in a cruel world, a world made cruel by the
stupidity and heartlessness of others. Nor does he allow a reader the
comforts of superior laughter" (2). One way in which West brings off this
extremely unlikely thematic development is by making his central characters as sick and violent as their peripheral peers. In *The Dream Life of
Balso Snell,* the title character deals with the pathetic Miss McGeeney by
"hit[ting] her a terrific blow in the gut"; then he "hove her into the foun-
tain" (33). Miss Lonelyhearts is just as vicious toward the "clean old man"
whom he and Gates encounter in the park. After Miss Lonelyhearts has
verbally pressed the elderly homosexual to reveal all his most intimate
secrets, "[w]hen the old man still remained silent, he took his arm and
twisted it. . . . The old man began to scream. Somebody hit Miss Lonelyhearts from behind with a chair" (78). Nothing has been accomplished
in these scenes, considerable pain has been inflicted, and the corruptible
body has emerged as obviously superior to any deeper human feelings.
Because Lemuel Pitkin is too naive to function as an agent of violence,
other characters in *A Cool Million* often fill that role. After the highly
inept volunteer fire department fails to quench the fire at Betty Prail's
childhood home, for example, Betty's parents die in the fire, their house
is vandalized, and Betty is raped by Bill Baxter, the fire chief. "In the
morning, she was found lying naked on the ground by some neighbors
and taken into their house. She had a bad cold, but remembered nothing of what Bill Baxter had done to her. She mourned only the loss of
her parents" (142). Lem is himself often the victim of violence, as when
he loses parts of his body or when a stereotypical Irish police sergeant
"struck him an extremely hard blow on the head with his club" (151). In
The Day of the Locust, Faye Greener dances provocatively with Miguel in
front of Tod Hackett and Earle Shoop. The consequences are, perhaps,
predictable in West's fictional universe: "Tod saw the blow before it fell.
He saw Earle raise his stick and bring it down on the Mexican's head. He

heard the crack and saw the Mexican go to his knees still dancing, his body unwilling or unable to acknowledge the interruption" (307). In this novel, a review of Harry Greener's vaudeville act observes that "[t]he pain that almost, not quite, thank God, crumples his stiff little figure would be unbearable if it were not obviously make-believe. It is gloriously funny" (263). West gives us no reason to believe that the violence in all of his novels is any more "make-believe" than anything else in what he obviously sees as a decidedly fallen world, but, for Calvinist reasons of his own, he continues to find it all "gloriously funny."

As Tod's sexual fantasies about Faye imply, West connects sex and violence more consistently in *The Day of the Locust* than in any of his other books. When Faye Greener dances lasciviously with her boyfriend Earle Shoop in that novel, the principal consequence is a very violent response from the dwarf, Abe Kusich, rather than any "healthy" sexual effect: "Just as Faye and Earle started to dance again, he charged between Earle's legs and dug upwards with both hands. Earle screamed with pain, and tried to get at him" (363). As if this is not enough, Earle's Mexican partner responds even more violently: "Lifting the little man free, Miguel shifted his grip to his ankles and dashed him against the wall, like a man killing a rabbit against a tree" (363). This is apparently what sex leads to in West's fictional world—on the personal or social levels. During the concluding riot, we read that an "old man" "had one of his hands inside her dress and was biting her neck. Tod freed his right hand with a heave, reached over the girl and brought his fist down on the man's head" (385). Tod therefore becomes a savior of sorts for this girl, suggesting his distance from the univocal obsessions of the other rioters. And yet Tod is not always able to separate sex and violence, as we see, not only in his sexual fantasy about Faye, but also when "Tod felt his fingers slipping from the rail [during the riot] and kicked backwards as hard as he could. The woman let go" (387). All of this apocalyptic sexual violence is triggered when Homer Simpson[13] violently kills little, androgynous Adore Loomis: "The boy turned to flee, but tripped and fell. Before he could scramble away, Homer landed on his back with both feet, then jumped again" (383). To West, this seems to be where we are all heading. John Calvin might well agree. As he writes in *The Institutes*, "As we are vitiated and corrupted in all parts of our nature, we are held rightly condemned on account of such corruption alone and convicted before God, to whom nothing is acceptable but righteousness, innocence, and purity" (1311).

In West's fiction, "righteousness, innocence and purity" are in short supply. *Miss Lonelyhearts* is the novel in which West most directly attacks religious orthodoxy, but this critical disposition surfaces throughout all his works. In *The Dream Life of Balso Snell*, Maloney the Areopagite "attempt[s] to crucify himself with thumb tacks" (11). Shrike gets to ridicule organized religion frequently in West's second novel, as when he mockingly claims, "The church is our only hope, the First Church of Christ Dentist, where He is worshipped as Preventer of Decay. The church whose symbol is the trinity new-style: Father, Son and Wire-haired Fox Terrier" (97–98). In *A Cool Million*, a lawyer named Barnes gets in the most telling jab against Christianity. When Lemuel Pitkin cries, "'I'm innocent!' a little desperately," Barnes rejoinders, "So was Christ . . . and they nailed Him" (197). In *The Day of the Locust*, when Tod Hackett hears Bach's "Come Redeemer, Our Savior" at Harry Greener's funeral, he reflects, "Perhaps Christ heard. If He did, He gave no sign. The attendants heard, for it was their cue to trundle on Harry in his box" (322). In a more extravagant satire later on, Tod "visit[s] the 'Church of Christ, Physical' where holiness was attained through the constant use of chest-weights and spring grips; the 'Church Invisible' where fortunes were told and the dead made to find lost objects; the "Tabernacle of the Third Coming' where a woman in male clothing preached the 'Crusade Against Salt'; and the 'Temple Moderne' under whose glass and chromium roof 'Brain Breathing, the Secret of the Aztecs' was taught" (337). Perhaps we might focus on West's satire of religious faddishness in these passages, but it is hard to avoid the conclusion that he sees all religion as just another (inadequate) simple answer. While West's narrator claims in *The Day of the Locust* that "[i]t is hard to laugh at the need for beauty and romance, no matter how tasteless, even horrible, the results of that need are" (243), we may observe that, though hard, it is not impossible for West.

Miss Lonelyhearts provides the most opportunities for such laughter. First of all, we read about the central character, "Even without a beard no one could fail to recognize the New England puritan" (61). And yet, unlike the Puritans we have read about in an earlier chapter, Miss Lonelyhearts is surrounded on the one side by honest inquirers like Desperate, the girl born without a nose, who writes, "What did I do to deserve such a terrible bad fate? Even if I did do some bad things I didn't do any before I was a year old and I was born this way. I asked Papa and he says he doesn't know, but that maybe I did something in the other world before I was born or that maybe I was being punished for his sins. I don't believe that because he is a very nice man. Ought I commit suicide?" (60); and on the other by Shrike, who advises, "Explain that man cannot live by bread alone and give them stones" (63).[14] Miss Lonelyhearts himself is adrift between these two incompatible positions, as we see when he reflects, "If he could only believe in Christ then adultery would be a sin, then everything would be simple and the letters extremely easy to answer" (88). The key word, of course, is *simple,* West's usual synonym for the most ludicrous solution possible. It is merely a sign of changed times that the simple solution advocated by John Calvin and his Puritan successors becomes a source of comedy to a later, secular Calvinist humorist. Instead of attaining a state of grace when he attains total communion with God at the novel's conclusion— "He submitted drafts of his column to God and God approved them. God approved his every thought" (125)—Miss Lonelyhearts seems to have become insane. In any event, West kills him off on the next page.

Because these developments seem (and are) so bleak, West also feels obliged to devote attention to the ways in which simple answers have failed his characters. Perhaps the most theoretical presentation of the problem occurs in *Miss Lonelyhearts* when we read, "Men have always fought their misery with dreams. Although dreams were once powerful, they have been made puerile by the movies, radio and newspapers. Among many betrayals, this one is the worst" (103). More directly, Chief Israel Satinpenny expresses the problem in this way in *A Cool Million* when he says about the civilization of the white man: "His final gift to us is doubt, a soul-corroding doubt" (217). Faye Greener articulates this disappointment in *The Day of the Locust:* "[S]he said that any dream was better than no dream and beggars couldn't be choosers. She hadn't exactly said this, but [Tod] was able to understand it from what she did say" (293). Concerning Homer Simpson in this same novel, the narrator observes,

"Only those who still have hope can benefit from tears. When they finish, they feel better. But to those without hope, like Homer, whose anguish is basic and permanent, no good comes from crying. Nothing changes for them. They usually know this, but still can't help crying" (291). West consistently shows the failure of dreams, hopes, beliefs, and simple answers of all sorts. As West wrote in a letter to Malcolm Cowley (May 11, 1939), "I have no particular message for a troubled world (except possibly 'beware') . . ." (794).

Messages aside, West imitates his own character Tod Hackett by painting a truly terrifying picture of what happens when people must abandon their dreams, however unsatisfactory these dreams may be. The crowds of disappointed Americans who riot at the end of *The Day of the Locust* "were savage and bitter, especially the middle-aged and the old, and had been made so by boredom and disappointment" (380). As would be appropriate in the 1930s, West puts the blame for this frustration squarely on the usual subjects, excoriated by the Frankfurt Group[15] among others: "Every day of their lives they read the newspapers and went to the movies. Both fed them on lynchings, murder, sex crimes, explosions, wrecks, love nests, fires, miracles, revolutions, wars" (381). Violence is the inevitable consequence. And yet, even as West brings us all of this bad news in the last chapter of his last novel, he makes a joke: "A super 'Dr. Know-All Pierce-All' had made the necessary promise and they were marching behind his banner in a great united front of screwballs and screwboxes" (388). Like Kafka, and Melville, and the other grim writers to whom he is so often compared, Nathanael West "says NO! in thunder; but the Devil himself cannot make him say *yes*."[16] Like Melville, the author who coined this formula, and Hawthorne, the writer whom it was intended to describe, West says "NO" primarily by exploiting Calvinist humor. And, this is true, even though West holds no religious tenets in common with John Calvin.

The final lesson seems to be that a humorous form of Calvinism runs so deeply in the American spirit that even patently irreligious writers like Ernest Hemingway and Nathanael West share it. There should be nothing funny, for example, about the letter that Miss Lonelyhearts receives from Desperate: "I am sixteen years old now and I don't know what to do and would appreciate it if you could tell me what to do. When I was a little girl it was not so bad because I got used to the kids on the block makeing fun of me, but now I would like to have boy friends like the other girls and go out on Saturday nites, but no boy will take me because I was born without a nose—although I am a good dancer and have a nice shape and my father buys me pretty clothes" (60). Somehow, though, we are tempted to laugh,[17] perhaps because West times the appearance of his punch line so effectively. We should not laugh when Lemuel Pitkin's parts fall off either, or when Adore Loomis is stomped to death, but we probably do laugh and then feel bad about it afterwards. If, after laughing at vicious and disgusting things, we go on to ask, "What kind of person am I anyhow?" we have assembled all of the ingredients of one kind of Calvinist humor—the kind that Nathanael West is so good at.

9 Flannery O'Connor

"Funny because It Is Terrible"

In a highly influential essay entitled "Flannery O'Connor's Devil" (1962), O'Connor's friend and fellow novelist John Hawkes connects the young, Roman Catholic southerner's work to the fiction of Nathaniel Hawthorne and Nathanael West, both of whom have been discussed earlier in this book. Hawkes is clearly onto something. There can be no doubt that Flannery O'Connor's work resembles Hawthorne's and West's and, furthermore, that she deserves a place among the American Calvinist humorists. Perhaps this is why O'Connor writes in a letter to "A." (September 24, 1955), "In my own experience, everything funny I have written is more terrible than it is funny, or only funny because it is terrible, or only terrible because it is funny" (957).

We may begin our examination by noting that O'Connor's fiction carries clear religious intonations. As Frederick J. Hoffman has written, "Her major subjects are the struggle for redemption, the search for Jesus, and the meaning of 'prophecy'; all of these in an intensely evangelical Protestant South . . ." (33). Specific examples bear out Hoffman's claim. In O'Connor's first novel, *Wise Blood* (1952), for example, her principal character, Hazel Motes, says to Mrs. Wally Bee Hitchcock in the book's first chapter, "I reckon you think you been redeemed" (6).[1] Later in the novel, Motes goes on to meet Asa Hawks, a false prophet, and Onnie Jay Holy, a religious hustler, before blinding himself in a desperate act of religious atonement. Since these are not the materials that occupied most significant American writers in the early 1950s—who were famously uninterested in prophets, preachers, and modes of atonement[2]—O'Connor's religious subject matter is all the more noticeable. In fact, O'Connor wrote in a letter to Carl Hartman (March 2, 1954) that *Wise Blood* was "written by some one who believes that there was a fall, has been a Redemption, and will be a judgment" (919)—distinctly Christian, if not exclusively Calvinistic, sentiments. The same may be said of O'Connor's other novel, *The Violent Bear It Away* (1960), which presents a fanatic elderly preacher, Mason Tarwater, who teaches his great-nephew, Francis Marion Tarwater, "[h]istory beginning with Adam expelled from the Garden and going on down through the presidents to Herbert Hoover and on in speculation toward the Second Coming and the Day of Judgment" (331); the old man's challenge to this great-nephew to baptize his idiot cousin, Bishop; and the great-nephew's conflict between his onerous religious destiny and the insistently secular vision of his uncle, George Rayber, Bishop's father. Although they are decidedly twisted, these folk are not obsessed Delta planters or nasty beauty shop patrons, as they might be in the fiction of other southern writers such as William Faulkner or Eudora Welty;[3] they are actors in the grand, enduring Christian drama of salvation and damnation.[4]

O'Connor's shorter fiction makes the same point, as Louis D. Rubin maintains in an essay aptly entitled "Flannery O'Connor and the Bible Belt": "Both her novels and most of her short stories are directly concerned with religion" (51). Consequently, in O'Connor's most popular story, "Good Country People," Joy/Hulga, the philosopher, announces, "I don't even believe in God," and Manly Pointer, the Bible salesman, responds, "That's very unusual for a girl" (277–78). Pointer also says, later on, "I hope you don't think . . . that I believe in that crap. I may sell Bibles but I know which end is up and I wasn't born yesterday and I know where I'm going!" (283). Clearly, this is not the usual ground for modern American fiction. Nor is it usual to create a character like Obadiah Elihue Parker, in "Parker's Back," who thinks that he will impress his wife by getting a tattoo of Jesus on his back, or one like Ruby (Mrs. Claud) Turpin, who yells at God in "Revelation," "If trash is what you wanted why didn't you make me trash?" (652). Even O'Connor's titles reveal her involvement with Christian ideas: "Revelation"; "Judgement Day"; "A Temple of the Holy Ghost"; *The Violent Bear It Away,* from the Gospel of Matthew; "Everything That Rises Must Converge," from the Catholic philosopher

Pierre Teilhard de Chardin. As C. Hugh Holman has accurately observed, "Flannery O'Connor's restless souls belong to people primitive in mind and Protestant in religion, who with all their difference, share a common, deep, and personal awareness of the awful and awesome presence and power of God in the world" (86). Here is plausible material for Calvinist treatment.

And yet, even though O'Connor resembles other Calvinistically inclined thinkers and writers, there is the palpable stumbling block of her Roman Catholicism to stand in the way of her absorption into the fold of Calvinist American humorists. As O'Connor wrote in a letter to John Lynch (November 6, 1955), "I feel that if I were not a Catholic, I would have no reason to write, no reason to see, no reason ever to feel horrified or even to enjoy anything" (966). Admittedly, there are doctrinal affiliations separating O'Connor from William Bradford and Michael Wigglesworth. However, we might ponder how this Catholic way of seeing suggests to O'Connor that she abandon Joy/Hulga in a hayloft at the end of "Good Country People" without her glasses, her wooden leg, and her delusion of superiority. How is this Catholic *raison d'écrire* responsible for the Misfit's murder of the whole family in "A Good Man Is Hard to Find," of Bevel's drowning in "The River," of Mrs. May's fatal goring in "Greenleaf"? We might ask whether these developments reveal even a Christian view of experience, much less the orthodox Roman Catholic commitment that O'Connor frequently professed.[5] The answer may be that O'Connor is having too much nasty fun in these stories to need any theological explanations of what she is up to. That is to say, as Josephine Hendin plausibly maintains, "O'Connor's assertions of Christian orthodoxy do not accurately describe her art" (16). When all is said and done, then, O'Connor's affiliation with the Catholic Church may be considered more of a private matter than as an informing source for her fiction.

In the judgment of Martha Stephens, moreover, "O'Connor's Christian faith was as grim and literalistic, as joyless and loveless a faith, at least as we confront it in her fiction, as we have ever seen in American letters—even, perhaps, in American theology" (41). Temporarily putting aside Stephens's terms *faith* and *literalistic,* we can glimpse in her analysis the resemblance of O'Connor's work not so much to that of other twentieth-century Catholic novelists but rather to her harsh nineteenth-century southern predecessors, the humorists of the Old Southwest. Miles Orvell is only one of many critics to draw such connections, in his *Invisible Parade: The Fiction of Flannery O'Connor* (54–56), where he derives O'Connor's technique from that of her predecessors and comments on her connections to William Faulkner and Erskine Caldwell. Louis Rubin agrees, in "Flannery O'Connor and the Bible Belt," claiming that what "makes Flannery O'Connor's fiction so gripping and memorable lies in the insight into religious experience afforded her by her double heritage as both Catholic and Southerner" (70–71). In other words, O'Connor reaches back as much to the Old Southwest tradition of cruel, violent humor as to the text of the Bible, whether it be the Protestant King James version or the Catholic Douay-Rheims translation. O'Connor claims to repudiate this literary tradition in her Georgetown University lecture, "The Catholic Novelist in the Protestant South," when she says dismissively, "In nineteenth century American writing there was a good deal of grotesque literature which came from the frontier and was supposed to be funny—such as *Sut Lovingood*" (860). In spite of her apparent scorn for these writers, O'Connor clearly derives authorial pleasure from the suffering of her fictional characters, as do the creators of the "grotesque literature which came from the frontier and was supposed to be funny."[6]

In illustration, we might consider the passage in Augustus Baldwin Longstreet's "The Horse Swap," from his *Georgia Scenes* (1835), in which the removal of a saddle blanket from the back of a horse named Bullet "disclosed a sore on Bullet's back-bone, that seemed to have defied all medical skill. It measured six full inches in length, and four in breadth; and had as many features as Bullet had motions." The heart of Longstreet's genteel narrator "sickened at the sight; and [he] felt that the brute who had been riding him in that situation, deserved the halter" (30). The local Georgians, however, laugh heartily. Furthermore, this laughter is not directed at the horse's physical misery but at the foolishness of Peter Ketch, who has apparently been seduced into trading for such a defective animal. Significantly, there is nothing warm and inclusive about this laughter: "The laugh became loud and general at the old man's expense, and rustic witticisms were liberally bestowed upon him and his late purchase" (30). When it is discovered that Kit, the horse that Ketch gave in trade, is both deaf and blind, the crowd's laughter is turned on Kit's new owner, Yellow Blossom. Even though these characters are not directly laughing at a horse's misery, they *are* laughing at another human being's embarrassment and misfortune. That Yellow Blossom has been shown to be an arrogant braggart complicates the joke somewhat, but it does not totally eliminate the joke's cruelty or its delight in another's (richly deserved) misfortune. Longstreet is surely a Calvinist humorist in this respect and thus one of O'Connor's potential literary ancestors. Consider merely this passage from "Good Country People": "Carramae, a blonde, was only fifteen but already married and pregnant. She could not keep anything on her stomach. Every morning Mrs. Freeman told Mrs. Hopewell how many times she had vomited since the last report" (264).[7]

Cruel Calvinist humor is equally evident in the episode from Mark Twain's *Roughing It* (1872), in which a drunken Jim Blaine tells about Becky Martin's daughter, Maria. Maria "married a missionary and died in grace," Blaine says, and he recounts that she was

> et up by the savages. They et *him*, too, poor feller—biled him. It warn't the custom so they say, but they explained to friends of his'n that went down there to bring away his things, that they'd tried missionaries every other way and never could get any good out of 'em—and so it annoyed his relations to find out that the man's life was fooled away just out of a dern'd experiment, so to speak. But mind you, there ain't anything ever reely lost; everything that people can't understand and don't see the reason of does good if you only hold on and give it a fair shake. Providence don't fire no blank ca'tridges, boys. That there missionary's substance, unbeknowns to himself, actu'ly converted every last one of them heathens that took a chance at the barbacue. Nothing ever fetched them but that. Don't tell *me* it was an accident that he was biled. There ain't no such thing as an accident. (*Complete Short Stories* 79–80)

Surely this episode is funnier in most ways than the horse trade depicted by Longstreet, and surely Twain's satire of the widely held theological belief in special providences contributes to this humor.[8] Just as surely, we cannot ignore the fact that the cruel fates of bodily infirmity and cannibalism stand as the basis of the principal joke.

We might also recall William Bradford's delight occasioned by the plight of the plague-stricken Indians. In this respect, O'Connor can be seen to belong to this grotesque Old Southwestern tradition as much, or more so, than to the tradition of Catholic, or even of Christian, fiction writers. We may all say amen to this possibility, recognizing the terrible physical and mental distortions of her characters even while howling at how funny she makes the whole thing. That is to say, we may recognize Flannery O'Connor as a true Calvinist humorist, either because of or despite her religious dispositions.

In keeping with John Hawkes's insight about the commonality in the authors, we might go on to note that the plot of *Wise Blood* patently demonstrates O'Connor's debt to Nathanael West and his personally inflected Calvinism. Like Miss Lonelyhearts, Hazel Motes has a Christ complex, but unlike Miss Lonelyhearts, Motes conceives of his mission in inverted terms. Instead of offering salvation, Motes typically preaches that "[n]obody with a good car needs to be justified" (64). Motes's church is the apparently unorthodox Church without Christ. And yet, his concerns are hardly secular or worldly. As I have already said, he *preaches* his unorthodox beliefs—from the hood of his rat-gray Essex. Characteristically, Motes reveals his actual immersion in the spiritual world that he claims to reject by saying, "If I was in sin I was in it before I ever committed any. There's no change come in me" (29). Like West's hero, Motes pursues spiritual goals in a secular world, best represented, perhaps, by Motes's landlady who thinks, "She was not religious or morbid, for which every day she thanked her stars" (119). Also like Miss Lonelyhearts, who is accidentally killed by Peter Doyle, the man he is trying to save, Hazel Motes comes to a tragicomic end. After learning that Asa Hawks did not actually blind himself with lime to prove his faith, Motes does blind himself with lime; he falls into the clutches of Mrs. Flood, the grasping landlady; and he ends up being beaten to death by some cops who are supposedly bringing him home to Mrs. Flood. O'Connor differs from West, however, in implying that Motes finally attains salvation in spite of his doctrinal dissent. As she describes Motes in her introductory note to the second edition of *Wise Blood,* he is "a Christian *malgré lui.*"[9] In spite of this supplementary judgment of her hero's "integrity" (2), black, vicious, Calvinist humor is omnipresent in the book.

Mrs. Flood, for example, concludes after Motes has adopted a regimen of bodily mortifications: "It's like one of them gory stories, it's something that people have quit doing—like boiling in oil or being a saint or walling up cats. . . . There's no reason for it. People have quit doing it" (127). In Mrs. Flood's view, the penitential Motes "might as well be one of them monks . . . he might as well be in a monkery" (123). Some satire is directed at Mrs. Flood's secularism in these passages, of course, but O'Connor's language is in comic excess of what is required to make her thematic point. The terms *walling up cats* and *monkery* are just too good for mere satire. They are as certain signs of Calvinist humor as Hawthorne's sentence in "The Minister's Black Veil": "One imitative little imp covered his face with an old black handkerchief, thereby so affrighting his playmates that the panic seized himself, and he well-nigh lost his wits by his own waggery" (377).[10]

Even though she often bears weighty thematic responsibilities, Mrs. Flood is just as often a happy occasion for Calvinist humor. Thus, while we encounter the symbolic judgment "The landlady stared for a long time, seeing nothing at all" (126), we also relish her response to Motes's initial declaration that he is a preacher by vocation: "'Protestant?' she asked suspiciously, 'or something foreign?'" (60). The joke is probably disposable in terms of the novel's overall thematic intentions, but O'Connor likes it too much to pass up the opportunity. And, Mrs. Flood is not the only comic temptation that O'Connor gives in to in this novel. Onnie Jay Holy, for example, says about the Church without Christ: "In the first place, friends, you can rely on it that it's nothing foreign connected with it. You don't have to believe nothing you don't understand and approve of. If you don't understand it, it ain't true, and that's all there is to it. No jokers in the deck, friends" (86). Holy also claims that "[t]his church is up-to-date! When you're in this church you can know there's nothing or nobody ahead of you, nobody knows nothing you don't know, all the cards are on the table, friends, and that's a fack!" (87). While these jokes obviously have something to do with Christianity—or at least with religion—they are assuredly jokes even so. And, as Marilyn Arnold reluctantly notes, "Probably most of us were attracted to Flannery O'Connor for her comic spirit" (244).

No wonder! in light of passages such as the one in which Sabbath Lily Hawks tells Motes about the time she wrote to advice columnist Mary Brittle: "Dear Mary, I am a bastard and a bastard shall not enter the kingdom of heaven as we all know, but I have this personality that makes boys follow me. Do you think I should neck or not? I shall not enter the kingdom of heaven anyway so I don't see what difference it makes." Mary replied, "Dear Sabbath, Light necking is acceptable, but I think your real problem is one of adjustment to the modern world. Perhaps you ought to re-examine your religious values to see if they meet your needs in Life. A religious experience can be a beautiful addition to living if you put it in the proper perspective and do not let it warp you. Read some books on Ethical Culture." A number of the Calvinist humorists considered in this book might have created this exchange of letters. Only O'Connor would conclude with Sabbath Lily's response: "Dear Mary, What I really want to know is should I go the whole hog or not? That's my real problem. I'm adjusted okay to the modern world" (67). Since "the modern world"—or what Mary Brittle calls "Life"—is the environment in which Calvinists like Jonathan Edwards see people deluding themselves that they will avoid hell—"No, I never intended to come here: I had laid out matters otherwise in my mind. . . ."—we can laugh a deep Calvinist laugh at both Sabbath Lily and Mary Brittle. I suspect that O'Connor then wants us to ask ourselves whether our own views are any more responsible. At the same time that she rings these serious thematic chimes, O'Connor can't keep from noting, as a descendant of the Old Southwest humorists, that Sabbath Lily was "scratching his ankle with the toe of her sneaker, and smiling" while saying all of this. This is the cruel streak that leads O'Connor to say about Manley Pointer in "Good Country People," "He had on the same suit and the same yellow socks sucked down in his shoes from walking" (277). Apparently, a writer does not need abused horses or cannibals to create cruel Calvinist humor.

O'Connor also expresses her Calvinist criticism through larger elements of *Wise Blood*. Enoch Emery experiences the impersonal coldness of an indifferent city until he is desperate for any touch of true Christian charity. In his desperation, Enoch hopes that shaking hands with what he takes to be a movie-star gorilla will bring him some semblance of the

love he is missing. After Enoch tumbles out a confused account of his pathetic loneliness, we read: "The star leaned slightly forward and a change
came in his eyes: an ugly pair of human ones moved closer and squinted
at Enoch from behind the celluloid pair, 'You go to hell,' a surly voice inside the ape-suit said, low and distinctly, and the hand was jerked away"
(102). The episode is simultaneously shocking, sad, and comic. It is also
thematically appropriate in light of O'Connor's overall theological commitment to the idea that human life is only a probationary period. Thematic seriousness aside, we must conclude that *Wise Blood* is definitely
funny—in a Calvinist way.

The same may be said of O'Connor's first collection of stories, *A Good
Man Is Hard to Find* (1955). The title story reflects O'Connor's quasi-reli-
gious humor when the homicidal maniac called the Misfit says that Jesus
should not have raised the dead: "Jesus thown everything off balance"
(151). Then he completes his massacre of a vacationing family by shooting
the grandmother three times, perhaps in fulfillment of his recognition
that "[s]he would have been a good woman . . . if it had been somebody
there to shoot her every minute of her life" (153). In a remote theological sense, the grandmother may just have had it coming, as we can see
in speeches of this sort: "In my time . . . children were more respect-
ful of their native states and their parents and everything else. People
did right then. Oh look at the cute little pickaninny!" (139). Racism like
this surely trumps social propriety, as most true moralists would see. In
another, nonthematic sense, the grandmother is simply funny because
she exemplifies a type so effectively, as when she says, "I believe I have
injured an organ" (145), or thinks, "In case of an accident, anyone seeing her dead on the highway would know at once that she was a lady"
(138). This grandmother does end up dead, and probably no one realizes
that she is a lady, but June Star ends up dead, too, although she gets to
deliver one of the story's funniest lines when she says on the first page
that the grandmother "wouldn't stay at home to be queen for a day" (137).
Later, when Red Sammy's wife praises June Star's tap dancing by asking
whether she would like to stay with them and live in the café, June Star
says, "I wouldn't live in a broken-down place like this for a million bucks!"
(141). Another victim of the Misfit is June Starr's brother, John Wesley,

who says hilariously, "Tennessee is just a hillbilly dumping ground, . . . and Georgia is a lousy state too" (139). Probably some thematic intention is fulfilled by the children's rudeness but, from the perspective of Calvinist humor, the speeches can stand firmly on their own comic nastiness. After all, bad kids are always funny—when they are someone else's. O'Connor may thus be seen to echo the Misfit's sentiment, "No pleasure but meanness" (152).

"The River" is a pretty serious story in every sense of the word since it aggressively attacks modern secularism and concludes with the drowning death of a little boy named Harry Ashfield, who pretends to be named Bevel after a fundamentalist preacher. Despite this weightiness, the story also contains a comic exchange involving Bevel's babysitter, Mrs. Connin, and a watercolor belonging to Bevel's seriously hung-over parents. First, Mrs. Connin says, "I wouldn't have paid for that. . . . I would have drew it myself" (154). Later, she concludes, "I wouldn't have drew it" (155). Some humor is directed at Bevel's parents' artiness and some at Mrs. Connin's lack of sophistication in this episode, but—as in other cases mentioned already—much of the humor derives simply from O'Connor's phrasing. We can detect the same stylistic technique in "A Late Encounter with the Enemy" when the narrator observes about a summer graduation in Georgia, "The graduates in their heavy robes looked as if the last beads of ignorance were being sweated out of them" (259).

Similar joking occurs at some points in "The Displaced Person." As the title perhaps suggests, O'Connor can say about this story, "Lady, I've come to speak of serious things" (270), like her character Manly Pointer. This is her friend Robert Fitzgerald's point when he says about "The Displaced Person," "In most O'Connor stories we are aware of the Roman or universal Church mainly by its absence. Here it is present from the start" (388). Fitzgerald is perceptive in this judgment. Mr. Guizak is the story's title character, and other characters' lack of Christian charity toward him is the narrative's chief thematic burden. Like the innocent Bevel, Mr. Guizak ends up dead at the conclusion of the story. Even so, there are a few comic highlights. Mrs. Shortley, Mr. Guizak's employer, is made as uncomfortable by the Polish language as Mrs. Connin is by the Ashfields' water color: "She saw the Polish words, dirty and all-knowing and unreformed, flinging mud on the clean English words until everything was equally dirty" (300). Another example of this incidental comic technique appears when we read: "Mr. Shortley said he had never cared for foreigners since he had been in the first world's war and seen what they were like" (318). "The Displaced Person" has several more integral Calvinist jokes, however, including: "Christ in the conversation embarrassed her [Mrs. Shortley] the way sex had her mother" (317) and "She had never given much thought to the devil for she felt that religion was essentially for those people who didn't have the brains to avoid evil without it" (294). Here O'Connor combines Calvinist subject matter with Calvinist jokes to create a deeper form of Calvinist humor.

Other stories in this collection occasionally touch on this religious territory also. In "A Temple of the Holy Ghost," O'Connor has the young female in the story reflect prayerfully, "Lord, Lord, thank You that I'm not in the Church of God, thank You Lord, thank You" (205). In "A Circle in the Fire," Mrs. Cope "began to tell the child [her daughter] how much they had to be thankful for, for she said they might have had to live in a development themselves or they might have been Negroes or they might have been in iron lungs or they might have been Europeans ridden in boxcars like cattle . . ." (247). Such thoughts, such speeches, attest to how far from perfection most of us are. We have already seen John T. McNeill's warning in his introduction to Calvin's *Institutes:* "Since all of us have faults and suffer from 'the mists of ignorance,' we should not renounce communion with others on slight grounds" (lxi). As these passages attest, O'Connor would agree with McNeill's premise but, significantly, her stories often make this point comically. This is one strain of Calvinist humor, even when her Calvinist vision does not encompass the whole story.

O'Connor operates within the full-body Calvinist arena in "The Life You Save May Be Your Own," however. In this story, Tom T. Shiflet tells Mrs. Lucynell Crater, "[T]he monks of old slept in their coffins!" and she replies, "They wasn't as advanced as we are" (176). After Shiflet begins to take advantage of Mrs. Crater—as she hoped to take advantage of him— the narrator observes, "He had an expression of serious modesty on his face as if he had just raised the dead" (178). When O'Connor can combine what Shiflet calls "a moral intelligence" (176) with really funny dialogue in this way, she scales the heights of Calvinist humor. Two other stories in her first collection particularly illustrate this point.

O'Connor writes in a letter to "A." (September 6, 1955), "I suppose The Artificial Nigger is my favorite" (953), and it is easy to see why. The story resonates with quasi-theological remarks. In this story about a trip to Atlanta, Nelson, the young boy, "connected the sewer passages with the entrance to hell and understood for the first time how the world was put together in its lower parts" (220). Mr. Head, Nelson's grandfather, reflects O'Connor's familiar Christian emphases even more directly, as when we read that "his true depravity had been hidden from him lest it cause him despair" (231) and that "[t]he speed of God's justice was only what he expected for himself, but he could not stand to think that his sins would be visited upon Nelson and that even now, he was leading the boy to his doom" (227). In such passages, though, O'Connor's thematic intentions seem almost to overwhelm her aesthetic conscience. Sarah J. Fodor admits that this story "stands out in her oeuvre because it directly states religious meaning" (222). Such suspicions about the story are surely correct. In fact, O'Connor wrote to Ben Griffith (May 4, 1955), "[I]n those last two paragraphs [of "The Artificial Nigger"] I have practically gone from the Garden of Eden to the Gates of Paradise" (931). That this is no formula for any sort of humor should be obvious. On the other hand, O'Connor also writes this about Mr. Head's plan for Nelson: "Mr. Head meant him to see everything there is to see in the city so that he would be content to stay at home for the rest of his life" (211–12). O'Connor also writes about Nelson that "the boy's look was ancient, as if he knew everything already and would be pleased to forget it" (212). We can hear Tom T. Shiflet in these passages and even the grandmother from "A Good Man Is Hard to Find." Also, in what is probably the best joke in the story, Nelson replies to Mr. Head's boast that Nelson has never seen him lost, "It's nowhere around here to get lost at" (211). Once again, it's the phrasing that makes the joke, even more than O'Connor's acerbic insight into human nature.

This jaundiced view controls O'Connor's approach to all of the characters in "Good Country People." In one of her most successful comic sentences, O'Connor writes that "Mrs. Hopewell had no bad qualities of her own but she was able to use other people's in such a constructive way that she never felt the lack" (264). The delicate Calvinist balance between recognizing ourselves in others and feeling superior to them determines our reading of this sentence. Less problematic are O'Connor's jokes concerning Mrs. Hopewell's feelings about her daughter Joy/Hulga's Ph.D. degree in philosophy: "Whenever she looked at Joy this way, she could not help but feel it would have been better if the child had not taken the Ph.D. It certainly had not brought her out any . . ." (267); "You could not say, 'My daughter is a philosopher.' That was something that had ended with the Greeks and Romans" (268). This perspective also underlies the brilliant passage in which O'Connor describes Mrs. Hopewell's response to one of Joy/Hulga's philosophy books: "These words had been underlined with a blue pencil and they worked on Mrs. Hopewell like some evil incantation in gibberish" (269). O'Connor's language is, again, brilliantly comic.

But, of course, Mrs. Hopewell is not the only Calvinistically comic figure in the story, as is evident in her exchange with her tenant, Mrs. Freeman: "'Everybody is different,' Mrs. Hopewell said. 'Yes, most people is,' Mrs. Freeman said. 'It takes all kinds to make the world.' 'I always said it did myself'" (265). In this way, the two characters are brilliantly encapsulated. We are thus unsurprised by Mrs. Freeman's account of her daughter Glynese's date with her chiropractor boyfriend, Harvey Hill. According to Mrs. Freeman, Harvey Hill told Glynese, "You just lay yourself down acrost the seat of that car and I'll show you" how to get rid of a pesky sty. And she naively continues: "So she done it and he popped her neck. Kept on a-popping it several times until she made him quit. This morning . . . she ain't got no sty. She ain't got no traces of a sty" (273). Speeches of this sort are hilarious enough to make us temporarily forget O'Connor's most comically damning indictment of this character: "Mrs. Freeman had a special fondness for the details of secret infections, hidden deformities, assaults upon children. Of diseases, she preferred the lingering or incurable" (267). One is inescapably reminded of Sally Fitzgerald's opinion, in her introduction to *Three by Flannery O'Connor*, that "the fiction, although more often than not dreadful in the surface resolution of her stories, was also extremely funny" (xviii).

The "surface resolution" of this story concerns Joy/Hulga and Manly Pointer rather than Mrs. Freeman and Mrs. Hopewell, and so it is appropriate that O'Connor also devotes "extremely funny" attention to both of them. At one point, for example, she summarizes this exchange between Mrs. Freeman and Joy/Hulga: "Glynese said she would rather marry a man with only a '36 Plymouth who would be married by a preacher. The girl asked what if he had a '32 Plymouth and Mrs. Freeman said what Glynese had said was a '36 Plymouth" (274). On a more serious note, O'Connor writes, "[T]he large hulking Joy, whose constant outrage had obliterated every expression from her face, would stare just a little to the left of her [Mrs. Hopewell], her eyes icy blue, with the look of someone who has achieved blindness by an act of the will and means to keep it" (264–65). This description is on the more serious side because of the theological implications of Joy/Hulga's disposition. As she says later on to Manly Pointer, "I'm one of those people who see *through* to nothing" (280). But not all of her remarks are so symbolically significant. When Mrs. Hopewell remarks that "a smile never hurt anyone," Joy/Hulga shouts in outrage: "Malebranche was right: we are not our own light. We are not our own light!" (268).[11] What fun! Manly Pointer is sometimes brimming with symbolic significance also, as when he tells Joy/Hulga, "I been believing in nothing ever since I was born!" (283). But, he can still say to Mrs. Hopewell, "I see you have no family Bible in your parlor. I see that is the one lack you got!" (270), and he can say, in answer to Joy/Hulga's confession that she is highly educated, "I don't care a thing about what all you done. I just want to know if you love me or don'tcher?" (280). That is to say "Good Country People" is most probably filled with fear, loathing, and other "dreadful" things, as Sally Fitzgerald observes, but as she also observes, it is also, like most of O'Connor's fiction, "extremely funny."

The Violent Bear It Away is less funny in almost every way—as most critical commentary attests. Martha Stephens maintains that the novel "attempt[s] to convey, in more realistic and persuasive terms, the anguish and beauty of true religious experience" (98). This hardly promises belly laughs, Calvinist or otherwise, perhaps because such ponderous intentions rule out such a reaction. This is Miles Orvell's view. While conceding that "[t]he novel was indeed long in the making," Orvell concludes that "it is not entirely successful . . . because there was in fact too much reason in making it" (125). This thematic motivation appears in Gilbert H. Muller's proposal that the novel characteristically probes "such moral and theological problems as the nature of good and evil, the origin of sin, the reality of temptation, and the burden of free will . . ." (61). Such critical insights hardly tempt one to echo Bobby Lee's exclamation in "Good Country People": "Some fun!" (153). Even so, as Muller also maintains, O'Connor's approach to all of these weighty theological concepts is by means of "grotesque action" (61), as was the approach of the Old Southwest humorists. One of the injunctions that Mason Tarwater lays on his great-nephew, for example, is to bury him in Christian fashion after his death. Since old Tarwater has grown rotund over the years, this task may prove too much of a challenge for the boy, as we see when Tarwater tries out his destined coffin. We read that the old man "had climbed into it where it stood on the back porch, and had lain there for some time, nothing showing but his stomach which rose over the top like over-leavened bread" (337). Description of this sort recalls Sut Lovingood's description of the title character in George Washington Harris's "Parson Bullen's Lizards": "He weighed ni onto three hundred, hed a black stripe down his back, like ontu a ole bridil rein, an' his belly wer 'bout the size an' color over a beef paunch, an' hit a-swingin out frum side to side; he leaned back frum hit, like a littil feller a-totin a big drum, at a muster . . ." (211). By accepting the grotesque body in this way, O'Connor obviously resembles her literary ancestors. But, most of the book is not written like this.

Admittedly, O'Connor sometimes plays with the rural eccentricities that give such pith to her other fiction, as when she presents, in indirect discourse, young Tarwater's thinking, "The old man had always impressed on him his good fortune in not being sent to school" (339). It should also be funny that, after seeing his Uncle Rayber's hearing aid, young Tarwater wonders whether "his head ran by electricity" (386), but somehow it isn't. O'Connor is so committed to rendering in this novel "the anguish and beauty of true religious experience," the "nature of good and evil, the origin of sin, the reality of temptation, and the burden of free will" identified by the critics that she forgets to be funny. In this book, O'Connor's characters may be as fallen as any in American literature, but there is nothing especially comic about their condition.

The demonic voice that often dogs young Tarwater's tracks is a potential source of Calvinist humor, as in this passage: "Shaw, you know yourself that it give him great satisfaction to admit she [Mason Tarwater's sister] was a whore, the stranger said. He was always admitting somebody was an ass or a whore. That's all a prophet is good for—to admit somebody else is an ass or a whore" (355). The characterization entails the kind of hyperbole popular with writers as diverse as Melville and West. Since the voice offering this judgment is identified as definitely demonic, however, we can hardly relish old Tarwater's failings in the way that we can relish those of the Confidence Man's victims or Miss Lonelyhearts's correspondents. F. H. Buckley defines such ethical dilemmas about being free to laugh: "Our mutual laughter seals a pact by which we participate in a community with similar tastes and aspirations" (187). In most cases, the choices of community offered by O'Connor in *The Violent Bear It Away* are too narrow to afford us opportunities for laughter.

Rayber, for instance, sounds like he was invented at a meeting of the Nashville Agrarians to stand as an epitome of all that is wrong with modern secular life. As Louis Rubin explains, in his very sympathetic introduction to *I'll Take My Stand: The South and the Agrarian Tradition,* "[The] headlong race for mastery over nature called Progress by some and Industrialism by others, stifled the aesthetic impulse, rendered impotent the religious impulse, and converted man's days into a frantic and frenzied drive for the often tawdry conveniences of modernism" (xxx). This sounds like Rayber's biography writ large, as does Ralph C. Wood's characterization of O'Connor's general disposition in these matters: "While others were noisily trumpeting the American Way of Life, O'Connor joined . . . in resisting all attempts to baptize individualist self-sufficiency and materialist well-being in the name of a sentimental religiosity" (76–77). Rayber's role as epitome of all that is wrong with this secular view is evident when he declares: "The great dignity of man . . . is his ability to say: I am born once and no more. What I can see and do for myself and my fellowman in this life is all of my portion and I'm content with it. It's enough to be a man." When O'Connor adds, "There was a light ring in his voice. He watched the boy closely to see if he had struck a chord" (437), we are likely to respond, "Please! Let us go! We promise not to be secular humanists!" Who is likely to choose to follow Rayber's path anyway, since he thinks about his love for his idiot son, Bishop, "He had kept it from gaining control over him by what amounted to a rigid ascetic discipline. . . . [H]e only knew that it was the way his life had to be lived if it were going to have any dignity at all" (402)? O'Connor writes in a letter to Cecil Dawkins (May 19, 1957), "[T]he people I write about certainly don't disgust me entirely though I see them from a standard of judgment from which they fall short" (1033). Her depiction of Rayber in this novel would seem to call this statement into question because her "standard of judgment" so patently determines her inverse fictional depiction. The ideal southern society, according to Rubin's introduction, is "one in which men could live as individuals and not as automatons, aware of their finiteness and their dependence upon God and nature, devoted to the enhancement of the moral life in its aesthetic and spiritual dimensions, possessed of a sense of the deep inscrutability of the natural world" (xxxi). Once again, we can glimpse Rayber standing somewhere back in the corner where he has been exiled for failing to live up to the Christian ideal. Surely there is some other way to represent non-Christian modes of life, a way that would leave room for humor as well as condemnation.

Returning to the short story form in her posthumously published collection *Everything That Rises Must Converge,* O'Connor again seems to regain her sense of Calvinist humor. In the title story, for example, the central male character, Julian, "standing with his hands behind him, appeared pinned to the door frame, waiting like Saint Sebastian for the arrows to begin piercing him" (485). Julian's mistaken sense of himself is captured brilliantly and comically in the allusion to Saint Sebastian. Of course, we do not share Julian's views in this story, especially when he believes that some sort of justice entitles him to think about his suffering mother, "Your punishment exactly fits your pettiness. This should teach you a permanent lesson" (496). At the same time, neither do we see him as epitomizing all that is wrong with the world today as O'Connor encourages us to see George Rayber. In the same way, we can laugh at the other mother-son relationship in "The Enduring Chill" when the mother hopes that her supposedly literary son, Asbury, has been spending all these years writing a blockbuster novel like *Gone with the Wind*: "Mrs. Fox hoped it wasn't going to be just a poem" (553). We feel that we know Mrs. Fox and Asbury—and probably that we know Julian and his mother—but nobody knows Rayber, and nobody would want to. We just might want to spend some time with Thomas's mother in "The Comforts of Home" because she thinks that the promiscuous Star Drake, nee Sarah Ham, is a "nimpermaniac" (574). Malapropisms are always good for a laugh to those who know the correct word.

"The Lame Shall Enter First" is, as many have observed, a displaced version of *The Violent Bear It Away*, an unsurprising development since—as we have seen—O'Connor worked on her second novel for many years. Sheppard, this story's version of Rayber, shares many of Rayber's shortcomings. He thinks, for example, that "[h]eaven and hell were for the mediocre, and he [his son, Norton] was that if he was anything" (613). Sheppard's repudiation of his son clearly puts him in the same leaky boat with Rayber, but his assumption that "[h]eaven and hell were for the mediocre," while doctrinally reprehensible, is at least funny. Even so, Rufus Johnson, this story's version of young Tarwater, is justified in saying to Norton: "God, kid, . . . how do you stand it? . . . He thinks he's Jesus Christ" (609). Overall, there is more opportunity for humor in O'Connor's shorter version of this moral exemplum, but the nature of the material confines the humor to small effects here and there, as when Rufus Johnson says about his grandfather, "He's gone with a remnant to the hills" (607). In this exaggerated commonplace, Rufus Johnson's grandfather seems, like the elder Tarwater, to rise above the narrative surrounding him to provide us with an occasional wry laugh.

Several other stories in *Everything That Rises* contain both great one-liners and probing satire, in the manner of *A Good Man Is Hard to Find* rather than of *The Violent Bear It Away*. In "Greenleaf," Mrs. May offers us a terrific one-liner when she recalls that "Wesley, the younger child had had rheumatic fever when he was seven" and concludes that "this was what had caused him to be an intellectual" (504). This is a merely amusing eccentricity, but Mrs. May is, at the same time, one of those awful, self-righteous people that O'Connor loves to hate. Typically, the narrator says about her, "She thought the word, Jesus, should be kept inside the church building like other words inside the bedroom. She was a good Christian woman with a large respect for religion, though she did not, of course, believe any of it was true" (506). Experienced readers can anticipate from this passage that something bad is going to happen to Mrs. May, but they can also anticipate some good laughs along the way to this tragic development. Mrs. May ends up gored to death by a bull, but O'Connor allows us to laugh frequently before this happens. One source of humor is Mrs. May's genteel disapproval of the extreme form of worship practiced by Mrs. Greenleaf, who clips stories about suffering out of the paper, buries the clippings in a hole, and then prays over them. When Mrs. May sees one of these orgies of religious feeling taking place in her own woods, she imagines saying to Mrs. Greenleaf: "Jesus . . . would be *ashamed* of you. He would tell you to get up from [the ground] this instant and go wash your children's clothes" (507). Her feelings about Mrs. Greenleaf's husband are similarly mean and similarly funny: "'I thank Gawd for everthang,' Mr. Greenleaf had drawled. You might as well, she had thought in the fierce silence that followed; you've never done anything for yourself" (514). People shouldn't talk this way about other people, we think, but then we think that Mrs. May is not entirely mistaken. And, perhaps, we remember that O'Connor is the one who made Mrs. May talk this way in the first place and made Mrs. Greenleaf roll around on the ground. As a result, we can only respond ambivalently to Mrs. May's summary judgment of herself: "Before any kind of judgement seat, she would be able to say: I've worked, I have not wallowed. At this very instant while she was recalling a lifetime of work, Mr. Greenleaf was loitering in the woods and Mrs. Greenleaf was probably flat on the ground, asleep over her holeful of clippings" (522). Mrs. May is admittedly a monster of uncharitable judgments, but she seems to take on literary ancestry by echoing Henry James's character Mrs. Costello in *Daisy Miller*. When Mrs. Costello's nephew, Frederick Winterbourne, says that Daisy is merely an innocent American girl, Mrs. Costello responds, "She goes on from day to day, from hour to hour, as they did in the Golden Age. I can imagine nothing more vulgar" (48). James is probably just making a joke about social snobbery here. O'Connor makes a similar joke, but she also works on her Calvinist condemnation of Mrs. May when she has this woman say about the Greenleafs that "[t]hey lived like the lilies of the field, off the fat that she struggled to put into the land" (509). In a certain sense, O'Connor is playing for even higher thematic stakes than Henry James. No matter how we decide thematically, however, while deciding we must laugh a deep Calvinist laugh at what O'Connor says.

In "Parker's Back," Obadiah Elihue Parker starts out sounding like another Mrs. May, as when he ominously thinks about religion, "I ain't got no use for that. A man can't save his self from whatever it is he don't deserve none of my sympathy" (669). Since O'Connor spreads her jokes more evenly over this story, however, other characters also become targets of her Calvinist humor. Thus we read about Parker's wife, "Sarah Ruth thought churches were idolatrous" (663). Surely this is one of O'Connor's grandest gestures of Calvinist humor. If Parker tends toward atheism, in other words, Sarah Ruth succumbs to religious extremity. Mrs. Greenleaf might have climbed into the same boat if O'Connor's intentions had been different in that story, but her desire to expose Mrs. May's religious shortcomings leaves no room for equal-opportunity abuse. Things are different in "Parker's Back," and so we can read Parker's rumination on his wife: "In addition to her other bad qualities, she was forever sniffing up sin. She did not smoke or dip, drink whiskey, use bad language or paint her face, and God knew some paint would have improved it . . ." (655). As is often the case in O'Connor's stories, there is no one entirely in the clear, and this is one great attraction of "Parker's Back." This evenhanded criticism enables comments like the following: "Parker did nothing much when he was at home but listen to what the judgement seat of God would be like for him if he didn't change his ways" (664). "Serious things" are, as Manly Pointer says, probably the only things really worth talking about, but that doesn't mean that you can't have a few Calvinist laughs while you're at it.

"Revelation" is a perfect illustration of this principle. In this story, Ruby Turpin shouts out to God at one point, "Who do you think you are?" (653). Even the creator and sustainer of the universe would have a lot of nerve asserting any sort of familiarity with Ruby Turpin—much less superiority—and that goes double for Mary Grace. After all, as Mrs. Turpin patiently explains to God, "It's no trash around here, black or white, that I haven't given to. And break my back to the bone every day working. And do for the church" (652). Like Mrs. May, Mrs. Turpin feels that she has met and passed any test that supernatural forces might put before her. Then, why don't things work out the way she thinks they should? Why does Mary Grace get to hit Mrs. Turpin square in the forehead with a social studies textbook and shout at her, "Go back to hell where you came from, you old wart hog" (646)? If things worked out the way they should—the way Mrs. Turpin thinks they should—then none of this would happen. But O'Connor is committed to keeping Mrs. Turpin from having what she thinks she deserves. Mrs. Turpin's low ranking on O'Connor's supernatural scale is epitomized in the passage in which she tries to contemplate being in any way different from how she already is. "If Jesus had said to her before he made her, 'There's only two places available for you. You can either be a nigger or white trash,'" Mrs. Turpin is sure that she would have responded, "Please, Jesus, please . . . just let me wait until there's another place available" so that she would not have to come to earth as anyone other than Ruby Turpin. Most likely, Jesus would have told her, "No, you have to go right now and I have only those two places so make up your mind." Given this divine either/or, Mrs. Turpin is sure that she would have "wiggled and squirmed and begged and pleaded" for some other option. In the end, though, she would have said to her savior, "All right, make me a nigger then—but that don't mean a trashy one" (636). The imaginary encounter is outrageous but it is perfectly consistent with her character and with the premises by which Ruby Turpin lives her life. As W. A. Sessions writes, "Ruby Turpin defines the negative aspect of her Calvinist world—a society seen in levels of election" (209). Clearly, O'Connor is saying, Mrs. Turpin is too self-righteous to be admirable from a religious point of view.

From a secular point of view, however, there is much to recommend her, at least as the subject of Calvinist humor. Since—unlike O'Connor—most of us do not get to decide who deserves heaven or hell,[12] we can appreciate both the author's jokes and those we might tell ourselves. Both kinds of jokes are captured in an exchange of dialogue that takes place before Mary Grace assaults Mrs. Turpin. A woman identified by Mrs. Turpin as "white trash" says about a clock displayed in the doctor's waiting room, "You can get you one with green stamps. . . . Save you up enough, you can get most anything. I got me some joo'ry." Mrs. Turpin thinks in response, "Ought to have got you a wash rag and some soap" (637). We are probably reminded of the way Mrs. May thinks about the Greenleafs, and we probably laugh all over again at evidence of the same cruel disposition. Mrs. May might say to God, as Ruby Turpin does, "If you like trash better, go get yourself some trash then . . . You could have made me trash. Or a nigger . . ." (652). O'Connor's term for Mrs. Turpin's tone in this encounter with the divine is *railed.* Of course, the stories tell us, we should disapprove of all this, but there is probably a part of most of us that laughs at what Mrs. Turpin says, as we might laugh at what Sut Lovingood or the Big Bear of Arkansas says. The fact that O'Connor's subject matter involves religion doesn't change this fact.

There is no doubt that O'Connor differs in her positive affirmation of Christianity from the other twentieth-century American writers I have been discussing. In fact, it is this affirmation that attracts the lion's share of critical attention devoted to her work. In a series of essays collected under the title *Flannery O'Connor and the Christian Mystery* (1997), Richard Giannone writes in summary: "Her writing is a *vade mecum* in how to live in desolate times, a handbook for constant use drawn from the words and example of the primitive monastics she admired" (187). One can hardly imagine praise of this sort lavished on Nathanael West, Ernest Hemingway, or William Faulkner. None of these writers would be likely to attract this judgment by Ralph C. Wood in the same collection: "I contend that O'Connor's Catholic faith—both as she practiced it in her life and as she made it the motive-force in her fiction—was set against the vaporized faith of a 1950s consensus religion" (82). And yet, as we have seen, O'Connor's fiction is more than the sum of its religious parts. In the same collection, Marilyn Arnold finds herself forced to admit, "Probably most of us were attracted to Flannery O'Connor for her comic spirit" (244). Arnold and other critics collected in *Flannery O'Connor and the Christian Mystery* and elsewhere believe that they have gone beyond this surface attraction to reach some deeper truth. From the point of view of Calvinist humor, however, Flannery O'Connor's "comic spirit" is reason enough to admire her work.

10 Calvinist Humor Revisited

To catch the spirit of Calvinist humor as it has been expressed by the authors treated here, we might consider Nathaniel Hawthorne's comment, in his late essay "Chiefly about War Matters," about the very idealistic behavior of John Brown: "Any common-sensible man looking at the matter unsentimentally, must have felt a certain intellectual satisfaction in seeing him hanged, if it were only in requital of his preposterous miscalculation of possibilities." Admittedly, this is a pretty awful thing to say about anyone, much less a martyr for the abolitionist cause. In Hawthorne's judgment, though, Brown deserved hanging in large part just because he thought that things could be different from what they were. But, to a Calvinistically inclined mind like Hawthorne's, things cannot be different from the way they are no matter what we wish to the contrary. This is how they have always been, and this is how they will continue to be because human nature has been the same ever since the Fall of Man. Unfortunately—or, from a literary point of view, fortunately—people will continue to act as if this is not the case. Therefore, we will continue to have Calvinist humor, as we have had Calvinist humor almost from the beginnings of what we think of as America.

As we have seen in an earlier chapter, William Bradford, Michael Wigglesworth, and Jonathan Edwards joyfully predicted the sufferings of the damned. The Puritan settler Mary Rowlandson differed from these hard-core Calvinists primarily in the sense that she admitted to sharing herself some of the pathetic shortcomings of these damned souls. Thus, these four Puritan writers can be seen to exemplify both of the forms of Calvinist humor that I have identified. By the same token, Hawthorne launches his fictional characters on pointless quests for happiness, and continues to do so although he surely knows that they will fail. Herman Melville continues to embroil his characters in situations that he deliberately makes them misapprehend. Then Hawthorne and Melville laugh at these characters and encourage us to do the same, largely defining themselves in William Bradford's terms as superior to those fallen creatures whom we laugh at. Mark Twain's characters, on the other hand, share common human foibles with their author and readers, and this (correctly) strikes Twain as reason enough for laughter. William Faulkner's characters act as if they are damned, sometimes being blissfully unaware of their fallen condition and sometimes being fully aware of it. Even so, their damnation, whether they understand it or not, can elicit chuckles, sneers, guffaws, and laughs even if we recognize some of our own failings in theirs. Twain and Faulkner thus belong in the other Calvinist humorists' camp. Like the most profoundly secular of Faulkner's characters, Ernest Hemingway's characters—like Nick Adams's father, the doctor, and like Robert Cohn—seldom acknowledge any Old Testament perspective on their behavior, and yet Hemingway's narrators assume these characters to be damned in some sense and laugh at them both for being in their basic situations and for their failure to understand them. Nathanael West's Miss Lonelyhearts is a ridiculously foolish character because he believes that he can do something to help the pathetic readers who write to him for advice. West's other characters, such as Lemuel Pitkin and Faye Greener, are just as foolish—and just as humorous—largely because they are willing to accept the validity of some universal principle that West rejects out of hand. As Shakespeare's Puck says in A Midsummer Night's Dream, "Lord, what fools these mortals be!" (3.2.115). Flannery O'Connor's southerners also act frequently as if they are not "sinners in the Hands of an Angry God," but they are ludicrous even when they do acknowledge their condition. O'Connor laughs spitefully at them in consequence, and invites us to do the same. In other words, despite the wide-reaching philosophical implications of all these texts, a definite strain of Calvinist humor is present in them all, as it is in Hawthorne's unsympathetic gibe at John Brown. Even while we concede that this sort of humor is usually bleak and unredeeming, we must understand that it arises from the perceptions of our most highly esteemed writers.

To put all of this into a literary context, we might ponder the following points. We are probably convinced that, as Hawthorne asserts, an actual abolitionist named John Brown was involved somehow in the attack on Harpers Ferry, and we are also quite possibly convinced that this man must have gravely miscalculated the potential effects of his behavior in order to have acted as he did.[1] That is to say, we know that there is some sort of historical basis for what Hawthorne says, no matter how nasty it is. We probably also assume in the same way that an actual sailor ridiculed the Puritans as they crossed the Atlantic, as William Bradford tells us a sailor did, and that Mary Rowlandson's Indian captors most probably laughed at her when she fell off a horse with her seriously wounded daughter. By consulting the relevant religious texts, we can easily conclude that all of the people reported on in these accounts behaved as John Calvin assumed that human beings usually behave, perhaps because these human beings were fallen from prelapsarian perfection. On the other hand, we probably know with equal certainty that there was no real person named Goodman Brown—or Jason Compson either—despite all that we read about their fictional antics. Surely, Hawthorne and Faulkner just made them up. But, these authors made their characters up in such a way as to make them behave like the real human beings reported on in Calvinistically influenced "historical" writing. The same is undeniably true about the characters created by Twain, O'Connor, West, Melville, and numerous other American authors. The crucial question is, why? Why—when authors are perfectly free to create fictional characters of any sort—do they create characters as obviously fallen from perfection as the actors in recognizable Calvinist accounts? Perhaps more challenging still is the question why amateur and professional readers alike continue to consider such characters and their authors the very apex of our national literature even as they laugh at their antics?

Much of the evidence that I used in my opening chapter to show a residual Calvinist spirit in American life can be summoned once again to structure a possible answer to this baffling question. Melville, we may recall from the foregoing chapters, wrote in "Hawthorne and His Mosses": "Certain it is . . . that this great power of blackness in [Hawthorne] derives its force from its appeal to that Calvinistic sense of Inner Depravity and Original Sin, from whose visitations, in some shape or other, no deeply thinking mind is always and wholly free. For, in certain moods, no man can weigh this world without throwing in something, somehow like Original Sin, to strike the uneven balance" (837). And Agnes McNeill Donohue adds, we may also recall, "[N]o American writer, conscious of his country's religious past, is able to ignore his Calvinist inheritance, despise it though he may" (342). Finally, the editors of the aptly titled *The Calvinist Roots of the Modern Era* conclude, "In this [twentieth] century, Calvinism appears as a psychological construct, a cultural institution or artifact, a habit of mind, or a sociopolitical structure" (xiii). In literary terms, this means, according to these editors, that "Catholic, Jewish, and African American writers . . . although not in direct lineage from the Puritans, engage Calvinism through their experience as Americans" (xiii). We Americans are all, in other words, Calvinists of a sort even when we are aggressively secular. Rather than fleeing from this discouraging discovery, moreover, American readers and writers seem to revel happily in it. Or, as Louis D. Rubin, Jr., explains, in "The Great American Joke," "The American literary imagination has from its earliest days been at least as much comic in nature as tragic" (255).

This willingness on the part of American authors and readers alike to find a nasty situation laughable exists probably because an impressive critical consensus attests to the presence in American literature of the element that we might identify by invoking the title of Constance Rourke's groundbreaking—and aptly titled—*American Humor: A Study of the National Character* (1931). As Rourke writes, "There is scarcely an aspect of the American character to which humor is not related" (ix). Generations of literary critics and historians have seconded her proposition. Too many books and articles treating American humor exist to be listed here, but some volumes, selected to show historical continuity, include: Walter Blair's *Native American Humor* (1937), Albert Cook's *The Dark Voyage and the Golden Mean: A Philosophy of Comedy* (1949), *The Comic Tradition in America: An Anthology of American Humor,* edited by Kenneth S. Lynn (1958), *An Anthology of American Humor,* edited by Brom Weber et al. (1962), *The Penguin Book of Negro Humor,* edited by Langston Hughes (1966), Jesse Bier's *The Rise and Fall of American Humor* (1968),

The Comic Imagination in American Literature, edited by Louis D. Rubin, Jr. (1973), *American Humor: An Anthology,* edited by Enid Veron (1976), Walter Blair and Hamlin Hill's *America's Humor: From Poor Richard to Doonesbury* (1980), Walter Blair and Ravin I. McDavid, Jr.'s *The Mirth of a Nation: America's Great Dialect Humor* (1983), *Russell Baker's Book of American Humor* (1993), Mel Watkins's *On the Real Side: Laughing, Lying, and Signifying—The Underground Tradition of African-American Humor* (1994), *What's So Funny? Humor in American Culture,* edited by Nancy Walker (1998), Gerald Nachman's *Seriously Funny: The Rebel Comedians of the 1950s and 1960s* (2003), and James H. Justus's *Fetching the Old Southwest: Humorous Writing from Longstreet to Twain* (2004). In addition to countless books of this sort, the journal *Studies in American Humor* has intermittently published scholarly articles on the subject since 1974. As Rourke also says—and as these books and articles attest—"Humor has always been a fashioning instrument in America, cleaving its way through the national life, holding tenaciously to the spread elements of that life" (297). Of course, the sources cited—and others that could be easily summoned—define and illustrate American humor in a dizzying variety of ways. However, when this instrument is wielded in the light of active or residual Calvinism, the result is what I have been calling Calvinist humor. As we have seen, writing of this sort continues to be highly respected.

Harry Levin, for example, writes perceptively about Hawthorne that by "[t]aking a limited view of the potentialities of human nature, Hawthorne remained a Calvinist in psychology, if not in theology" (55). And Miles Orvell says about O'Connor, "The blackness of darkness that Melville discovered in Hawthorne and which finds its source of Puritanic gloom in the human heart's Original—and ongoing—Sin is a darkness that is most importantly at the center of O'Connor's conception of Man" (33). It is no wonder, given the disposition that Orvell discerns, that O'Connor would write in a letter to Ben Griffith (June 8, 1955), "*Understanding Fiction . . . is a book that has been of invaluable help to me*" (938), especially since the Calvinistic gloom that pervades this book's thematic/stylistic assumptions is manifest and, as many will attest, very long-lasting in its effects. The authors, Cleanth Brooks and Robert Penn Warren, explain, for example, that "[c]omedy, including even warm humor as well as savage satire, has to do with disappointment and surprises, confusions and miscarriages, the criticism and defeat of aspirations, contrasts of pretensions and reality, failure of expectations, inability to adjust to the changing demands of life" (275). And, this is what these esteemed critics think about comedy![2] This standard presumes that, without question, life is a constant struggle in which high aims are seldom achieved and frustration is the normal human lot. Or, that in literature, as well as in theology, a Calvinistic perspective displays a kind of "seriousness" missing, for example, in the writing of Ralph Waldo Emerson, Walt Whitman, Emile Coué, and Norman Vincent Peale, writing in which aspiration and optimism control the text. In fact, aspiration and optimism are often funny enough in themselves to provide the basis for Calvinist humor. The way things "just are" provides the rest.

In illustration, and as a happy reprise of some Calvinist jokes gone by, we might recall Jonathan Edwards's description of the damned but self-satisfied Puritan sitting upright in one of Edwards's pews: "[H]e flatters himself that he shall escape it; he depends upon himself for his own security; he flatters himself in what he has done, in what he is now doing; or what he intends to do. Every one lays out matters in his own mind how he shall avoid damnation, and flatters himself that he contrives well for himself, and that his schemes will not fail" (100). This salvific plan seems laughably inadequate to Edwards simply because "[t]he greater part of those who heretofore have lived under the same means of grace, and are now dead, are undoubtedly gone to hell; and it was not because they were not as wise as those who are now alive; it was not because they did not lay out matters as well for themselves as to secure their own escape. If we could speak with them, and inquire of them, one by one, whether they expected, when alive, and when they used to hear about hell, ever to be the subjects of that misery: we doubtless, should hear one and another reply, 'No, I never intended to come here: I had laid out matters otherwise in my mind . . .'" (100). This vision of eternal damnation for the blissfully unaware Puritan is awful, of course, but it is funny even so. Also funny is the narrator's sad-but-true reflection about the new Adam and Eve in Hawthorne's story of that title: "In the energy of new life, it appears no such impracticable feat to climb into the sky! But they have already received a woful lesson, which may finally go far towards reducing them to the level of the departed race, when they acknowledge the necessity of keeping the beaten track of earth" (748–49). Given the way things are, the new Adam and Eve will assuredly have the same experiences as all their predecessors, and their possibly thinking that things might turn out otherwise is a source of Calvinist humor. The narrator ironically implies the same sad lesson in Hawthorne's "Earth's Holocaust" (1844): "And now the drums were beaten and the trumpets brayed all together, as a prelude to the proclamation of universal and eternal peace, and the announcement that glory was no more to be won by blood; but that it would henceforth be the contention of the human race, to work out the greatest mutual good . . ." (894–95). The narrator believes that none of these noble intentions will be realized simply because of the way things are and have always been, and he assumes (probably correctly) that we share his beliefs. Melville's fictional spokesmen are equally unillusioned and equally disposed to laugh a Calvinist laugh. Consider the question raised by Melville's narrator concerning Amaso Delano's tendency, in "Benito Cereno," to assume that everything will work out fine: "Whether, in view of what humanity is capable, such a trait implies, along with a benevolent heart, more than ordinary quickness and accuracy of intellectual perception, may be left to the wise to determine" (67). The "wise" will surely adopt the less sunny, Calvinist view of human nature, at least in part because of the lessons taught by the "natural" observations available everywhere, as they are in *The Encantadas*: "That these tortoises are the victims of a penal, or malignant, or perhaps a downright diabolical enchanter, seems in nothing more likely than in that strange infatuation of hopeless toil which so often possesses them" (191). These tortoises continue to press fruitlessly against the immovable masts of ships just as human beings continue to act as if they will be the very first ones to escape the inescapable limits of human experience. What can we do but laugh at the tortoises and the human beings?

Leslie Fiedler uses the phrase "secularized Calvinism" in *Love and Death in the American Novel* to describe Twain's philosophical orientation (228), and this formula can be applied to Twain's literary successors also. In one of his Calendar entries in *Pudd'nhead Wilson*, for example, Twain writes, "There is this trouble about special providences—namely, there is so often a doubt as to which party was intended to be the beneficiary. In the case of the children, the bears and the prophet, the bears got more real satisfaction out of the episode than the prophet did, because they got the children" (17). It is religiously unorthodox to question the usual morals attached to Bible stories, but it is sometimes funny to do so. At the same time, questioning orthodoxy is evidence that one has profited from experience instead of simply taking the traditional explanation for granted, as Amaso Delano does. This sort of sadder-but-wiser wit also guides the following Calendar entries from *Following the Equator:* "It takes your enemy and your friend, working together, to hurt you to the heart; the one to slander you and the other to get the news to you" (2: 84); "Man is the Only Animal that Blushes. Or needs to" (1: 238). There is an undeniable sadness about these comic reflections, but Twain differs from some of his historical predecessors in implying that this sadness is occasioned by his own behavior as well as by that of other people. Faulkner, as we have seen, also tends to include himself and his readers among those who exhibit a fallen kind of behavior. Quentin Compson, the narrator of "That Evening Sun," for instance, says that his mother talks "[l]ike she believed that all day father had been trying to think of doing the thing she wouldn't like the most, and that she knew all the time that after a while he would think of it" (*Collected Stories* 294). "Aren't mothers—aren't people—just like that," we observe with a Calvinist chuckle. The next Faulknerian example, from *Light in August,* is admittedly more macabre, but it is also rooted in someone's perception of the way things undeniably are. After Joanna Burden has been murdered by having her throat slit, her body lies out in the open for all to see: "Because the cover fell open and she was laying on her side, facing one way, and her head was turned clean around like she was looking behind her." A volunteer, supposedly committed, as volunteers are, to making things better, says, "[I]f she could just have done that when she was alive, she might not have been doing it now" (92). This remark almost belongs in Nathanael West's territory; at least it connects Faulkner to the Old Southwest humorists. And, if we laugh at them, then we can laugh at this countryman's grim reflection about Joanna Burden's corpse. This willingness to find the corruptible human body humorous also explains the Calvinist humor contained in Jody Varner's annoyed description of his sister Eula's deter-mined inactivity in *The Hamlet:* "At the rate she's going at it, there aint a acorn that will fall in the next fifty years that wont grow up and rot down and be burnt for firewood before she'll ever climb it" (107). There is a resigned acceptance defining all of these remarks and comments, an ac-ceptance of the way things "just are" for fallen human nature. This recog-nition especially governs the last example of Faulkner's Calvinist humor that I will have space for here. The subject is the farmer from whom Ike Snopes has been stealing fodder for his beloved cow in *The Hamlet:* "[H]e experienced a shocking bewilderment followed by a furious and blazing wrath like that of a man who, leaping for safety from in front of a run-away, slips on a banana skin" (211). Just how "secularized" any of this is can best be decided by someone like Leslie Fiedler. For our purposes, it is enough to say that it is all somehow Calvinist and all somehow humorous.

Ernest Hemingway also can be thought to practice "secularized Cal-vinism." His sinners can be easily represented by Robert Cohn from *The Sun Also Rises,* about whom Jake Barnes says, "As he had been thinking for months about leaving his wife and had not done it because it would be too cruel to deprive her of himself, her departure was a very healthful shock" (4). Then, there is the Turkish officer from *In Our Time,* about whom we read, "Then I told the Turk the man was being sent on board ship and would be most severely dealt with. Oh most vigorously. He felt topping about it" (11). Cohn and the Turkish officer are clearly laughable because of their secular concupiscence, because of what Hawthorne might call their "preposterous miscalculation of possibilities." Hemingway's saints are equally easy to spot. Nick Adams, for example, "took the ax out of the pack," in "Big Two-Hearted River," "and chopped out two projecting roots. That leveled a piece of ground large enough to sleep on. He smoothed out the sandy soil with his hand and pulled all the sweet fern bushes by their roots. His hands smelled good from the sweet fern. He smoothed the uprooted earth. He did not want anything making lumps under the blankets. When he had the ground smooth, he spread his three blankets" (138). Insofar as secular salvation is possible in Hemingway's world, Nick is likely to attain it. The unhappy fates of those who fail to abide by Hemingway's "code" are just as easy to predict, and so they are laughable from a Calvinistic perspective.

In a letter to Malcolm Cowley (May 11, 1939), Nathanael West wrote, "But I'm a comic writer and it seems impossible for me to handle any of the 'big things' without seeming to laugh or at least smile" (794). The same could be said of any of the writers covered in this brief survey of Calvinist humor. West himself illustrates the point in *The Dream Life of Balso Snell* when Saniette says: "I won't die! I am getting better and better. I won't die! The will is master o'er the flesh. I won't die!" and Death replies, "Oh, yes you will" (24). Although Jonathan Edwards and Nathaniel Hawthorne seem to be operating on a completely different philosophical level from Nathanael West, we might easily imagine any of the three writing some version of this exchange. West is on his own 1930s high horse, however, in mocking the univocal economic thinking of Lemuel Pitkin in *A Cool Million*. Lem's Horatio Alger-like economic optimism is probably "secularized" in Fiedler's sense, but West looks at it with a disdain that he shares with his more religious literary ancestors: "At this rate of pay, he calculated, he would earn ninety-six dollars for an eight-hour day or five hundred and seventy-six dollars for a six-day week. If he could keep it up, he would have a million dollars in no time" (165). To laugh at this calculation—as to laugh at the unwary assumptions of the predictably damned Puritan in Edwards's congregation—it is probably necessary to have some ideas in common with the joker, as all the literary critics of American Calvinism assume. Tod Hackett's observation of Harry Greener's corpse in *The Day of the Locust,* however, can stand, even without ideological underpinning, unexplained, on its own: "He looked like the interlocutor in a minstrel show" (318). Generally, we must be willing to put our finer feelings to sleep when laughing at West's humor; in the words of Henri Bergson, we must attain "a temporary anesthesia of the heart" (557). We must view Saniette's death, and Lem's pathetic foolishness, and Harry Greener's corpse without any sense that these fictional characters are human—as we all are. When we can make this stretch, however, West emerges as a true American Calvinist humorist. O'Connor asks us to view her characters from an emotional distance, too, even though her language is often patently religious. Hazel Motes's landlady, for example, concludes after Motes has adopted a regimen of bodily mortifications: "It's like one of them gory stories, it's something that people have quit doing—like boiling in oil or being a saint or walling up cats. . . . There's no reason for it. People have quit doing it" (127). In "The Displaced Person," Mrs. Shortley thinks that "[s]he had never given much thought to the devil for she felt that religion was essentially for those people who didn't have the brains to avoid evil without it" (294). In "The Life You Save May Be Your Own," Tom T. Shiflet tells Mrs. Lucynell Crater, "[T]he monks of old slept in their coffins!" and she replies, "They wasn't as advanced as we are" (176). Average, everyday people's willingness to live without any religious consciousness is the specific target of O'Connor's satire in all of these cases, but the author's evident pleasure in skewering them for these apparently common failings is what turns their behavior into Calvinist humor. More of a piece with the examples that we have drawn from other authors is O'Connor's harsh comment in "Good Country People": "Mrs. Freeman had a special fondness for the details of secret infections, hidden deformities, assaults upon children. Of diseases, she preferred the lingering or incurable" (267). This is more like what we might expect from Melville or West, but it is also quintessential Flannery O'Connor. She laughs at her own, individually created characters and expects us to laugh at them too. That is to say, she is a true Calvinist humorist.

From an easily conceivable moral position, there should be nothing funny about the conditions of O'Connor's characters. It shouldn't be funny either that Jonathan Edwards and most of his congregants think that some of them will soon end up in everlasting hellfire or that Melville's human beings and tortoises are condemned to butt their heads fruitlessly against circumstance. But it is. And it is probably funnier than some far more benign forms of humor. Perhaps Calvin is correct to assume, as he writes in *The Institutes,* that "the uncleanness of the parents is so transmitted to the children that all without any exception are defiled at their begetting" (248). Perhaps Nathanael West is correct to assume, in more secular language, that "[t]here is nothing to root for in my work . . ." (qtd. in Reid 11). Whether the absolute is revealed in religion, however, or merely projected by the inquiring mind, the answer is the same: no sale! We Americans often find our literary humor in the fact that we cannot achieve what we can easily imagine. And that is what Calvinist humor is all about.

Notes

1. Calvinist Humor

1. As Calvin characteristically writes in *Institutes of the Christian Religion:* "Original sin, therefore, seems to be a hereditary depravity and corruption of our nature, diffused into all parts of the soul, which first makes us liable to God's wrath, then also brings forth in us those works which Scripture calls 'works of the flesh'" (251), and also, "[T]he uncleanness of the parents is so transmitted to the children that all without any exception are defiled at their begetting" (248).

2. In an essay in the *Wilson Quarterly* in which he defends the design of American bipartisan foreign policy through several administrations, John Ikenberry characterizes the more critical perspective on American foreign policy as follows: "To hear critics tell it, the American preoccupation with promoting democracy around the world is the product of a dangerous idealistic impulse" (56).

3. Wimsatt and Phillips agree—perhaps unawares—when they write in union with Rickels, "[A] strict Presbyterian, Harris unrolled in Sut a demonic energy and apocalyptic fury perhaps inspired by the Calvinistic strain in his religious heritage" (156).

4. William J. Bouwsma explains, in *John Calvin: A Sixteenth-Century Portrait,* that in Calvin's system "the human body was "[l]owest of all . . . , the primary source of human wickedness." He adds that "Calvin suggested that God had displayed his own disdain for it by creating it from the dust to keep us humble. . . . At times, then, the body seemed to him not only the prison of the soul but worse: 'carrion, dirt, and corruption,' full of a 'stinking infection' that defiles the rest of the personality" (80). Later on, Bouwsma balances the scales somewhat by writing, "He also praised the body. Noting a tendency in himself to refer to it 'grossly,' he apologized to his congregation for implying that it might be intrinsically corrupt" (134). In any event, the human body emerges in this system, both directly and in terms of residual influence, as corrupt.

5. Neil Schmitz shares Wilson's view, in the *Columbia Literary History of the United States:* "Sut's tales, proudly presented, barely bracketed, relate sadistic pranks, acts of vandalism, practical jokes that humiliate and injure victims, and they are vividly told in a mean hard voice" (322).

6. William Shurr approaches a similar perspective when discussing a letter from Oliver Wendell Holmes to Harriet Beecher Stowe. "In the present letter," Shurr writes, Holmes "picks over the points of this old calvinism one by one: reprobation, predestination, inherited guilt, the just and angry God, infant damnation, and the pleasure of God and the saints at witnessing God's just retribution against the wicked" (23).

7. Writing about Hart Crane, in the collection of essays *Voices and Visions: The Poet in America,* Alan Williamson observes in passing, "Like almost every other American writer, [Crane] finds by experience that the ravages of Puritanism have been worse in America than elsewhere" (343). Again, the writer feels no need to explain what is meant by "Puritanism."

8. "Or what man is there of you, whom if his son ask bread, will he give him a stone?" (Matt. 7.9).

9. Lowell's membership in this Calvinistic fraternity might also be signified by his poem "Mr. Edwards and the Spider" (1946), especially by the line "What are we in the hands of the Great God?" (l. 10).

10. In "Memories of West Street and Lepke" (1959), Lowell describes himself at the time of World War II as "a fire-breathing Catholic C.O." (l. 14).

11. For one searching discussion, among many others, of these doctrines, see Gerald J. Goodwin, "The Myth of 'Arminian-Calvinism' in Eighteenth-Century New England."

12. Lawrance Thompson, *Melville's Quarrel with God* (1952).

13. As in the case of Twain, many other stories and novels might be cited in support of Faulkner's membership in this dark literary fraternity.

14. In *Nathanael West: The Art of His Life,* Jay Martin quotes Matthew Josephson's testimony on this point: "We might be of mixed English, German, Irish, or French ancestry or, as in my own case, Jewish, yet the prevailing 'Protestant Ethic' of middle-class America seemed to possess all our parents alike" (24).

2. Calvinist Humor and the American Puritans

1. For some cinematic treatments of the problems involved in this sociological transition, see *What's Cooking* (2000), directed by Gurinder Chadha, and *Pieces of April* (2003), directed by Peter Hedges.

2. See Hawthorne's "The May-Pole of Merry Mount" (*Tales and Sketches* 360) and *The Education of Henry Adams* (269).

3. This passage in Adams's autobiography so affected T. S. Eliot, who grew up in St. Louis but attended college in Massachusetts, at Harvard, that he alluded to it in his poem "Gerontian" (1920).

4. In his article "'And Laughter Holding Both His Sides': Milton as Humorist," Roger B. Rollin captures the stereotypical view of John Milton as "the quintessential Puritan Poet—dour to the point of unapproachableness [and] religious to the point of zealotry" (136). The same characterization might be misapplied to all of the writers I consider in this chapter.

5. See my article "Geographic Irony and the New England Literary Imagination" (1983) for a fuller discussion of these issues.

6. See, among other New Testament texts, Matthew 23.25: "Woe unto you, scribes and Pharisees, hypocrites! for ye make clean the outside of the cup and of the platter, but within they are full of extortion and excess."

7. "And why beholdest thou the mote that is in thy brother's eye, but perceivest not the beam that is in thine own eye?" (Luke 6.41).

8. Neal Salisbury, editor of the text of *The Sovereignty and Goodness of God* that I have used, writes, "[T]aken at face value, the narrative vividly dramatizes the Puritans' belief in the inherently sinful nature of human beings, even the relatively few whom God has chosen to save from hell" (6).

9. "But many that are first shall be last, and the last first" (Mark 10.31).

10. In *Comedy, Tragedy, and Religion,* John Moreall asks about those damned in the Calvinist system, "Will everything work out for the best in the end?" According to Moreall, the true Calvinist will reply, "No, for the damned, everything will work out for the worst, and that condition will last forever" (117).

11. To Moses Coit Tyler, also, Wigglesworth is "the explicit and unshrinking rhymer of the Five Points of Calvinism" (284).

12. As Weber explains, "This consciousness of divine grace of the elect and holy was accompanied by an attitude toward the sin of one's neighbour, not of sympathetic understanding based on consciousness of one's own weakness, but of hatred and contempt for him as an enemy of God bearing the signs of eternal damnation" (122).

13. George Marsden writes that "[t]he Edwards family . . . produced scores of clergymen, thirteen presidents of institutions of higher learning, sixty-five professors, and many other persons of notable achievements" (500–501), including Aaron Burr, Jr., third vice president of the United States.

14. In his essay "Calvinist Earthquake: *Moby Dick* and Religious Tradition," Walter T. Herbert, Jr., explains this certainty by writing, "Orthodox Calvinists believed that the sacred truths they dispensed from the pulpit were obtained not through human efforts to understand the godhead but from God's own disclosure of himself in the scriptures" (116–17).

15. See Dryden's "Preface to Fables, Ancient and Modern" (1700), 167.

3. Nathaniel Hawthorne

1. Throughout this book, I am using the Library of America volume *Nathaniel Hawthorne: Tales and Sketches* as my text for his shorter works.

2. Goodman Brown also hears—or thinks he hears—the forest in which he is sojourning produce "a broad roar around the traveler, as if all Nature were laughing him to scorn" (283–84).

3. Edwin Haviland Miller speaks for many when he identifies Sophia Hawthorne's "almost incredible powers of idealization" (9) in *Salem Is My Dwelling Place.*

4. In a letter to Hawthorne, written probably on April 16, 1851, Herman Melville writes, "There is this grand truth about Nathaniel Hawthorne. He says NO! in thunder; but the Devil himself cannot make him say *yes*" (125).

5. Elsewhere in the story, Hawthorne writes that persons "who claimed a superiority to popular prejudice" interpreted Hooper's very strange decision as "merely an eccentric whim, such as often mingles with the sober actions of men otherwise rational, and tinges them all with its own semblance of insanity" (380)—a brilliant example of what the rhetoricians call "apophasis" (assertion through denial).

6. Concerning Hawthorne's stylistic indirection, see—among many other analyses— my *Hawthorne's Narrative Strategies* (22–46).

7. According to G. R. Thompson's *The Art of Authorial Presence*, "Brown . . . may be seen to epitomize in Hawthorne's world the extreme Calvinist world view of the Puritans . . ." (64).

8. When Robin joins in the laughter of the townspeople in "My Kinsman, Major Molineux" (1832), he abandons his sense of exceptionality and joins a guilty compact with them.

9. See Winters's *Maule's Curse, or Hawthorne and the Problem of Allegory* (1938).

10. Melinda M. Ponder and John L. Idol, Jr., write, in *Hawthorne and Women,* that "Hawthorne's works appealed to women readers partly because he knew about and respected the complexity of women's lives . . ." (4).

4. Herman Melville

1. In this story, collected in *The Piazza Tales* (19–65), Bartleby's employer asks him, most sympathetically, to "say now, that in a day or two you will begin to be a little reasonable:—say so, Bartleby"; Bartleby comically offers, "At present I would prefer not to be a little reasonable," as his "mildly cadaverous reply" (44).

2. According to Andrew Delbanco, Delano is "a white New Englander too stupid to realize that he is being manipulated by an African slave of brilliance and wit" (157).

3. See the passage in Edwards's "Sinners in the Hands of an Angry God" running: "Unconverted men walk over the pit of hell on a rotten covering, and there are innumerable places in the covering so weak that they will not bear their weight, and these places are not seen" (99).

4. Kenneth S. Lynn says that Delano is "sappy" because he "considers the master-slave relationship, as he first encounters it on board the *San Dominick,* a beautiful one" (102).

5. In *American Renaissance,* F. O. Matthiessen calls Delano "trusting and obtuse" (476).

6. See John 16.8: "[F]or the children of this world are in their generation wiser than the children of light," an apt citation in view of Lawrance Thompson's observation, in *Melville's Quarrel with God,* "He took wry pleasure in the irony of disguising his riddle-answers behind the self-protective riddle-masks of ingenious art; behind various subterfuges of rhetoric and symbol; behind naughty uses of Bible quotation or allusion which may have one meaning in a Christian context and quite a different meaning as controlled by Melville's anti-Christian context" (3).

7. See "My Kinsman, Major Molineux," *Tales and Sketches* 68–87.

8. According to Leon Howard, "The river, the confidence man, and the theme provided the only continuity which ran through the book . . ." (288).

9. These verses occur in Ecclesiasticus 13, also called the Apocryphal Book of Sirach.

5. Mark Twain

1. Calvin writes, in the *Institutes*, "No one who wishes to be thought religious dares simply deny predestination, by which God adopts some to hope of life, and sentences others to eternal death" (926).

2. Although the expression is conventionally associated with Twain, it actually appears first as a quotation in William Dean Howells's *My Mark Twain:* "He had begun before that to amass those evidences against mankind which eventuated with him in his theory of what he called 'the damned human race'" (76).

3. Note also, this episode from "The Story of the Old Ram": "There ain't no such thing as an accident. When my Uncle Lem was leaning up agin a scaffolding once, sick, or drunk, or suthin, an Irishman with a hod of bricks fell on him out of the third story and broke the old man's back in two places. People said it was an accident. Much accident there was about that. He didn't know what he was there for, but he was there for a good object. If he hadn't been there the Irishman would have been killed. No one can ever make me believe anything different from that. Uncle Lem's dog was there. Why didn't the Irishman fall on the dog? Becuz the dog would 'a' seen him a-coming and stood from under. That's the reason the dog wasn't appointed. A dog can't be depended on to carry out a special prov'dence" (*Complete Short Stories* 80).

4. In the comic tale "Mrs. McWilliams and the Lightning," Twain seems to (safely) mock the whole idea of Providence when he has Mrs. McWilliams say to her husband during an apparent storm that "there is not a lightning-rod on the place, and your poor wife and children are absolutely at the mercy of Providence" (*Complete Short Stories* 154).

5. According to Kenneth S. Lynn, *Following the Equator* "is noteworthy only for the mordant maxims from 'Pudd'nhead Wilson's New Calendar' which it contains . . ." (277).

6. It seems to me that the best biographical/critical introduction to Bakhtin is Michael Holquist's *Dialogism: Bakhtin and His World.*

7. Hamlin Hill writes on this topic: "'Classic' New England literature . . . was elitist and idealistic, didactic and uplifting. A savage was acceptable as long as he was noble and a farmer if he acted like a gentleman" (viii).

8. A comparable incident occurs in chapter 10 of *Huckleberry Finn*, probably to make a comparably physical joke: "Old Hank Bunker done it once, and bragged about it; and in less than two years he got drunk and fell off of the shot tower and spread himself out so that he was just a kind of layer, as you may say; and they slid him edgeways between two barn doors for a coffin, and buried him so, so they say . . ." (81).

9. Samuel Johnson writes, in his "Preface to Shakespeare," "The delight of tragedy proceeds from our consciousness of fiction; if we thought murders and treasons real, they would please no more" (211).

10. Thompson's most sincere, yet still comic observation about the supposed corpse is: "He's pretty ripe, *ain't* he" (*Complete Short Stories* 189).

11. Calvin writes, in the *Institutes*, "If all are drawn from a corrupt mass, no wonder they are subject to condemnation!" (950–51).

6. William Faulkner

1. On the other hand, Nancy is still alive at the time of *Requiem for a Nun* (1951). This problem arises for readers because Faulkner says, in *Faulkner in the University*, that the two women are "the same person actually" (79).

2. In *The Sound and the Fury*, Jason says about his father, "I reckon the reason all the Compson gave out before it got to me like Mother says, is that he drank it up" (197).

3. In *The Sound and the Fury*, Mrs. Compson spends Easter Sunday in bed while Dilsey takes Benjy to church. When Dilsey returns, Mrs. Compson, without rising from the bed, asks Dilsey to pick up her Bible which has fallen to the floor: "You laid it there on the edge of the bed. How long did you expect it to stay there?" (300).

4. Blotner is somewhat discreet about these matters, but Jay Parini is scathing, especially in his account of the Faulkners' wedding (137–43).

5. Joanna's grandfather was named Calvin Burden.

6. In *The Yoknapatawpha Country*, Cleanth Brooks writes about this incident and the onlooker's comment, "This is comic and we may call it a grotesque and savage comedy, but we miss the point if we think the countryman is being rude or cynical" (71).

7. The classic analysis of Faulkner's misogyny appears in Albert J. Guerard's chapter of that title in *The Triumph of the Novel* (109–35).

8. When Christmas first approaches Joanna Burden sexually, "he appeared to be watching his body, seeming to watch it turning slow and lascivious in a whispering of gutter filth like a drowned corpse in a thick still black pool of more than water" (107). Christmas is a walking collection of psychological problems, admittedly, but this feeling still should strike most readers as badly askew.

9. In "The Unity of Faulkner's *Light in August*," C. Hugh Holman explains Hightower's function in a Calvinist context: "Significantly, organized religion is represented by the Presbyterian Church rather than the Baptist or Methodist, both of which are numerically superior in Faulkner's country" (161). This is because, as Holman writes, "the Presbyterian Church is the doctrinal church of the Protestant sects, the church of unrelenting Calvinism" (161).

10. In *God and the American Writer*, Alfred Kazin writes that Faulkner is like Nathaniel Hawthorne, "another Calvinist obsessed by the past of his homeland" (34).

11. Hyatt Waggoner, for example, concludes that Sutpen's "error had been ultimately, of course, in the moral sense, that he had always treated people as things" (183).

12. As John Calvin writes in the *Institutes*, "And truly God claims, and would have us grant him, omnipotence—not the empty, idle, and almost unconscious sort that the Sophists imagine, but a watchful, effective, active sort, engaged in ceaseless activity" (200).

13. Calvin writes, in the *Institutes*, "Now as the superiority of the male sex is conceded in the fact that children are reckoned noble or ignoble from their father's status, conversely, in slavery, 'the offspring follows the womb,' as lawyers say" (479). For an amusing exposition of how such ideas operate in American literature, see *Love and Death in the American Novel*, by Leslie A. Fiedler (1959, 1997).

14. Mr. Compson says about Sutpen that he was "a man who to my certain knowledge was never in a Jefferson church but three times in his life" (20).

15. Calvin writes, in the *Institutes*, "Now, through the condition of our nature, and by the lust aroused after the Fall, we, except for those whom God has released through special grace, are doubly subject to women's society" (406).

16. Edmond L. Volpe claims that I. O. "is more a comical scoundrel than an incarnation of the repulsiveness Snopesism generally conveys" (308).

17. Edmond Volpe writes about characters like this: "It is as if these people have known and suffered all the blows that outrageous fortune can heap upon them, accepted their fate as inevitable, and accepted a status quo arrangement in which they contain their anger so long as no further injustice is inflicted upon them. Then any occurrence, no matter how minor in comparison to their standard afflictions, is enough to upset the balance and trigger their pent-up fury. Overcome by rage, they move close to madness" (314). It is not part of Volpe's critical project to identify these developments as fuel for Calvinist humor.

18. For an earlier example of the Calvinist humor to be derived from corpses, see Twain's "The Invalid's Story," especially this passage in which Thompson, the expressman, observes about the box that they assume to hold the corpse of John B. Hackett: "Sometimes it's uncertain whether they're really gone or not—*seem* gone, you know—body warm, joints limber—and so, although you *think* they're gone, you don't really know. I've had cases in my car. It's perfectly awful, becuz *you* don't know what minute they'll rise up and look at you!" Then, after a pause, and slightly lifting his elbow toward the box—"But *he* ain't in no trance! No, sir, I go bail for *him*" (189).

19. The boy's name came about in this way: "I.O. read about that one in the paper. He figured if we named him Wallstreet Panic it might make him get rich like the folks that run the Wallstreet panic" (295).

20. In *The Yoknapatawpha Country*, Cleanth Brooks agrees, proposing definitively that Faulkner's "attitude is closest, of course, to that of Ratliff, and Ratliff significantly views the world with a good measure of detachment and has his own joy in observing the behavior of human beings and the parade of human folly" (172).

7. Ernest Hemingway

1. Richard Fulkerson writes, "There can scarcely be a greater incongruity in marriage than to have a devout Christian Scientist married to a doctor . . ." (152).

2. In *The Sun Also Rises*, Robert Cohn says, "Nobody ever lives their life all the way up except bullfighters" (10). According to James Mellow (310), the remark was originally intended for Jake.

3. See Young's *Ernest Hemingway* (1952) and *Ernest Hemingway: A Reconsideration* (1966), the latter of which substantially reproduces the 1952 study.

4. James Mellow complains, to the contrary, about "the numbing detail" of "Big Two-Hearted River" (273).

5. James Mellow proposes a similar conclusion in his biography of Hemingway: "He announced themes [in *In Our Time*] that would carry him through a lifetime of work: the disappointments of family life, the disaffections of early love, the celebration of country and male companionship, a young man's initiation into the world of sex, the complications of marriage" (267).

6. See Bakhtin's *Rabelais and His World*, esp. "The Grotesque Image of the Body and Its Sources" (303–67). See also Wallace Stevens's poem "Dance of the Macabre Mice," *The Palm at the End of the Mind* (117).

7. According to Philip Young's *Ernest Hemingway: A Reconsideration*, Hemingway "wrote to his editor Maxwell Perkins [that] the point of his novel is, as the Biblical lines say in part, that 'the earth abideth forever'" (87).

8. Nathanael West

1. The collection of West's four published novels issued by Farrar, Straus Cudahy (1957), which was long accepted as the standard edition, has been superseded by *Nathanael West, Novels and Other Writings* (2000) published by the Library of America. The latter will be my text.

2. Jay Martin quotes Matthew Josephson's testimony on this point: "We might be of mixed English, German, Irish, or French ancestry or, as in my own case, Jewish, yet the prevailing 'Protestant Ethic' of middle-class America seemed to possess all our parents alike" (24).

3. In a screenplay of *A Cool Million* that West wrote with Boris Ingster, we read that the hero, Joe Williams, is "a hero out of Horatio Alger," and the script continues ironically: "Only fools laugh at Horatio Alger, and his poor boys who make good. The wiser man who thinks twice about that sterling author will realize that Alger is to America what Homer was to the Greeks" (745).

4. In *Love and Death in the American Novel* , Leslie Fiedler writes, "If Nathanael West appears to us from our present vantage point the chief neglected talent of the age, this is largely because he was immune to the self-deceit which afflicted his contemporaries; he knew what he was doing. Despite his own left-wing political sympathies and the pressure of friends more committed than he, he refused to subscribe to the program for proletarian fiction laid down by the official theoreticians and critics of the Communist movement" (485).

5. Randall Reid, *The Fiction of Nathanael West: No Redeemer, No Promised Land* (Chicago: U of Chicago P, 1967).

6. In *Love and Death in the American Novel,* Leslie Fiedler uses, as the formula for West's Calvinist humor, "a perilous borderline between jest and horror" (486).

7. In Flannery O'Connor's story "Good Country People," she seems greatly amused at the exchange in which Manly Pointer says, "I may die," and Joy/Hulga answers, "I may die too" (276). To O'Connor, as to West and John Calvin, it is certain that all of these fictional characters—like all real ones—will die.

8. As the novel reports, "Through his martyrdom the National Revolutionary Party triumphed, and by that triumph this country was delivered from sophistication, Marxism and International Capitalism" (238).

9. In a July 2006 review of a new edition of West's work in *Harper's,* David Gargill writes, "West seems to suggest that in the mouth of a demagogue, any collective dream, even if only faintly remembered, can serve to rouse the masses once more—not out of belief this time but out of nostalgia for a golden age of certainty and conviction" (88).

10. The falseness, and thus the emptiness, of Faye's dream is underscored when we see Tod on the back lot of the movie studio: "On the porch of the 'Last Chance Saloon' was a rocking chair. He sat down on it and lit a cigarette" (324).

11. See Hawthorne's "The Minister's Black Veil" (374).

12. Probably the most extreme statement of this position occurs in Norman Mailer's *The Naked and the Dead* when Red Valsen says, "There damn sure ain't anything special about a man if he can smell as bad as he does when he's dead" (217).

13. Homer's sexual maladjustment is evident even in his repulsion at Miguel's "dirty black hen": "The roosters have torn all the feathers off its neck and made its comb all bloody and it has scabby feet covered with warts and it cackles so nasty when they drop it into the pen" (344). Homer's squeamishness seems to be because the chicken sexually services several fighting cocks.

14. Cf. the passage from Matthew cited earlier: "Or what man is there of you, whom if his son ask bread, will he give him a stone?" (Matt. 7.9).

15. Writing in *Cultural Theory and Popular Culture: A Reader,* John Storey explains the rationale of the Frankfurt School theorists: "Mass culture, they claim, is uniform, predictable, and to the untrained ear or eye, transparent. Unfortunately, for most people it is culture. The culture industry produces culture which the masses consume unthinkingly and are thus confirmed as unthinking" (188).

16. See Herman Melville's letter to Nathaniel Hawthorne (April 16, 1851?): "There is this grand truth about Nathaniel Hawthorne. He says NO! in thunder; but the Devil himself cannot make him say *yes*" (125).

17. Enid Veron reproduces this passage to represent West's "particular kind of joking" in *Humor in America* (38–41).

9. Flannery O'Connor

1. Although all of O'Connor's work is readily available in various inexpensive editions, the Library of America volume collects nearly everything in one place, and so I have used this edition—except for two cases, noted below—when referring to O'Connor's works.

2. In a letter to "A." (July 5, 1958), which appears in *The Habit of Being,* O'Connor writes, "The setting in which most modern fiction takes place is exactly a setting in which nothing is so little felt to be true as the reality of a faith in Christ" (290). For a good sampling of American literary opinion during these times, see *The Bit between My Teeth: A Literary Chronicle of 1950–1965* by Edmund Wilson.

3. See Faulkner's *Absalom, Absalom* (1936) and Welty's "Petrified Man" (1941).

4. John Calvin writes in his *Institutes of the Christian Religion:* "But they do not realize that true religion ought to be conformed to God's will as to a universal rule; that God ever

remains like himself, and is not a specter or phantasm to be transformed according to anyone's whim" (49).

5. For a sampling of these professions, see O'Connor's letters to Carl Hartman (March 2, 1954): "Wise Blood is about a Protestant saint, written from the point of view of a Catholic" (919) and to Thomas Mabry (March 1, 1955): "I am a Catholic (not because it's advantageous to my writing but because I was born and brought up one) and at some point in my life I realized that not only was I a Catholic but that this was all I was, that I was a Catholic not like someone else would be a Baptist or a Methodist but like someone else would be an atheist" (930).

6. Milton Rickels discovered in conversation with Flannery O'Connor that she had read the work of George Washington Harris (141, n. 13).

7. In *The Enduring Legacy of Old Southwest Humor,* Ed Piacentino maintains that "O'Connor was particularly adept at using the grotesque humorously . . ." (20).

8. See Calvin's argumentative premise in the *Institutes;* "Therefore we must prove God so attends to the regulation of individual events, and they all so proceed from his set plan, that nothing takes place by chance" (203).

9. Reprinted in *Three by Flannery O'Connor* 2.

10. In addition to John Hawkes's contention regarding the connection to Hawthorne and West, see O'Connor's characteristic remark in a letter to Ben Griffith (March 3, 1954): "[M]y opinion of Hawthorne is that he was a very great writer indeed" (924).

11. To get at O'Connor's grim joke, it may be helpful to consult this information from George M. Marsden's biography of Jonathan Edwards: "Nicholas Malebranche (1638–1715), [was] a French Augustinian Catholic philosopher and theologian who held that things are really God's ideas and that the unity of the soul with God is the Proper source of knowledge" (73).

12. As a sign of the religious censoriousness that O'Connor practiced in her fiction and that she continues to elicit from her critics, let us consider this very confident pronouncement by Marilyn Arnold: "Thus Ruby Turpin, Hulga, the grandmother in 'A Good Man is Hard to Find,' Mrs. May, Mrs. Shortley, and a host of others are to be considered redeemable. Tom Shiflet and Mr. Shortley, however, are not, and Rayber and Julian are questionable" (257).

10. Calvinist Humor Revisited

1. In his *New Yorker* review of David S. Reynolds's book *John Brown, Abolitionist,* Adam Gopnik writes, about Brown's proposed raid on Harpers Ferry, "The plan was, to say the least, quixotic" (93).

2. Tragedy is even more forbidding. As Brooks and Warren write, "[S]urely this much is true: the tragic hero is always defeated—his sin, by the way, is usually an overweening pride—but he always manages to wrest something from the defeat and from death" (23).

Works Cited

Adams, Henry. *The Education of Henry Adams*. Ed. Ernest Samuels. Boston: Houghton Mifflin, 1973.

Arnold, Marilyn. "Sentimentalism in the Devil's Territory." In Murphy et al., 243–58.

Bakhtin, Mikhail. *Rabelais and His World*. Trans. Helene Iswolsky. Bloomington: Indiana UP, 1984.

Barnard, Rita. *The Great Depression and the Culture of Abundance: Kenneth Fearing, Nathanael West, and Mass Culture in the 1930s*. New York: Cambridge UP, 1995.

Barnstone, Aliki, Michael Tomasek Manson, and Carol J. Singley. Introduction. *The Calvinist Roots of the Modern Era*. Ed. Barnstone, Manson, and Singley. Hanover and London: UP of New England, 1997. xiii–xxv.

Berger, Sidney E., ed. *Pudd'nhead Wilson and Those Extraordinary Twins*. A Norton Critical Edition. New York: Norton, 1980.

Bergson, Henri. "Laughter: Essay on the Meaning of the Comic." Trans. Maurice Charney. *Classic Comedies*. Ed. Charney. New York: Meridian, 1985. 557–64.

Berthoff, Warner. Introduction. *Great Short Works of Herman Melville*. New York: Harper and Row, 1969. 9–18.

Bewley, Marius. *The Eccentric Design: Form in the Classic American Novel*. New York: Columbia UP, 1963.

Bier, Jesse. *The Rise and Fall of American Humor*. New York Holt, Rinehart and Winston, 1968.

Blair, Walter. *Native American Humor*. New York: American Book Company, 1937.

Blair, Walter, and Hamlin Hill, eds. *America's Humor: From Poor Richard to Doonesbury*. New York: Oxford UP, 1980.

Blotner, Joseph. *Faulkner: A Biography*. New York: Random House, 1974.

Bouwsma, William J. *John Calvin: A Sixteenth-Century Portrait*. New York: Oxford UP, 1988.

Bowden, James H. "No Redactor, No Reward." In Madden, 283–97.

Bradford, William. *Of Plymouth Plantation, 1620–1647*. Ed. Samuel Eliot Morison. New York: Knopf, 1963.

Brand, John M. "A Word Is a Word Is a Word." In Madden, 57–75.

Braswell, William. *Melville's Religious Thought: An Essay in Interpretation*. 1943. New York: Octagon, 1973.

Brodwin, Stanley. "Blackness and the Adamic Myth in Mark Twain's *Pudd'nhead Wilson*." In Berger, 332–42.

Brooks, Cleanth. *William Faulkner: The Yoknapatawpha Country*. New Haven: Yale UP, 1963.

Brooks, Cleanth, R. W. B. Lewis, and Robert Penn Warren, eds. "Jonathan Edwards and the Great Awakening." *American Literature: The Makers and the Making*. 2 vols. New York: St. Martin's, 1973. 1: 82–87.

Brooks, Cleanth, and Robert Penn Warren. *Understanding Fiction*. 2nd ed. New York: Appleton-Century-Crofts, 1959.

Brooks, Cleanth, and William K. Wimsatt, Jr. *Literary Criticism: A Short History*. New York: Vintage, 1967.

Buckley, F. H. *The Morality of Laughter*. Ann Arbor: U of Michigan P, 2003.

Calvin, John. *Institutes of the Christian Religion*. Ed. John T. McNeill. Philadelphia: Westminster P, 1960.

Cash, W. J. *The Mind of the South*. 1941. New York: Knopf, 1965.

Chase, Richard. *The American Novel and Its Tradition*. Garden City, NY: Doubleday, 1957.

Clemens, Samuel Langhorne. *Adventures of Huckleberry Finn*. Centennial Facsimile edition. Ed. Hamlin Hill. New York: Harper and Row, 1987.

———. *The Complete Short Stories of Mark Twain*. Ed. Charles Neider. New York: Bantam, 1981.

———. *Following the Equator: A Journey Around the World*. 2 vols. New York: P. F. Collier, 1897.

———. *Pudd'nhead Wilson and Those Extraordinary Twins*. Ed. Sidney E. Berger. A Norton Critical Edition. New York: Norton, 1980.

Cohen, Hennig, and William B. Dillingham, eds. *Humor of the Old Southwest*. 3rd ed. Athens: U of Georgia P, 1994.

Covici, Pascal, Jr. *Mark Twain's Humor: The Image of a World*. Dallas, TX: Southern Methodist UP, 1962.

Cowley, Malcolm. "A Natural History of the American Writer." *The Literary Situation*. New York: Viking, 1969. 132–51.

Cox, James M. "Regionalism: A Diminished Thing." In Elliott et al., 661–784.

Delbanco, Andrew. *Melville: His World and His Work*. New York: Knopf, 2005.

Donohue, Agnes McNeill. *Hawthorne: Calvin's Ironic Stepchild*. Kent, OH: Kent State UP, 1985.

Dryden, John. "Preface to Fables, Ancient and Modern." 1700. *Criticism: The Major Texts*. Ed. Walter Jackson Bate. Enlarged ed. New York: Harcourt, 1970. 160–71.

Dunne, Michael. "Geographic Irony and the New England Literary Imagination." *Border States: Journal of the Kentucky-Tennessee American Studies Association* 4 (1983): 41–49.

———. *Hawthorne's Narrative Strategies*. Jackson: UP of Mississippi, 1995.

Edwards, Jonathan. "Sinners in the Hands of an Angry God." In Brooks, Lewis, and Warren, 97–105.

Elliott, Emory, et al., eds. *Columbia Literary History of the United States*. New York: Columbia UP, 1988.

Emerson, Ralph Waldo. *The Portable Emerson*. Ed. Carl Bode and Malcolm Cowley. New York: Penguin, 1981.

Faulkner, William. *Absalom, Absalom!* The corrected text. New York: Vintage, 1987.

———. *Collected Stories*. New York: Random House, 1950.

———. *Faulkner in the University*. Ed. Frederick L. Gwynn and Joseph L. Blotner. New York: Vintage, 1965.

———. *Light in August*. 1932. The corrected text. New York: Viking, 1985.

———. *The Hamlet*. 1940. The corrected text. New York: Viking, 1990.

———. *The Portable Faulkner*. Ed. Malcolm Cowley. Revised and expanded edition. New York: Viking, 1967.

———. *The Sound and the Fury*. 1929. New York: Vintage, 1990.

———. *The Unvanquished*. 1938. New York: Vintage, 1991.

Fiedler, Leslie A. "'As Free as Any Cretur . . .'" 1955. In Berger, 220–29.

———. *Love and Death in the American Novel*. 1959. Intro. Charles B. Harris. Normal, IL: Dalkey Archive P, 1997.

Fisher, Marvin, and Michael Elliott. "*Pudd'nhead Wilson:* Half a Dog Is Worse Than None." In Berger, 304–15.

Fitzgerald, F. Scott. *The Great Gatsby*. In *The Cambridge Edition of the Works of F. Scott Fitzgerald*. Ed. Matthew J. Bruccoli. New York: Cambridge UP, 1991.

Fodor, Sarah J. "'A world apparently without comment' or Shouting at the Reader: Narrative Guidance in O'Connor's Fiction." In Murphy et al., 217–29.

Foerster, Norman, ed. *American Poetry and Prose*. 4th ed. Boston: Houghton Mifflin, 1947.

Ford, Thomas W. "Pudd'nhead Wilson's Calendar." *Mark Twain Journal* 14 (Summer 1978): 15–19.

Fowler, Doreen, and Ann Abadie, eds. *Faulkner and Religion*. Jackson: UP of Mississippi, 1991.

Fulkerson, Richard. "The Biographical Fallacy and 'The Doctor and the Doctor's Wife.'" Michael S. Reynolds, ed. *Critical Essays on Ernest Hemingway's In Our Time*. Boston: G. K. Hall, 1983. 150–54.

Gargano, James W. "*Pudd'nhead Wilson:* Mark Twain as Genial Satan." *South Atlantic Quarterly* 74 (1975): 365–75.

Gargill, David. "Master of the Convincing Lie: Nathanael West's Brilliant Distortions." *Harper's* July 2006: 83–88.

Geismar, Maxwell. *Mark Twain: An American Prophet*. 1970. Abridged edition. New York: McGraw-Hill, 1973.

Gerber, John C. "*Pudd'nhead Wilson* as Fabulation." *Studies in American Humor* 2.1 (Apr. 1975): 21–31.

Giannone, Richard. "Warfare and Solitude: O'Connor's Prophet and the Word in the Desert." In Murphy et al., 61–89.

Goodwin, Doris Kearns. *Lyndon Johnson and the American Dream*. New York: Harper and Row, 1976.

Goodwin, Gerald J. "The Myth of 'Arminian-Calvinism' in Eighteenth-Century New England." *New England Quarterly* 41 (1968): 213–37.

Gopnik, Adam. "John Brown's Body." Rev. of *John Brown, Abolitionist*, by David S. Reynolds. *New Yorker* 25 Apr. 2005: 90–95.

Guerard, Albert J. *The Triumph of the Novel: Dickens, Dostoevsky, Faulkner*. New York: Oxford UP, 1976.

Hall, Lawrence Sargent. *Hawthorne: Critic of Society*. New Haven: Yale UP, 1944.

Harris, George Washington. "Blown Up with Soda." In Cohen and Dillingham, 212–17.

———. "Contempt of Court—Almost." In Cohen and Dillingham, 240–45.

———. "Mrs. Yardley's Quilting." In Cohen and Dillingham, 224–31.

———. "Parson John Bullen's Lizards." In Cohen and Dillingham, 206–12.

———. "Sut Lovingood's Daddy, Acting Horse." In Cohen and Dillingham, 201–6.

Hart, James D. *The Oxford Companion to American Literature*. 4th ed. New York: Oxford UP, 1965.

Hawkes, John. "Flannery O'Connor's Devil." *Sewanee Review* 70 (1962): 395–407.

Hawthorne, Nathaniel. *The Blithedale Romance*. 1852. New York: Norton, 1958.

———. "Chiefly About War Matters." http://www.eldritchpress.org/cawm.html.

———. *The English Notebooks*. Ed. Randall Stewart. New York: Russell and Russell, 1962.

———. *Tales and Sketches*. Library of America College Editions. New York: Library of America, 1996.

Heimert, Alan. "Jonathan Edwards, Charles Chauncey, and the Great Awakening." In Elliott et al., 113–26.

Hemingway, Ernest. "The Gambler, the Nun, and the Radio." *The Snows of Kilimanjaro and Other Stories*. New York: Scribner's, 1961. 37–53.

———. *In Our Time*. 1925. New York: Scribner's 1970.

———. *The Sun Also Rises*. 1926. New York: Scribner's, 1954.

Hendin, Josephine. *The World of Flannery O'Connor*. Bloomington: Indiana UP, 1970.

Herbert, T. Walter, Jr. "Calvinist Earthquake: *Moby Dick* and Religious Tradition." *New Essays on* Moby Dick. Ed. Richard H. Brodhead. Cambridge: Cambridge UP, 1986. 109–40.

———. Moby Dick *and Calvinism: A World Dismantled*. New Brunswick, NJ: Rutgers UP, 1977.

Hill, Hamlin. Introduction. *Adventures of Huckleberry Finn*. By Samuel Langhorne Clemens. Centennial Facsimile edition. Ed. Hill. New York: Harper and Row, 1987. vii–xviii.

Hoffman, Frederick J. "The Search for Redemption: Flannery O'Connor's Fiction." *The Added Dimension: The Art and Mind of Flannery O'Connor*. Ed. Melvin J. Friedman and Lewis A. Lawson. New York: Fordham UP, 1977. 32–48.

Holman, C. Hugh. *A Handbook to Literature*. 4th ed. Indianapolis: Bobbs–Merrill, 1981.

———. "The Unity of Faulkner's *Light in August*." *PMLA* 73 (June 1958): 155–66.

Holquist, Michael. *Dialogism: Bakhtin and His World*. London: Routledge, 1990.

Howard, Leon. "The Quest for Confidence." In Parker, 286–98.

Howells, William Dean. *My Mark Twain: Reminiscences and Criticisms*. New York: Harper and Brothers, 1910

Ikenberry, John. "Why Export Democracy?" *Wilson Quarterly* 23.2 (Spring 1999): 56–92.

Irwin, John T. *Doubling and Incest / Repetition and Revenge: A Speculative Reading of Faulkner*. Baltimore, MD: Johns Hopkins UP, 1975.

Isabelle, Julanne. *Hemingway's Religious Experience*. New York: Vantage, 1964.

James, Henry. *Daisy Miller*. 1878. New York: Dover, 1995.

Johnson, Claudia. *The Productive Tension of Hawthorne's Art*. Tuscaloosa: U of Alabama P, 1981.

Johnson, Samuel. "Preface to Shakespeare." 1765. In Kaplan and Anderson, 200–231.

Johnson, Thomas H. "Jonathan Edwards." *Literary History of the United States*. 3rd ed. revised. Ed. Robert E. Spiller et al. London: Macmillan, 1963.

Justus, James H. *Fetching the Old Southwest: Humorous Writing from Longstreet to Twain*. Columbia: U of Missouri P, 2004.

Kaplan, Charles, and William Davis Anderson, eds. *Criticism: Major Statements.* 4th ed. Boston: Bedford/St. Martin's, 2000.

Kaul, A. N. "*The Blithedale Romance* and the Puritan Tradition." *Nathaniel Hawthorne; Modern Critical Views.* Ed. Harold Bloom. New York: Chelsea House, 1986. 59–70.

Kazin, Alfred. *God and the American Writer.* New York: Knopf, 1997.

King, Richard H. "World-rejection in Faulkner's Fiction." In Fowler and Abadie, 65–84.

Leary, Lewis. Introduction. *Home As Found.* By James Fenimore Cooper. New York: Capricorn, 1961. v–xxvi.

Leavis, F. R. "Mark Twain's Neglected Classic: The Moral Astringency of *Pudd'nhead Wilson.*" In Berger, 229–42.

Levin, Harry. *The Power of Blackness: Hawthorne, Poe, Melville.* New York: Knopf, 1958.

Lewis, R. W. B. *The American Adam: Innocence, Tragedy, and Tradition in the Nineteenth Century.* Chicago: U of Chicago P, 1955.

Lewis, Robert W. "Hemingway's Concept of Sport and 'Soldier's Home.'" *Critical Essays on Ernest Hemingway's In Our Time.* Ed. Michael S. Reynolds. Boston: G. K. Hall, 1983. 189–98.

Longley, John Lewis, Jr. "Thomas Sutpen: The Tragedy of Aspiration." *William Faulkner: A Collection of Criticism.* Ed. Dean Morgan Schmitter. New York: McGraw-Hill, 1973. 110–21.

Longstreet, Augustus. "The Fight." *Georgia Scenes.* 1835. Uppersaddle, NJ: Literature House/Gregg Press, 1969. 53–64.

———. "The Gander Pulling." *Georgia Scenes.* 1835. Uppersaddle, NJ: Literature House/Gregg Press, 1969. 110–19.

———. "The Horse Swap." In Cohen and Dillingham, 30–36.

Lowell, Robert. *Collected Poems.* Ed. Frank Bidart and David Gewanter. New York: Farrar, Straus and Giroux, 2003.

Lowance, Mason I., Jr. "Biography and Autobiography." In Elliott et al., 67–82.

Lynn, Kenneth S. *Mark Twain and Southwestern Humor.* Boston: Little Brown, 1959.

Madden, David, ed. *Nathanael West: The Cheaters and the Cheated, A Collection of Critical Essays.* Deland, FL: Everett/Edwards, 1973.

Mailer, Norman. *The Naked and the Dead.* 1948. New York: Modern Library, n.d.

Marsden, George M. *Jonathan Edwards: A Life.* New Haven: Yale UP, 2003.

Marshall, Ian. "Humor and the Techniques of Humor in William Bradford's *Of Plymouth Plantation.*" *Studies in American Humor* NS 5.2–3 (Summer/Fall 1986): 158–67.

Martin, Jay. *Nathanael West: The Art of His Life.* New York: Farrar, Straus and Giroux, 1970.

Martin, Wallace. *Recent Theories of Narrative.* Ithaca, NY: Cornell UP, 1986.

Matthiessen, F. O. *American Renaissance: Art and Expression in the Age of Emerson and Whitman.* 1941. New York: Oxford UP, 1968.

McNeill, John T. Introduction. *Institutes of the Christian Religion.* By John Calvin. Philadelphia: Westminster P, 1960. xxix–lxxi.

Mellow, James R. *Hemingway: A Life without Consequences.* New York: Houghton Mifflin, 1992.

Meltzer, Milton. *Mark Twain Himself: A Pictorial Biography.* Hannibal, MO: Becky Thatcher Bookshop, 1960.

Melville, Herman. *The Confidence Man: His Masquerade.* Ed. Hershel Parker. A Norton Critical Edition. New York: Norton, 1971.

———. "Hawthorne and His Mosses." 1850. In Brooks, Lewis, and Warren, 834–42.

———. *The Piazza Tales.* 1856. New York: Russell and Russell, 1963.

———. "To Nathaniel Hawthorne." 16? April? 1851. *The Letters of Herman Melville.* Ed. Merrell R. Davis and William H. Gilman. New York: Yale UP, 1960. 123–25.

Mencken, H. L. "Puritanism as a Literary Force." *A Book of Prefaces.* 1917. New York: Octagon, 1977. 197–283.

Meyers, Jeffrey, ed. *Hemingway: The Critical Heritage.* London: Routledge and Kegan Paul, 1982.

Miller, Edwin Haviland. *Salem Is My Dwelling Place: A Life of Nathaniel Hawthorne.* Iowa City: U of Iowa P, 1991.

Miller, James E., Jr. *A Reader's Guide to Herman Melville.* New York: Farrar, Straus and Giroux, 1962.

Mirella, Loris. "T. S. Eliot's Calvinist Modernism." In Barnstone, Manson, and Singley, 20–35.

Moore, Margaret B. *The Salem World of Nathaniel Hawthorne.* Columbia: U of Missouri P, 1998.

Morreall, John. *Comedy, Tragedy, and Religion.* Albany: State U of New York P, 1999.

Muller, Gilbert H. *Nightmares and Visions: Flannery O'Connor and the Catholic Grotesque.* Athens: U of Georgia P, 1972.

Murphy, John J., et al., eds. *Flannery O'Connor and the Christian Mystery.* Provo, UT: Brigham Young U, 1997.

Neider, Charles. Introduction. *The Comic Mark Twain Reader.* Ed. Neider. New York: Doubleday, 1977. xv–xxx.

Noble, David W. *The Eternal Adam and the New World Garden.* 1968. New York: Grosset and Dunlap, 1971.

O'Connor, Flannery. *Collected Works*. New York: Library of America, 1988.

———. *The Habit of Being: Letters*. Ed. and with an intro. by Sally Fitzgerald. New York: Farrar, Straus, Giroux, 1979.

———. *Three by Flannery O'Connor*. Intro. Sally Fitzgerald. New York: New American Library, 1983.

Orvell, Miles. *Invisible Parade: The Fiction of Flannery O'Connor*. Philadelphia: Temple UP, 1972.

Parini, Jay. *One Matchless Time: A Biography of William Faulkner*. New York: HarperCollins, 2004.

Pearce, Roy Harvey. *The Continuity of American Poetry*. 1961. Middletown, CT: Wesleyan UP, 1987.

Piacentino, Ed. "Intersecting Paths: The Humor of the Old Southwest as Intertext." *The Enduring Legacy of Old Southwest Humor*. Ed. Piacentino. Baton Rouge: Louisiana State UP, 2006. 1–35.

Pieces of April. Dir. Peter Hedges. Perf. Katie Holmes, Derek Luke. United Artists, 2003.

Pitavy, François. *Faulkner's* Light in August. Trans. Gillian E. Cook. Bloomington: Indiana UP, 1973.

Ponder, Melinda M., and John L. Idol, Jr. Introduction. *Hawthorne and Women: Engendering and Expanding the Hawthorne Tradition*. Ed. Ponder and Idol. Amherst: U of Massachusetts P, 1999. 1–19.

Reid, Randall. *The Fiction of Nathanael West: No Redeemer, No Promised Land*. Chicago: U of Chicago P, 1967.

Richards, Jeffrey H. "Samuel Davies and Calvinist Poetic Ecology." *Early American Literature* 35 (200): 29–50.

Rickels, Milton. *George Washington Harris*. New York: Twayne, 1965.

Robinson, Edwin Arlington. "The Man against the Sky." *The Oxford Book of American Verse*. Ed. F. O. Matthiessen. New York: Oxford UP, 1962. 496–505.

———. "New England." *The Oxford Book of American Verse*. 509.

Rollin, Roger B. "'And Laughter Holding Both His Sides': Milton as Humorist." *South Carolina Review* 35.1 (Fall 2002): 133–48.

Rosenfeld, Paul. Review of *In Our Time*. In Meyers, 67–69.

Rourke, Constance. *American Humor: A Study of the National Character*. New York: Harcourt, 1931.

Rowlandson, Mary. *The Sovereignty and Goodness of God*. Ed. Neal Salisbury. Boston: Bedford, 1997.

Rubin, Louis D., Jr. "Flannery O'Connor and the Bible Belt." *The Added Dimension: The Art and Mind of Flannery O'Connor*. Ed. Melvin J. Friedman and Lewis A. Lawson. New York: Fordham UP, 1977. 49–72.

———. "The Great American Joke." In Veron, 255–65.

———. Introduction. *I'll Take My Stand: The South and the Agrarian Tradition.* By Twelve Southerners. [1930] Baton Rouge: Louisiana State UP, 1977. xi–xxxv.

———, ed. *The Comic Imagination in American Literature.* New Brunswick, NJ: Rutgers UP, 1973.

Schmitz, Neil. "Forms of Regional Humor." In Elliott et al., 306–23.

Schorer, Mark. Rev. of *For Whom the Bell Tolls.* In Meyers, 337–41.

Schuldiner, Michael, ed. *Calvinism and Nineteenth-Century American Women Authors.* Lewiston, NY: Mellen, 1997.

Schwartz, Delmore. Rev. of *To Have and To Have Not.* 1938. In Meyers, 243–56.

Sessions, W. A. "How to Read Flannery O'Connor: Passing by the Dragon." In Murphy et al., 191–215.

Shakespeare, William. *A Midsummer Night's Dream. The Bedford Introduction to Literature.* Ed. Michael Meyer. 7th ed. Boston: Bedford/St Martin's, 2005. 1405–59.

Shroeder, John W. "Sources and Symbols for Melville's *Confidence Man.*" In Parker, 298–316.

Shurr, William. *Rappaccini's Children: American Writers in a Calvinist World.* Lexington: UP of Kentucky, 1981.

Smith, Henry Nash. *Mark Twain: The Development of a Writer.* 1962. New York: Atheneum, 1967.

Smith, Henry Nash, and William M. Gibson, eds. *Mark Twain–Howells Letters: The Correspondence of Samuel L. Clemens and William D. Howells.* Cambridge, MA: Harvard UP, 1960.

Steiner, T. R. "West's Lemuel and the American Dream." In Madden, 157–70.

Stephens, Martha. *The Question of Flannery O'Connor.* Baton Rouge: Louisiana State UP, 1973.

Stevens, Wallace. *The Palm at the End of the Mind: Selected Poems and a Play.* Ed. Holly Stevens. 1967. New York: Vintage, 1972.

Stonum, Gary Lee. *Faulkner's Career: An Internal Literary History.* Ithaca, NY: Cornell UP, 1979.

Storey, John, ed. *Cultural Theory and Popular Culture: A Reader.* 2nd ed. New York: Pearson/Prentice Hall, 1998.

Thompson, G. R. *The Art of Authorial Presence: Hawthorne's Provincial Tales.* Durham: Duke UP, 1993.

Thompson, Lawrance. *Melville's Quarrel with God.* Princeton, NJ: Princeton UP, 1952.

Thoreau, Henry David. *Walden and Civil Disobedience.* Ed. Sherman Paul. Boston: Houghton Mifflin, 1960.

de Tocqueville, Alexis. *Democracy in America*. 1835–39. Trans. George Lawrence. Ed. J. P. Mayer. Garden City, NY: Anchor, 1969.

Turner, Arlin. Introduction. *The Blithedale Romance*. By Nathaniel Hawthorne. New York: Norton, 1958. 5–23.

Twain, Mark. *Pudd'nhead Wilson*. New York: Grosset and Dunlap, n.d.

Tyler, Moses Coit. *A History of American Literature, 1607–1765*. 1878. New York: Collier Books, 1962.

Vatai, Frank L. "John D. McDonald and Calvinism: Some Key Terms." *Clues: A Journal of Detection* 11 (1990): 9–19.

Veitch, Jonathan. *American Superrealism: Nathanael West and the Politics of Representation in the 1930s*. Madison: U of Wisconsin P, 1997.

Veron, Enid, ed. *Humor in America: An Anthology*. New York: Harcourt Brace Jovanovich, 1976.

Volpe, Edmond L. 1964. *A Reader's Guide to William Faulkner*. New York: Farrar, Straus and Giroux, 1971.

Wadlington, Warwick. "Nathanael West and the Confidence Game." In Madden, 299–322.

Waggoner, Hyatt. "Past as Present: *Absalom, Absalom!*" *Faulkner: A Collection of Critical Essays*. Ed. Robert Penn Warren. Englewood Cliffs, NJ: Prentice-Hall, 1966. 175–85.

Wagner, Linda Welshimer. *Hemingway and Faulkner: Inventors/Masters*. Metuchen, NJ: Scarecrow P, 1975.

Wain, John. Obituary for Ernest Hemingway. In Meyers, 426–29.

Walker, Nancy, ed. *What's So Funny? Humor in American Culture*. Wilmington, DE: Scholarly Resources, 1998.

Warren, Robert Penn. *All the King's Men*. 1946. Restored edition. Ed. Noel Polk. New York: Harcourt, 2001.

Watkins, Mel. *On the Real Side: Laughing, Lying, and Signifying—The Underground Tradition of African-American Humor*. New York: Simon and Schuster, 1994.

Weber, Brom, et al., eds. *An Anthology of American Humor*. New York: Thomas Y. Crowell, 1962.

Weber, Max. *The Protestant Ethic and the Spirit of Capitalism*. Trans. Talcott Parsons. 1930. New York: Scribner's, 1958.

West, Nathanael. *Novels and Other Writings*. New York: Library of America, 1997.

What's Cooking. Dir. Gurinder Chadha. Perf. Mercedes Ruehl, Joan Chen. Flashpoint, 2000.

Widmer, Kingsley. "The Last Masquerade: *The Day of the Locusts*." In Madden, 179–93.

Wiggins, Robert A. "The Flawed Structure of *Pudd'nhead Wilson*." In Berger, 255–59.

Wigglesworth, Michael. *The Day of Doom; Or, a Poetical Description of the Great and Last Judgment, with Other Poems.* [1662] Ed. Kenneth Murdock. 1929. New York: Russell and Russell, 1966.

Williamson, Alan. "Hart Crane." *Voices and Visions: The Poet in America.* Ed. Helen Vendler. New York: Random House, 1987. 312–51.

Wilson, Charles Reagan. "William Faulkner and the Southern Religious Culture." In Fowler and Abadie, 21–43.

Wilson, Edmund. *The Bit between My Teeth: A Literary Chronicle of 1950–1965.* New York: Farrar, Straus and Giroux, 1965.

———. *Patriotic Gore.* New York: Oxford UP, 1962.

———.*The Shores of Light: A Literary Chronicle of the Twenties and Thirties.* New York: Farrar, Straus and Young, 1952.

Wilson, James D. *A Reader's Guide to the Short Stories of Mark Twain.* Boston, MA: G. K. Hall, 1987.

Wimsatt, Mary Ann, and Robert L. Phillips. "Antebellum Humor." *The History of Southern Literature.* Ed. Louis D. Rubin, Jr., et al. Baton Rouge: Louisiana State UP, 1985. 136–56.

Wineapple, Brenda. *Hawthorne: A Life.* New York: Knopf, 2003.

Winters, Yvor. *Maule's Curse, or Hawthorne and the Problem of Allegory.* 1938. *In Defense of Reason.* 3rd ed. Chicago: Swallow, 1947. 157–75.

Wood, Ralph C. "Flannery O'Connor's Strange Alliance with Southern Fundamentalists." In Murphy et al., 75–98.

Wylder, Deb. Rev. of *Across the River and into the Trees.* In Meyers, 395–400.

Young, Philip. *Ernest Hemingway.* New York: Rinehart, 1952.

———. *Ernest Hemingway: A Reconsideration.* University Park: Penn State UP, 1966.

Index